Difficult Personalities

•

THE EXPERIMENT

BECAUSE EVERY BOOK IS A TEST OF NEW IDEAS

Difficult
Personalities

●

Difficult Personalities

A Practical Guide to Managing
the Hurtful Behavior of Others
(and Maybe Your Own)

•

HELEN McGRATH, PhD
and HAZEL EDWARDS, MEd

THE EXPERIMENT

NEW YORK

The Experiment, LLC
260 Fifth Avenue
New York, NY 10001-6425
www.theexperimentpublishing.com

Library of Congress Control Number: 2009937037
ISBN 978-1-61519-013-3

Cover design by Michael Fusco | michaelfuscodesign.com
Design by Pauline Neuwirth, Neuwirth & Associates, Inc.

Manufactured in the United States of America
First printing January 2010
10 9 8 7 6 5 4 3 2 1

Contents

Difficult
Personalities

●

Introduction

GENERAL PRINCIPLES
UNDERPINNING THIS BOOK

DO YOU HAVE a difficult personality in your life? Would others consider that you are their difficult person? In this book we have turned the microscope on difficult types of personalities and patterns of behavior, which range from annoying and confusing to the seriously damaging.

Like most of us, you have probably encountered situations with family, friends, coworkers, or associates who have hurt you. Either they have damaged you emotionally or financially, or their behavior has caused ongoing distress or worry. Understanding how people think and knowing some of the reasons for their patterns of hurtful behavior will take you part of the way toward handling your difficult relationships more successfully.

People sometimes do not reciprocate our feelings, fail to appreciate our worth, fall out of love with us, betray, leave, retrench, or disappoint us. These are all part of the pain of being human and do not necessarily reflect people being difficult. But some people have ongoing behavior patterns that hurt many others. They leave behind more than one hurt or troubled person because of their difficult personalities.

What exactly is "personality"? Each person has a unique personality. It is best described as a relatively enduring and predictable collection of personal qualities (traits) and patterns of behavior. We can also talk about "personality types." These are categories of personality that are very similar and are composed of predictable combinations of traits and behavior patterns.

Some people have a mildly difficult behavior pattern while others have moderate or very difficult behavior patterns, and the effect of these patterns on others may also range from minor to severe.

Here are some of the guiding principles we have used in identifying and elaborating on these difficult patterns.

Nobody's Perfect

All of us have people in our lives who hurt, frustrate, or annoy. But most of us occasionally hurt others as well. An understanding of the reasons for our *own* behavior means we are in a better position to improve relationships. Skills can be learned and strategies applied to help you deal more effectively with both the distressing behavior of others and your own hurtful behavior.

Don't feel distressed when you recognize yourself in one or more of the patterns or anecdotes. Weaknesses and limitations are universal. Probably everyone who reads this book will fit a pattern, at least in a mild way. As Sigmund Freud once said, even normal people are not all that normal!

Some People Hurt You Because Some of Their Personality Traits Are Incompatible with Yours

Some people cause us frustration and annoyance because their behavior differs so much from our own. Their hurtful behavior is an indirect outcome of perceiving the world differently and/or having different interpersonal styles. By implication, of course, we cause them distress, too. In general, the more we are alike, the easier it is to get along. Too much "alikeness," though, can lead to stagnation. How extroverts and introverts cope with each other and how, from different perspectives, "thinkers" and "feelers" work things out, is explored in this book. We also look at what happens when "planners" try to work and live with people who like to be more spontaneous and "go with the flow."

Some People Upset You Because Their Behavior Patterns Annoy and Frustrate

The intentions of people with annoying personalities are usually not selfish, mean-spirited, exploitive, or hostile. The categories of annoying personalities in this book are based on different combinations of ignorance, interpersonal difficulties, selfishness, coldness, insensitivity, immaturity, faulty thinking, pettiness, and low self-esteem. These are:

- bossy people
- people who consider themselves superior
- negative people.

Some People Cause Trouble and Confuse Themselves and Others Because of Their Personality

Two kinds of personalities are discussed in this category. Those with anxious personalities can sometimes confuse, hurt, and distress as a result of their attempts to deal with their own emotional difficulties, which have a strong biological component. Demanding personalities are so terrified and affronted by rejection or what they see as abandonment that they behave in outrageously demanding ways and sometimes take spiteful revenge on those whom they see as having denied them.

Some People Hurt You Because Their Behavior Patterns Are Very Damaging

Some personality types have toxic behavior patterns that frequently damage many others or cause pain, usually to an intense degree. Either their intention is to harm, or they are prepared to hurt you in order to get what they want. The personality types discussed in this category include:

- passive-aggressive people
- bullies
- everyday sociopaths.

People with these personalities find it difficult to change, and often they don't want to. They are getting what they want, but at your expense. As a result of their painful behavior, they alienate others, but that doesn't worry them. They are not generally distressed by their own behavior. These personality types usually show up from late adolescence onward, although there are exceptions in which there are earlier signs of the pattern. These patterns can be most easily identified in close relationships.

Some People Hurt Others Because They Have Poor Relationship and Coping Skills

Lack of effective relationship skills can indirectly cause pain. If our own relationship skills are also poor, we double the distress. Our lives are spent learning and refining the skills we need in relationships. Managing angry feelings, handling conflict constructively, not personalizing things too much, negotiating, validating, being empathic, respecting, and staying positive and optimistic are all such skills. Unskilled people may be simultaneously wrestling with behavior patterns, such as anxiety, which make it harder. Others may have had poor family models and need more opportunity to learn elsewhere. People don't change easily, but once the intention has been formed, they can. In Part V there are practical guidelines for improving your own relationship skills. They may also be a useful offering to someone you care about who needs to improve their relationship skills.

The DSM-IV-TR Is the Guide

Much of the material in this book is based on the categories of behavior disorders outlined in the DSM-IV-TR. The full title of the DSM-IV-TR is the *Diagnostic and Statistical Manual of Mental Disorders,* Fourth Edition, Text Revision (2000), and it is published by the American Psychiatric Association. It represents the results of the research and clinical experience of over one thousand psychologists and psychiatrists, as well as the contributions of numerous professional organizations involved with emotional health issues.

The DSM-IV-TR is a guide to diagnosing mental disorders. These are behavioral patterns and personality disorders that an individual displays and that are associated with distress or dysfunction. Dysfunction is about how much the pattern of behavior interferes with an individual's life, work, schooling, social activities, partner, and family. It can range from minor to very severe, and it inhibits maturity, progress, and day-to-day functioning.

The DSM-IV-TR is the basic reference for psychiatrists and psychologists when trying to diagnose patients with problems. In court, it is the most common basis of expert testimony. It lists behavioral characteristics that are typical of particular disorders and some personality types. The DSM-IV-TR stresses that the intensity and frequency of behaviors are also important in determining whether a person has a disorder. Often there are significant behavioral variations within a category. An individual may not have all the behaviors outlined but can still be diagnosed as having a particular disorder. Some people have the symptoms needed for a diagnosis but only in a mild way. People are complex and can be diagnosed as having more than one syndrome or disorder at a time.

The disorders outlined in the DSM-IV-TR are not all forms of mental illness. A few are about mental illness and what, in court, would be termed "insanity." An example would be schizophrenia, a disorder that involves an inability to differentiate between what is real and what is imagined. But there is a huge range of disorders outlined, from the crippling Bipolar I and Bipolar II disorders to the more common nicotine-related disorders, sleep disorders, caffeine-related disorders, and male erectile disorder. So, the DSM-IV-TR is not just about mental illness, or necessarily about behavior that has a huge impact on oneself or others. For example, although drinking too much coffee can be a problem, it is hardly comparable to depression or agoraphobia.

Within psychiatry and psychology, there are disputes over a few categories, as well as the indicators or criteria for some of them. The diagnosis of a disorder through the application of the criteria requires specialized training. Ultimately, the psychologist or psychiatrist will also rely on clinical experience and judgment, not just on these guidelines.

Behavior Can Be Viewed as a Continuum

People are complex. Few can be neatly categorized into just one kind of behavioral pattern or personality type. Many people have behavior that could fit into several categories. Most of us have a bit of this and a bit of that.

Imagine behavior as a continuum rather than as a simple category. Most people demonstrate some aspects of all the behaviors described in this book. They just differ in terms of combinations, how much, across how many situations, and with what intensity the behavior is shown. So we are all at different points on each behavioral continuum. This is the approach taken in this book. Each of the personality types, traits, and behavior patterns outlined are seen as a continuum. Most people are on the lower end of each continuum, but they still show some of the behavior patterns. Another group is in the middle and its members show a moderate degree, enough to significantly hurt themselves and/or others. A small number is at the higher end of each continuum. These people show such a severe pattern that they can be said to have a "disorder" in that they act this way, frequently, across many areas of their life (that is, pervasively), and their behavior hurts many others or themselves a great deal.

Behavior Always Has a Positive and a Negative Side

Behaviors usually have two sides: positive and negative. People who see things in extremes can be difficult to deal with because their thinking is rigid, narrow, and unrealistic. They fail to realize that most issues are fuzzy rather than sharply defined. Sometimes, though, their ability to reduce an issue to simple black-and-white terms, however unrealistic, can be helpful. Similarly, anxious people, always apprehensive about what might go wrong, can be wearying, but their vigilance can pick up potential dangers others miss. Where possible, the "bright side," as well the challenging aspects of each personality type and pattern, has been covered.

• • •

We All Have Working Hypotheses to Explain What Happens in Our Lives

Each of us has some basic working hypotheses that direct our thinking, feelings, interpretations, and behavior. These help us to make sense of the world as we see it and what happens to us in that world. Some working hypotheses are more helpful than others. A key way to change behavior is to adopt a more realistic working hypothesis as a guide. This book identifies the working hypotheses of particular personality types and offers alternatives.

Behavior Is Never "Simply" Caused

Oversimplification can be harmful. There is no single "right" way of looking at people's behavior or its causes. Unfortunately, an overly simplistic view of what causes behavior is perpetuated in movies, TV programs, and books in an effort to entertain and to fit the media time limits and budgets.

Genetic inheritance probably contributes between 25 and 50 percent toward how we behave and what kind of personality we develop. In some cases it is more than 50 percent. Scientists have been able to identify the influence of specific genes on behavior by studying transgenic mice that have had certain genes removed or replaced, so we have a clearer idea of the impact of genetic predispositions. But environment also matters. Behavior is caused by different factors interacting. Rarely is it just the result of one factor, such as what parents did or didn't do, an event at school, or a trauma. All those factors play a role, but a genetic predisposition can interact with any or all of them. And even if behavioral patterns stem in part from genetic biological predispositions, psychological intervention and learning to behave differently can still alter them enough to reduce some of the distress and hurt caused to oneself and others.

A genetic predisposition involves inherited physiological factors that influence behavior. These include brain chemistry and the neurological structure with which we are born. A genetic predisposition directs, but does not necessarily control, our behavior. It predisposes us to behave in specific ways. The combined action of several different genes, each with small additive effects, can produce a genetic predisposition. Some genetic predispositions remain latent until a triggering event or set of circumstances occurs—for example, moving away from home or facing a loss. Others are activated by puberty, trauma, illness, or the use of toxic substances such as marijuana, Ecstasy, or heroin.

It is known that many aspects of "temperament" are present at birth or shortly after. These characteristic ways of behaving and responding are remarkably consistent until late adolescence and probably into adulthood. Some factors are:

- activity level
- distractibility and the tendency to get bored easily
- persistence in the face of frustration and obstacles
- sociability (as opposed to shyness)
- adaptability to change (as opposed to inflexibility and non-adaptivity)
- predominantly positive or negative mood
- intensity of reactions and emotions.

Ultimately, most behavior is caused by the interaction of experiences and any genetic predispositions. Positive and negative experiences can moderate or exaggerate predispositions. Experiences may alter aspects of the brain's chemistry and functioning, temporarily or permanently. Age also affects the chemistry and functioning of the brain, with our capacity for dealing with stress declining with age. Our behavior patterns are like a symphony—many instruments play together with ongoing themes or patterns. But at certain times, one instrument dominates or influences others. However, we can with some certainty say that there is a reduced focus in psychology on "bad parenting" as a major causative factor in behavior patterns. We now look at "dysfunctional brain chemistry" as more significant than we used to, so there is less blame directed at our parents. All of us have to take responsibility for our behavior, and if biological factors can be identified as contributing significantly, we need to seek strategies and support for modifying these predispositions.

Incompatible
Personality
Traits

1

What Are Incompatible Personality Traits?

THE MYERS-BRIGGS TYPE INDICATOR* (commonly referred to as the MBTI) is an instrument used by many psychologists and organizations to get some idea of people's preferred style of operating, and their resultant behavior patterns, needs, strengths, and limitations. With a sound research base, it is probably the most widely used psychological test of the last decade.

The MBTI was developed by Isobel Myers and Katherine Briggs, and is based on the personality theory of Carl Jung, a Swiss psychiatrist of the 1920s. It identifies people's preferences for ways of dealing with their world and those in it. Many researchers since have identified typical behaviors, or personality traits, for each of the four kinds of "preferred style" dimensions identified, and have shown how those behaviors can have an impact on relationships. By having some idea of your styles and those of your significant others and colleagues, you gain an insight into yourself and them. Such information also helps to identify where both synergy and potential clashes might occur.

In this section, three of the four "style" dimensions, which are the basis of the MBTI, are discussed. In parts, the terminology is different from that used by the MBTI. The three discussed here are:

- whether you are more extroverted or more introverted
- whether you have a preference for a planned orderly life over a more flexible one where options are kept open

- whether you have a greater preference for logic or emotions as the basis for your decision making. We have not looked at the fourth dimension identified in the MBTI, namely, whether you prefer to focus more on the big picture or the details. Research suggests that this dimension has less direct impact on relationships.

For a fuller self-picture, ask your Human Resources department to arrange for you (and perhaps your coworkers) to take the test under the control of a trained administrator. If you are seeing a counselor about relationship issues, consider asking to fill out an MBTI record sheet. Otherwise, select from the titles in Books You Might Like to Read (page 271). The books listed don't give you the chance to take the test or give it to your partner or coworker, but they do elaborate on the styles.

1. EXTROVERSION OR INTROVERSION

This style dimension determines where you get your psychological energy. If you are more energized by people, variety, and external events, you probably have an extroverted style. If you are more energized by predictable routine, private reflections, and ideas, you probably have more of an introverted style. The MBTI is neither the first nor the only psychological test to identify the dimension of extroversion/introversion. This trait is one of the most common characteristics to be studied in psychological research.

2. PLANNING OR OPTIONIZING

This style dimension reflects whether you prefer to have a structured and organized lifestyle, in which you plan and "close off" by making decisions relatively quickly, or a lifestyle characterized by spontaneity and flexibility, which allows you to make fewer commitments so that you can remain "open" to other possibilities.

• • •

3. THINKING OR FEELING

This dimension reflects the basis on which you prefer to make your decisions. Some people's patterns suggest that they prefer to decide mostly on logic. Other people's patterns reflect a preference for deciding more on the basis of feelings, personal values, and emotional impact in the situation.

There are key points about these styles:

- Although they can be studied separately, your three preferred styles can also be looked at in terms of how they operate together. The overall effect is more than just the three added together (or the four added together, which is the case with the full MBTI). Again, a reminder that only three of the four are discussed here. The combination of the four preferences results in your "psychological type."
- Your styles reflect your natural preferences, not permanent facts about how you always behave. Just like your preferred hand, your preferred response comes naturally and requires little effort. When the situation demands, however, you can choose to behave in ways that are typical of the opposite style, the one that comes less naturally. For example, we all behave in extroverted *and* introverted ways at various times and in various situations. However, our pattern is that we tend to behave in one way more than the other—that is, we are more likely to be extroverted than introverted, or vice versa.
- "Styles" are not rigid categories containing a set of unchanging and unchangeable characteristics. Variations exist within each "style." Some people have extreme or "rampant" styles. Others have "middle-of-the-road" or "half-and-half" styles in which they seem to use one style as much as its opposite.
- No particular style in each of the three dimensions is "better." In many cases, what is better is a reasonable balance of styles.
- In general, romantic relationships are more successful when the partners have significant style similarities. If there are extreme differences, it can be difficult to bridge the gap. The greatest relationship difficulties are most

likely to occur for couples in which the man is extremely introverted and the woman is extremely extroverted.

Since people tend to think that others see the world their way, misinterpretation can lead to frustration and conflict. You can become so caught up in your differences that you lose sight of the common ground. So, understanding and respecting differences and trying to accommodate and negotiate is important. Understanding how another thinks will reduce potential conflict at home and in the workplace. Accepting that another person whose style is different from yours will think and operate differently, but with equal validity, will help you to deal with their behavior and help them deal with yours.

Reframing conflict as "difference" rather than something intolerable can be useful. For example:

Susie and Aaron often found themselves arguing within the first hour of arriving home. Aaron has an extroverted style and a boring job that involves spending a lot of time alone. When he gets home, he needs conversation. Susie is more introverted and feels overwhelmed by the demands made upon her at work. When she gets home, she needs peace and space to think. If one perceives the other to be "wrong" in how they behave at home, then they are more likely to fight, each taking the moral high ground. ("You're wrong. I'm right. How could you do this to me?") But if they frame it as difference and negotiate, then it doesn't have to create tension. ("We each have different needs when we come home. How about we each have 15 minutes of recovery time, and then come together to talk about our day for another 15 minutes?")

2

Variety Plus or a Rich Inner Life?

EXTROVERTS AND INTROVERTS

KEY WORDS FOR EXTROVERTS	KEY WORDS FOR INTROVERTS
outward	inwards
breadth	depth
variety	sameness
talkative	reflective
people oriented	private; likes own company
impulsive	controlled
trusting and open	reserved and cautious

"EXTROVERT" AND "INTROVERT" are labels people use casually without being certain of their exact definitions. They are oversimplified shorthand for psychological differences in the way people prefer to operate.

All of us tend to favor either an extroverted or an introverted style. A preference for extroversion or introversion can be seen in nearly everything we do. None of us is exclusively one or the other. Also, our preferred style, whether predominantly extroverted or introverted, is only one part of who we are and is modified by other characteristics.

Neither way is superior. They are just different preferences for operating and being energized. Since extroverts predominate in our society (they represent 75 percent), we tend to believe that the extroverted way is the "normal" way, but this is not the case. They are just in the majority.

Some of us are strongly introverted or extroverted and can be described as having a "rampant" style of extroversion or introversion. Some have a good balance of both and are best described as having a half-and-half style. With experience, we modify our extroverted or introverted characteristics and do not seem to be quite the same as we were when we were younger.

The stereotype of an extrovert is someone who is a "party animal." But that is an oversimplification. An extrovert's main stimulation comes from the outer world of people and things. Extroverts are more energized by their interactions with others and their external experiences. They appreciate and seek variety and prefer others' company to their own. They tend to respond quickly and enjoy a fast pace. Everyone who is more extroverted in their style, though, also has times and situations in which they prefer more introverted ways of acting.

Introverts' main stimulation comes from their inner world of thoughts and feelings. Introverts are more energized by their own reflections and interpretations than by external events or people. They appreciate and seek private time for reflection and like to do things in depth. But everyone who is mainly introverted in their style also has times and situations in which they prefer more extroverted ways of behaving.

Extroverted Style

People who more closely fit the profile of an extrovert are likely to have many of these characteristics:

- often friendly, talkative, and easy to get to know. They easily express emotions, and what you see is what you get.
- often take action and then think about it afterward
- use dramatic language for effect
- tend to think out loud. In talking, they find out what they think. They often change their minds after discussing things with others. They prefer to talk problems over.
- like variety. They often have a wide circle of friends and acquaintances, and like to socialize to relax.

- relatively comfortable being the center of attention
- tend to talk more than listen and often interrupt without realizing that they are doing it.

Introverted Style

People who more closely fit the profile of an introvert are likely to have these characteristics:

- fairly self-sustained and are often happy with their own company
- tend to think first and then act
- often very loyal to a few close friends, rather than have a wide circle of friends
- prefer constancy and routine, and prefer depth to breadth
- a strong need for privacy and a preference not to be the center of attention
- often feel drained by meeting too many people and need privacy to mentally rehearse before speaking. They like to relax by being alone.
- tend to listen more than talk and may get interrupted by the nearest extrovert
- what you see is not always what you get
- reserved, but have a rich inner world of ideas, emotions, and impressions. They prefer to keep their thoughts and feelings inside so that others need to ask directly about them rather than try to work them out.

EXTROVERTS SAY	INTROVERTS SAY
Talk to me. Spend time with me. I need company.	I want to be alone and think.
Tell me how you really feel.	My thoughts are private.
I'm happy to tell you how I feel.	I don't know if I can trust you with my feelings. Besides, I haven't reflected enough yet to know what they are.

EXTROVERTS SAY	INTROVERTS SAY
Let's discuss our problem and solve it now so I can find out how I feel about it.	I want to go away by myself and think so I can find out how I feel about it. Perhaps we can talk later?
What's wrong? Did I do something wrong? Are you annoyed? Have I upset you?	Just because I'm not talking to you doesn't mean there's something wrong.
Let's have a meeting tomorrow.	Do we have to? Couldn't we just circulate position papers? Or do it by e-mail?
How can you understand my viewpoint if I don't tell you how I think and feel?	Have you ever had a thought or feeling that remained unspoken?
We've been home all day. Why don't you call Jeff and Sue and see if they'd like to have dinner?	I'd rather stay home tonight and watch a video or read a book.
It's boring doing the same thing all the time.	You're shallow, you jump all over the place. Find something meaningful to do by yourself.
Why do you think all the time instead of acting?	Why don't you think before you act?
You are avoiding me.	I like my own company and this is not the same as not liking yours.
You are being secretive.	I'm not into hiding anything. I just don't find it easy to voluntarily expose my feelings.
You drive me mad because you don't speak up until the last minutes of the meeting and then you criticize everything we have decided so far.	I don't speak up until I have something to say. Why do you have to "fill up the silence" all the time?

Potential Problems and Ways of Dealing with Them

Here are areas of potential conflict and some possible solutions. Remember that these are *differences*, not *defects*. They need to be understood, valued, accepted, and accommodated, not condemned or scorned.

Pacing and Conflict

Extroverts and introverts working or living together have pacing difficulties, especially regarding conflict. Extroverts want to work things out immediately and will pursue an introvert in an attempt to discuss things and start problem solving right away. They want to keep discussing the problem until a solution is found. Introverts don't like confrontation and will avoid it. The introvert is likely to react by feeling "cornered" by the more confrontational extrovert and then respond by "shutting down," refusing to discuss the issue immediately and attempting to escape in order to postpone and reflect. Often, though, they don't come back to the problem. The extrovert, in not being sensitive to the introvert's need to withdraw and think, may interpret their "escape" as lack of concern or lack of courage. The introvert resents feeling trapped.

The extrovert wants information about how an introvert is thinking and feeling (especially after a conflict). Because they don't know, they "mind-read" and then imagine that the introvert is angry or upset with them. Without "data" to help them judge a situation, they assume the worst. This can activate fears of rejection and loss. The introvert may develop an unhealthy sense of power when they realize that their withdrawal and/or failure to express feelings upsets the extrovert.

What You Can Do

- The extrovert should be prepared to summarize their perspective briefly and then allow the introvert time to deliberate. They can ask the introvert for a deadline when the discussion can take place. The extrovert should use the time in between to reflect and rehearse. Don't nag.
- The introvert must reassure the extrovert of their good faith, and honor their commitment to resume the discussion after

their reflection period and not just allow the situation to drift. It is their responsibility to reestablish contact on the problem.

- Introverts need to risk stating how they are feeling when the relationship is a more personal one. They need to be aware of how excruciating it can be for an extrovert not to know how a loved one is thinking and feeling about an issue that is important to both of them. Reassure them. Say, "No, I'm not angry. I'm feeling a little bit hurt and taking time to recover, but I'm not angry."

- An extrovert needs to practice being comfortable and rational about an emotionally ambiguous situation. It goes like this:

Well, I'm still feeling a little bit upset over the argument we had about the budget restrictions and the other person probably is, too. But I know from experience that they pull away after conflict and need to be inside their own head for a while. I can stand it if I have to wait for a while to feel reassured that all is okay with our working relationship. It's not rational to assume that their withdrawal and silence are automatically a bad sign. They just need longer to reflect and more space to deal with things.

Conversational Style

Extroverts want more of the conversational space. Their quicker, more confrontational, and less reflective style may overwhelm or freeze out the introverts. Extroverts may interrupt and not allow the introverts to finish their sentences. The introvert may say too little and appear not to respond to what the extrovert says.

The extrovert may be convinced that the introvert doesn't care and isn't listening. The less the introvert says in response, the more the extrovert panics and talks to fill the space. In return, the introvert is convinced there is no point in trying to say anything because there will be no space, and the extrovert only wants to tell, not listen, anyway. The introvert feels very resentful.

Extroverts' words are in process and are not necessarily the final thought. They are talking to work out how they think and feel, therefore they often appear to jump all over the place and change their minds as they go. When introverts make up their minds, after reflection, they can be hard to shift. An introvert's words, especially after time to reflect, are usually the product of considerable thought. (Not that this makes them any more correct!)

Introverts may believe their process is superior and that extroverts are shallow and superficial. Extroverts may believe that introverts have already made up their minds and are not prepared to discuss it.

What You Can Do

The extrovert needs to use more self-discipline and give the introvert a chance to talk. Sit back and listen more. Trust that there will be a chance to say more so that you can work out how you feel and think. This is the extrovert's fear. They can't work things out unless they talk it out. They have so many things jumping around in their heads that they want to say and get a response to that they are scared they will "lose" them before they can speak them. They fear silence.

The introvert needs to be more assertive, to insist on having a chance to speak without being interrupted. Do not do this in a nasty fashion. Don't say in a hostile voice: "Do you mind!," or "If you'd let me finish my sentence!"

Instead, you can use "Protective Assertion," that is, protect your own rights, but protect the relationship as well. In Protective Assertion, a version of the "When you . . . I feel . . . because. . . " format is used (see page 53) plus low-key emotion words coupled with I-messages, such as: "I'm feeling frustrated about having no space to say what I feel. Could we take turns more?"

If, however, you are more concerned about protecting your own rights than the relationship, you can assert firmly: "Please allow me to finish what I started to say."

Leisure time and variety

Extroverts want fewer routines and sameness, and more variety and excitement. Introverts want more routines and chances to deepen an interest, and crave less external variety. The extrovert may want to go out and socialize more than the introvert. Although they enjoy socializing and are prepared to go out, introverts dont like to do it as often. The extrovert may get frustrated and resentful, believing that the introvert is boring and limiting. The introvert may feel overwhelmed and exhausted and believe that the extrovert is being superficial and demanding.

What You Can Do

- Negotiate about leisure time. Extroverts need to settle for less partner socialization and introverts need to agree to socialize and go out more than they would choose to do on their own. Extroverts may need to find additional sources of social stimulation, such as friends and family.
- Negotiate how much variety and how much sameness you both want. Extroverts need to settle for a little more routine than they like, and introverts need to agree to a bit more variety and less routine than they would prefer. Extroverts may need to develop other sources of varied stimulation through work, sporting interests, etc.

Intimacy

Introverts need intimacy just as much as extroverts, but they need it in different ways and amounts. Extroverts want a lot of intimacy through being with the other person, and sharing deep thoughts and feelings. Introverts want some of that, but are intimate with another in their own heads. Extroverts need intimacy more through external contact and actions.

Often it is hard for an extrovert to develop intimacy with an introvert. Extroverts disclose a lot about themselves and this is a first step toward intimacy. But with introverts who are more reserved and less trusting, it is hard to know what they are thinking or feeling because they tend not to volunteer that information. Introverts may disclose little about themselves and bottle up emotions.

Extroverts usually want more contact, time, and conversation and may stress an introvert with their seemingly constant demands. Consistent talking can be exhausting and overwhelming to an introvert. Extroverts' demands may drive introverts into escaping their requests for company, attention, and deep conversation by more withdrawal into time alone.

What You Can Do

- Extroverts have to go slowly with introverts and wait until they are ready to talk more intimately. Interestingly, introverts are often very encouraging of extroverts being self-disclosing even though this may receive little reciprocity. It is almost as if they need the extrovert to do a lot of it "first," and then they can slowly follow. But they will never reveal as much as the extrovert.
- The extrovert must follow through on a commitment to be more self-disciplined and not interrupt the introvert's mental privacy more than necessary.
- "Needy" extroverts can use their relationships with friends and family to fulfill intimacy needs and not feel resentful at having to do it that way. There is no "correct way" in which intimacy needs must be catered to.
- Introverts can move a bit more out of their comfort zone, learn to reach out to their partners more, and tolerate more contact and deep discussion of feelings.

Workplace Contact

Extroverts like lots of meetings and can waste time talking on the phone. Introverts prefer to spend more time on their own and do not like excessive meetings or phone conversations.

What You Can Do

- Extroverts can use e-mail to avoid wasting working time or placing too many demands on the introvert. Phone calls to introverts should be relatively short.
- Introverts can accept that some workplace conversation and contact may not be strictly "necessary" but still be an important aspect of workplace community and morale. They can be more available than they currently are.

Action versus Reflection

Extroverts often fail to think in advance and act too impulsively. On the other hand, introverts may reflect too much and act too little.

What You Can Do

- A bit of humor can be helpful in personal relationships. Instead of scorning the other, laugh with them and against yourself. Be the other's best support and give them a signal when you think that the outcome will be "Too little thought" or "Too much thought."
- In both the workplace and in personal relationships, the introvert may attempt to "slow down" the action process if more time is needed for reflection. The introvert needs to remember to slow things down only a little to allow for reflection, not stop them. Continually blocking the other person creates resentment, and the introvert often misses out on the benefits that might have accrued from their actions.

Debra, who is 29, and Allie, who is 32, have both recently started work as instructors at a suburban fitness center. Debra, a triathlete in training, is a very private person with a more introverted style, and she sometimes feels overwhelmed by Allie's more extroverted behavior. Allie, who is the captain of the most successful community basketball team, seems to be on the go all the time and often spends time working out new routines and needs to talk to Debra about possible changes to the center. When Debra seems less than enthusiastic about one of Allie's ideas, Allie is like a "dog with a bone" and just keeps going on about why it would be a good idea. Debra feels a strong urge to retreat into her own space when this happens. Allie has complained to Jeff, their supervisor, that working with Debra is very frustrating because it is so hard to get to know her. She explains that even though she often suggests that they have lunch together or run together, Debra always rebuffs her. When Jeff takes up the issue with Debra, she bitterly replies that if Allie put as much time into her work as into trying to socialize with the customers, the center might make a profit.

3

Let's Get Organized or
Go with the Flow?

PLANNERS AND OPTIONIZERS

KEY WORDS FOR PLANNERS	KEY WORDS FOR OPTIONIZERS
organization	looseness
structure	flexibility
controlling options	putting off decisions
decisiveness	spontaneity
planning	staying open to possibilities
closure	change
predictability	

SOME PEOPLE PREFER a relatively decisive lifestyle in which events are ordered and predictable. For the purpose of simplification, we have called them "Planners." Planners prefer to have closure and structure in their lives and make reasonably speedy decisions in most areas. Deadlines are kept. They like structure, routine, and order, and they plan to make their lives reasonably predictable.

Others have a preference for a less structured and ordered lifestyle, characterized by keeping their options open. We have called them "Optionizers." Optionizers are reluctant to make decisions, always feeling they have insufficient information and that something better might come along. An optionizer prefers a lifestyle that is flexible, adaptable, and spontaneous, and not limited by unnecessary restrictions, structure or predictability.

Many people have an obvious and "rampant" planner or optionizer pattern across many areas of their lives. Others are half-and-half, and they are probably the easiest to live with. In some contexts, all choose to do it the "less preferred" way. And as we get older, changes occur. Planners begin to value more flexibility and "hanging loose," and optionizers see more advantages in organization and structure.

These preferred styles are only one aspect of a person. Neither way of operating is better. They both offer advantages and disadvantages, and the "best" way is undoubtedly a combination of the two.

Planning style

People who more closely fit the "Planner" profile are likely to show the following characteristics in their personal and work life:

- prefer to have life under control with structure, set procedures, and established routines
- collect information for decisions in an orderly fashion
- make decisions relatively quickly
- meet deadlines with little trouble
- use "to do" lists as a way of life
- usually give work priority over play.

Optionizing style

People who more closely fit the "Optionizer" profile are likely to show these characteristics:

- prefer a flexible lifestyle
- often meet deadlines by last-minute rush (but usually get there)
- like "going with the flow" to see what might happen
- delay deciding in case something better turns up
- make last-minute changes
- feel there is never enough information to make decisions
- often give play priority over work.

• • •

PLANNERS SAY	OPTIONIZERS SAY
Let's make a list.	Let's wait and see what we need when we get there.
We need to book our vacation for the end of the year.	Why don't we get some brochures and think some more about where we want to go. We might find something better.
We need a system to make sure that all frozen foods in the fridge are used up in time.	It will be fine. I'll try to use them up.
But we decided on that weeks ago.	Let's change our mind and do this instead.
We need to finish the tax returns by the end of the week. Let's work on it tonight.	I would rather go to dinner with Sue tonight. There's plenty of time to do the taxes.
You're chaotic, disorganized, messy, irresponsible, evasive, and indecisive.	You're rigid, uptight, a control freak, boring, and won't adapt.

Potential Problems and Ways of Dealing with Them

Here are areas where potential clashes might occur when you work or live with someone who has an opposite style. There are also some ideas for accommodating a different style from your own.

Decision Making

Optionizers often accuse planners of jumping to conclusions without checking with them. They can feel left out of the decision-making process because closure has arrived too fast. Optionizers may feel "nailed down" by planners, and planners see optionizers as evasive.

What You Can Do

- Allow for different attitudes to decision making and don't misjudge. Planners make decisions that they believe will be final. Optionizers like to look for other alternatives and resist settling things. They regard decisions as tentative and are likely to suggest changing at the last minute if a better solution arises. Unless this truly does cause problems, remind yourself that better decisions can often be made this way.

- If you are a planner, make sure that you always consult with others before making a decision.
- If you are a planner, explain how it feels to you. You can say, for example, "I feel really uncomfortable when things go on hold indefinitely. I can wait awhile, but I need reassurance that a decision will be made within a realistic time frame."

Stress and Pressure

Planners can be rigid and cause stress to themselves and others by wanting more structure and planning than is needed—for example, extra meetings, lists, systems, overorganizing others, and being demanding. If you are an optionizer, go along with what you can but assert limits, too. Say, for example, "Look, I know you prefer to have every meeting for the next six months locked in, but that doesn't give me enough flexibility," or "I realize that you like to know in advance what we will be doing over Easter, but it's five months away. I would like to give it a bit more thought before we commit ourselves."

What You Can Do

- Provide a list or agenda for planners, or give them goals. They like lists. An agenda will reassure them that the meeting is organized. It will reassure them that things are under control.
- Optionizers should try to avoid blocking in response to planners' demands for closure. It is tempting to be uncooperative. Instead, be assertive. Say something like, "I'm feeling a little bit hassled over this. I need some space to think about it. If I have to decide how I feel now, I won't make a good decision."
- Planners should try to avoid acting "parentally" toward optionizers and so avoid activating rebellion. Trust them to do as they promised unless you have evidence that this is unlikely.

- If you are an optionizer, don't put the planners under stress by being too casual or saying things such as "Let's just see how things work out." Be conscious of the language you use. Planners like specific action words, like "implement," "start," "finish."
- If you are a planner, relax more and worry less. Focus on the positives of an optionizer's style.
- If you are an optionizer, see the planners in your life as keeping you on track and helping you to organize yourself.

Punctuality

Optionizers are very relaxed about time and often annoy planners who take it more seriously. Planners can make an atmosphere very tense by insisting on absolute punctuality and deadlines.

What You Can Do

- Optionizers should try to be more punctual when dealing with a planner. Time matters to planners. They do not like interruptions, cancelled dates, or missed deadlines.
- Planners should remind themselves that optionizers are not being deliberately thoughtless if they are late, it is just that time matters less to them. Planners need to be more flexible and relaxed about the less important deadlines.

Progress

An optionizer may lose interest in a project before finishing, and leave a planner feeling frustrated and angry about "wasted time." Sometimes a planner decides too quickly and poor decisions result, making an optionizer cross about having to "wear" the poor outcome of the decision. Since optionizers tend to dislike routine, they may have bursts of energy with slack in between. Apparent inactivity and running close to deadlines can frustrate and stress planners. An optionizer can feel stressed by a planner's constant focus on "our progress."

What You Can Do

- Planners may need to make periodic checks on how optionizers are doing and give feedback to keep them encouraged.

- Optionizers should consider giving periodic updates, saying, "This is where I am now," to reassure the planner that the project will be completed.
- For optionizers, delegate the "action list" after the meeting, but build in some choice in the way it can be done.
- If you are a planner, discuss prospective plans with the optionizer to get feedback before committing either or both of you.
- Introduce a deadline. Planners can give optionizer partners some room to consider options but still ask for a deadline.
- Build in a 10 percent contingency factor with an optionizer. Allow extra time to complete a project or task. Monitor deadlines and have a private deadline later than the one you give the optionizer.

Fun

Planners can seem rigid and boring to optionizers because they will often put work ahead of fun.

What You Can Do

- Optionizers should respect this focus but override it now and then by putting more fun into the situation.
- An optionizer should ensure that a planner doesn't close off too many "fun" opportunities by not being prepared "at the drop of a hat" to do something that is fun. Use gentle encouragement.

Conflict

Planners may press for a quick decision or resolution of a conflict, whereas optionizers will prefer to put things on hold. Both will be frustrated.

What You Can Do

- The optionizer needs to reassure the planner that the conflict will be addressed.
- The planner can also ask for such reassurance: "Okay, we won't try to figure this out now, but I need your assurances that we will get back to it by Friday."

- Planners may need to handle more ambiguity and uncertainty than they are comfortable with.

The deadline for the major project was nine o'clock Monday morning. Lea (an optionizer) had not completed her share of the work by late Friday and said she would work on it over the weekend. Jo, one of her coworkers, was furious because Lea had been out for a long Friday lunch and didn't get back until three PM, insisting that there was plenty of time to make the deadline. Other staff who had already finished their portions were annoyed as she called them frequently from the office over the weekend to check on details or make suggestions about last-minute changes that would involve them coming in on Sunday to implement her suggestions. There was a blow-up between Lea and the graphic designer at noon on Sunday, when Lea had had a "brainstorm" about altering the color and the font of the report cover. Eventually Lea did finish her work by 8:45 on Monday morning, but since she'd been up all Sunday night working, she was useless for the rest of Monday. Other staff resented her shirking her responsibilities, even though they agreed that her final work was brilliant and the client was delighted. But the client did not have to handle Lea's grumpy tiredness the way the office staff did. Lea didn't have the domestic responsibilities of children or a partner that the other staff had, and they felt she should have organized herself better.

4

Which Rules,
the Head or the Heart?

THINKERS AND FEELERS

KEY WORDS FOR THINKERS	KEY WORDS FOR FEELERS
logic	feelings and values
objective analysis	appreciation of others
head rules	heart rules
principles and rules	empathy
facts	personal values
justice	kindness and caring
direct	harmony

"THINKING" IS THE style preference that relates to organizing and structuring information in order to make a decision in a logical and objective way. "Feeling" is the style preference that relates to organizing and structuring information to make a decision in a personal, values-oriented way.

The terms "thinker" and "feeler" here are oversimplified. Some people have extreme or "rampant" preferences for one or the other of these styles, but many operate on a half-and-half style. Nobody is exclusively one or the other, and your preferred style is modified by your other characteristics.

Neither style is superior. Both ways of looking at a situation are valid, and the best way undoubtedly combines elements of both.

Being a "thinker" is not the same as being insensitive or unfeeling. Thinkers are often just as warm, caring, and sensitive as feelers. But when it comes to making decisions, they prefer to use logic. They give more weight to facts, rational implications, and the logic behind actions, and less weight to their personal values and possible feelings of the people involved.

Being a "feeler" is not the same as being illogical. Feelers have the same capacity for logic as others—they just prefer to focus on emotional reactions and personal values when making decisions. They give more weight to what their emotions and values tell them about a situation and how aspects of the situation have an impact on the emotions of those involved.

As people experience more in life, they try to balance emotions and logic in dealing with the world. Sometimes, though, especially in family and romantic relationships, they need to be reminded about that balance.

Research into this dimension suggests that thinkers often marry feelers, probably to get the balance right. Men tend to find it easier to have a successful relationship with women who have a thinking or half-and-half style, and women have more successful relationships with men who have a feeling or half-and-half style.

Thinking Style

In their personal and work lives, people who more closely fit the "thinker" profile are likely to:

- refer frequently to the facts and logic of a situation or idea, and not talk much about feelings
- consider fair, honest criticism as a natural and acceptable process. They do not avoid conflict.
- be blunt and focus on what they believe to be the "truth" and see truth as more important than tact
- focus strongly on fairness and justice
- seem cold or insensitive and may accidentally hurt others' feelings
- get upset and irritated if "rules" are not followed or enforced, because rules represent logical order
- enjoy the process of "debate" and see it as a thinking exercise rather than an argument
- assume that people know that they like and value them,

because it "goes without saying." Similarly, they often will not say, "I love you," "You look great," or "You did well," because they think it is obvious.

- see flaws and tend to be critical
- want to be treated fairly.

Feeling Style

People who more closely fit the "feeler" profile are likely to:

- prefer to give more weight to personal convictions and subjective values
- decide with the heart
- be more concerned with relationships and harmony
- try to see things as though a participant within a situation, that is, to try to empathize
- dislike telling people unpleasant facts and so find it difficult to confront or fire people
- like to please others
- believe people work better if they know that you understand their feelings
- imagine others' feelings are hurt, because theirs would have been in the same situation
- want to be treated kindly
- tend to avoid conflict, criticism, and confrontation.

THINKERS SAY	FEELERS SAY
Look at the logic of the situation.	But what about their feelings?
That doesn't make any sense.	But that's how it feels to me.
Let's look at the facts here.	What good are facts if you don't consider how people respond to the facts?
You haven't convinced me with your argument.	It just feels like the right thing to do.

THINKERS SAY	FEELERS SAY
Let's list the pros and cons.	I have a good feeling about this.
I can see no good reason to do this so let's say no.	Let's keep the peace and say yes.
I'm sorry but I have to fire you. I will give you a good reference.	Due to some cost cutting, we may have to let you go, but I am trying to find another position for you.
But it isn't logical. How can you ignore the facts and be so illogical?	I wouldn't be comfortable doing it the other way. How can you be so cold and callous?

Looking on the Bright Side

STRENGTHS OF THINKERS	STRENGTHS OF FEELERS
Brave about conflict ("It has to be faced.")	Concern for relationships and harmony
More direct and up front	Shows kindness and compassion toward others
Logical analysis	Boosts others' morale and self-confidence
Can reprimand and fire more readily ("I know this will distress his family, but we simply need to cut costs and that's all there is to it.")	Checks up on people who might be upset and monitors the emotional and social "temperature" of situations.

What about Gender?

There are more thinkers in the population than feelers. More males are thinkers, partly due to socializing factors that help decide our gender identity. Evidence suggests that women's brains function more effectively in terms of empathy.

• • •

Potential Problems and Ways to Deal with Them

Accept that you are dealing with differences, not better or lesser ways. Differences need to be respected and not seen as defects. If you are a thinker, accept that there is a place for the emotional perspective in any argument or decision. Acknowledge the validity of both approaches; keep an open mind and don't misjudge.

There are some predictable areas where thinkers and feelers might be at odds. Here are a few, followed by suggestions as to how to deal with them.

Communication

Thinkers do not talk about emotions, and can seem cold and uncaring to feelers. Feelers may seem illogical and too emotional if you are a thinker.

What You Can Do

- Watch your language if you are a feeler. Remind yourself that thinkers' focus on logic can be misleading and that they may still have deep feelings about the issue being discussed. Listen for implied emotions in the conversation of thinkers. Ask directly, "But what are your personal feelings on this?" You often get a different response when you ask directly about how they feel. Thinkers are not necessarily deliberately withholding their feelings, but they are using a different language to discuss their reactions.
- Feelers should use more facts and cause-and-effect explanations. Refer to the logic and facts of the situation, as well as reminding thinkers about other ways of seeing a situation. You can say, for example, "Yes, I can see that there is an inconsistency in part of what I am saying, but people's feelings matter, too."
- Thinkers can pay more attention in conversations that refer to feelings.

Conflict and Problem Solving

Feelers may focus too much on the emotions of the situation, and thinkers will focus on them too little. Each may see the other as inept or handling a situation in the "wrong" way.

What You Can Do

- Anticipate. With a romantic partner who has a different style from yours, expect problems over potentially emotional issues such as disciplining children or dealing with money. In a working situation, expect problems over such issues as unions, management, friendships, idealistic areas, promotions, and salaries.
- Thinkers want to discuss issues objectively, and they analyze, clarify, and strategize solutions. Feelers, therefore, need to listen to this way of seeing things and acknowledge the equal validity: "Yes, what you are saying makes sense in lots of ways, but there is another side to this, too."
- Feelers should respect and value thinkers' ideas but point out that there is an emotional perspective, too. Be assertive about the importance of balancing the emotional and logical perspective. Do not always back down because the thinker has convinced you that logic is the only way to go.
- Thinkers need to accept that certain decisions can be made effectively on the basis of emotions and values, even if they are less logical. Give in on those issues.
- Thinkers should stop and listen to feelings, not just rush into problem solving. Be tactful. Ask, "How you feel about . . . ?" rather than, "What do you think about. . . ?" Validate feelings first. This simply means saying aloud that you have heard their feelings and are accepting them rather than telling the person that they shouldn't have them. Say, for example, "Yes, I know you feel angry about what happened last time we went there."
- Thinkers will tend to confront more, and feelers will tend to shy away more from conflict in order to maintain harmony. Each needs to move toward the center. Feelers should be more prepared to deal with conflict (see chapter 21), and thinkers should understand that not everything needs to be confronted.

Sensitivity

Thinkers often hurt others' feelings without realizing why. ("Why would that upset you? It wouldn't have upset me if you had said it.") They can be blunt and focus on "truth" and are often tactless. They may also spontaneously criticize, find flaws, and forget to balance their negative comments with positive ones.

What You Can Do

- Use more positives and cut back on the negatives if you are a thinker.
- Thinkers enjoy the process of debate and can become "logically competitive." If you are a thinker, use this rational self-statement both at work and in your personal life: "The relationship is more important than being right."
- Thinkers are less likely to compliment or make statements of appreciation, which feelers need more than others.
- Thinkers assume you realize that if you have been working well together, they must appreciate your input. As they see it, why should you need to be told? It is not logical. Similarly, they often fail to tell their partner that they love them, that they appreciate a special effort, that they look good, etc. For example, "Why don't you realize I love you, think you're attractive, etc. I'm still here, aren't I?" Feelers may assume that thinkers' failure to do this means they do not care. Instead, ask them directly. If the thinkers hedge, say something like, "Yes, I know I am probably a bit insecure and in need of reassurance, but I like to know how you feel/that I look good, etc."

Alysha was a fairly extreme feeler and David a very extreme thinker. This difference caused them a few problems. When they couldn't agree on something, David felt frustrated because of what he saw as Alysha's inability to be logical. Alysha grew increasingly angry because she couldn't make him see that there were other ways to make a decision apart from logic. One situation that caused them a lot of anger was related to Paul, her son from her first marriage. David felt that Paul, now 19, expected too much from his mother.

Paul was in college in another state and, unlike David's two children, didn't have a part-time job. He constantly called his mother for money and expected her to drop everything and change her plans if he had a problem or crisis.

Alysha usually did this and it made David very angry. He believed this was not helping Paul mature and learn to take responsibility. He was angry, too, that Paul was not respecting Alysha's right to her own life.

Alysha, however, realized that Paul was slow to mature. He had always needed more support than others, and she sensed that if she didn't support him he might not stay in college. His marks were not great and he was struggling to develop a social network.

Heated arguments occurred, with Alysha calling David "unfeeling" and "too tough," and David saying that Alysha would ruin her son if she didn't look more objectively at what was happening. Finally, after many exhausting and angry encounters, they sought help from a counselor about this issue, which was threatening their relationship. It didn't take long, just three sessions. After realizing that both perceptions were legitimate ways to look at the situation and that neither way was right or wrong, they were able to make accommodations. Alysha accepted that David could be very helpful to her in setting some firmer limits about what Paul could and could not expect. David also accepted that Alysha's "emotional" reading of the situation was probably accurate. She did need to give Paul more support than his children required of him.

PART

II

Frustrating and Annoying Personality Patterns

5

Built-in Flaw Detectors

NEGATIVITY

What is Typical of Most People

Can anyone honestly claim that they never badmouth, spread rumors, look on the gloomy side, make nasty or sarcastic comments, criticize, or complain? We all do it, but when the frequency and intensity of this kind of negativity becomes a personality pattern, it can turn into a major headache for us and others.

What is Typical of Negative People

A person can be considered to have a pattern of negativity if their approach to many areas of their life is characterized by criticizing, finding the flaw, being pessimistic, badmouthing, damaging reputations or using putdowns. Usually, there will be agreement by others that this pattern goes across people and situations. This personality pattern arises mainly because of low self-esteem and petty, irrational thinking.

Negative people alienate others. They find it hard to develop good relationships and maintain them over the long term. They wear people out, and can be very destructive in an organization and to individuals in many ways. First, others recognize the low self-worth that negativity signals, and they try to avoid working with that person. Second, negativity is contagious, and if you're nearby, you can start doing it, too, and then you don't like yourself. Or you become so artificially and unrelentingly positive, and Pollyannaish to counteract their negativity, that it is a strain. Third, people who are always negative signal that they are going through life hyper-critically, which means that they are doing it to you, too. It doesn't feel safe to be around them in case you make a mistake, or show a weakness and they broadcast it or file it away for later use. What they do to others, they are likely to do to you.

Negative people do these things in different combinations.

They Psychologically "Maim" as They Name, Shame, or Blame

They name-call, put down, insult, or use derogatory terms when talking about someone, or directly to them. For example: "John's really tight with money," or "Gail is always right, aren't you, Gail?"

They try to make others feel ashamed if they have made a mistake, or even when they haven't. For example: "Surely you realized the impact that would have on the budget?," or "How can you live with yourself, after saying what you did?" Often, though, their "shaming" tactics are much more subtle than this.

They allocate blame whenever they can and ensure that you and everyone else knows when something was, or might have been, "your fault." Often, they are very good at blaming you for everything that goes wrong in their life.

They Engage in "Negative Inflation"

They take one negative or apparently negative fact about you and turn it into a generalization. For example, if they observe that you are late to work one morning (even though you may have already attended a breakfast meeting), this becomes, when they report it to others, "He is frequently late to work."

They jump from a suspicion to a fact. For example, Tammi believed that her boss and his counterpart in another department were possibly having an affair. She had seen them having coffee together on a Saturday morning and this became, in the retelling, "They are having an affair."

They "negatively inflate" or "puff up" any bad news, so it sounds more dramatic.

They Happily Spread Rumors and Stories against Other People

Speaking in a hushed, conspiratorial tone, they say, "Of course, you know what really happened, don't you...?" Also, they make sure that everyone is told more than once.

They never keep a secret or act in a loyal fashion toward colleagues.

They "Doom and Gloom"

Focusing on whatever might go wrong, they assume that the worst will happen. Then they verbalize this over and over. Their most frequently used expression is, "Probably what will happen is . . ." (refer to the section on protective pessimism on page 111).

They "Bitch and Snitch"

They make nasty remarks about others and their motivations. What they say may contain some grain of truth, but it is usually said in a sneering way designed to ruin reputations and leave others with a negative impression of the target.

They "Moan and Groan"

They complain all the time, even about trivial things. Finding the unpleasant or annoying aspect, they will focus on this, and then communicate their unhappiness and intolerance.

They Carry an "Automatic Flaw Detector" Wherever They Go

If there is a flaw or an error, they will find it. For example, if a name is captioned under the wrong photo in the annual report, they will notice it. If you forgot to do one thing, they will harp on it to the exclusion of the many things you did accomplish.

Their working hypothesis is: "Mistakes and flaws are the most interesting things to focus on. Identifying them in others' lives can bring them down and make you feel superior."

They Often Act as Martyrs

Sometimes negative people publicly paint a picture of themselves as being the victims of uncaring or lazy others whom they have to tolerate or "carry" without thanks or reward.

Why They Do It

When it is a pattern of negativity across situations, time and people, it might be for the following reasons:

- Many have a marked sense of inferiority and low self-esteem. They believe others don't recognize or acknowledge their worth and that they have not received the recognition they deserve. So they draw attention to themselves by acting in a critical or self-sacrificing manner, which they make apparent to all in a painful way.
- Being negative brings people down, forcing them to acknowledge their mistakes, and this damages reputations. They believe that this makes the successes of their victims less impressive to others.
- For some, it is one way of being passively hostile to others or a specific person (see chapter 13).
- This is the main way they have learned to get social recognition. They know things that others don't. Since they "own" the bad news, they have status as the teller, and it makes them the center of attention.
- Rumor, bad news, or complaints can all be antidotes to boredom.
- They may have influential role models who showed them by example. Or did it to them.
- Some people with unrecognized mild levels of depression can be very negative and critical.

The Gender Factor

Gender is not a factor. Despite the belief of some men that women "gossip" more and are more "bitchy," this is unsupported by research. Men seem to do it just as much, but they give it a different label, such as "office politics" or "power games."

• • •

What about the Kids?

At school, children with a pattern of negativity usually have low levels of social acceptance. Popular kids are positive more than they are negative.

Strategies for Dealing with Another's Negativity

- Don't reinforce the negativity. Respond by raising your eyebrows, saying, "Really?" and then changing the topic.
- Walk away, without being offensive.
- Try not to be alone with them. Dilute them with other people's company.
- If you have to work with them, remind yourself not to succumb to their negativity, and find ways to stay positive about the work you are doing.
- Let others know that the negative person should be only "half-believed" because of their negativity (but try not to do this in a negative way!).
- Be assertive when necessary and say something like, "Let's break out of the doom and gloom mode. It's bringing us down." Or "Yes, you may be right about her, but none of us is perfect."
- Counterbalance every negative with a positive in conversation and action.
- If the negativity is related to boredom, increase and vary the workload.
- Where possible, provide other ways for them to feel important and to be the center of attention. They will be less negative if they feel they are being acknowledged for their "real worth."
- If the person is elderly, distract them with diversions such as new hobbies and other attentions.

Strategies for Dealing with Your Own Negativity

- Identify your own pattern. Be brutally frank with yourself.
- Do a reality check and ask someone close to you: "Do you think I am a negative person?"

- Don't ignore feedback from people who act toward you with goodwill—for example, close friends, family, or coworkers who drop hints that you are being negative about a few people or things in your life.
- Remind yourself about the damage it will do to your relationships with your partner, family, friends, or colleagues. Getting a reputation as "negative" or a "moaner" may be damaging to your career or home life.
- Try rational self-talk.
- Make and use a prompting card (see page 265) that says something like: "I need to focus on the good things instead," or "Being negative will damage my relationships and my acceptance."
- Double up on the positives. Make a resolution to praise rather than disparage. Look for assets rather than liabilities. Have an "optimistic week" in which you stress the positives, in your head and aloud.

Our neighbor, who was in her forties, was known locally as "The Whiner." She had lived in the area for quite a while, but the neighbors in the street tended to change. She wrote letters to the local paper complaining about the dogs who "did their business" in her front yard. She called the mayor's office frequently to pick up strays. When the teenagers from the house on the other side told her in advance about their end-of-school party, which would finish at one AM, she complained to everybody beforehand, and on the night of the party called three times to complain about the noise. Every day she walked to the local shop for the paper, and spoke to any customers and the owner about how rundown the neighborhood was becoming. Newcomers to the row of houses across the street were greeted with an introductory summary of each resident's flaws. For example, they didn't take their trash cans in, let their dog roam, should paint their fence, etc. She volunteered as a street organizer for Neighborhood Watch and kept an eye on everything. In charitable moments, neighbors said, "She was lonely" and "just loved to gossip," but after a while the barrage of negative comments got them down. They would cross the street if they saw her delivering

Neighborhood Watch pamphlets. While agreeing that the "watch" concept was excellent, they wished she wouldn't keep criticizing the neighbors. Her family didn't visit often anymore, and she complained that they had all turned out to be selfish and thoughtless. The reality was that they didn't enjoy her company because her conversation and focus were always negative and complaining. She always made them feel as if they hadn't done the right thing by her, even when they had!

6

I'm Better Than You!

SUPERIORITY

What Is Typical of Most People?

Smugness and arrogance may characterize our behavior occasionally. On meeting certain people, we may feel superior, assuming we look after our health better, are better educated, etc. A sense of self-satisfaction in particular parts of our life can become our "armor" in a challenging world. Occasionally we go past being pleased with ourselves, into feeling smug and superior. With maturity, though, we temper this with the lessons from life. Experiences teach us that we are all imperfect, there is much we don't know, can't do or control, and misfortune or good fortune can strike randomly.

What Is Typical of Those with a Superiority Pattern?

This pattern of behavior gives a strong message of superiority ("I'm better than you") across many areas and causes significant distress to others. It is a very alienating pattern. Youth is characteristically arrogant and smug simply because young people have not lived long enough to learn those humbling lessons of life. So the older person with this pattern is of greater concern.

There are three main categories of behavior demonstrated by people who act as if they are superior to you. Interestingly, people who may genuinely be considered superior do not necessarily feel nor act this way. Allowing for some overlap, the categories are: smugness, arrogance, and superiority by osmosis.

Smugness

The *Oxford Dictionary* defines a person who is smug as "self-satisfied, complacent, respectable, and narrow-minded." Colloquially, they are described as a "pain in the neck."

The smug person thinks, "I've got it right," or "My attitude is the correct one," or "I know what's right and others don't," or "I've been able to do things other people haven't." Smug persons are not just pleased with themselves, they are also judgmental, implying that others are inferior, even when such an assessment is unfounded.

Their working hypothesis is: "I am better than you because I have made the right choices and behaved in the right ways. My way is the only way."

Smug people are sure that they know more about what is right and what is important than others do. They feel superior and slightly sorry for you. They are glad they are not you and their need to "hint" at this, or rub it in, is overwhelming. Reminding you of their correct choices and behavior makes them feel even more superior.

It never occurs to them that they might be wrong, limited, or possess only one way of looking at a situation. It does not cross their mind that they may have been luckier or more advantaged than others. Often, irrational or ignorant comments are made, but they are done with such assurance that they are difficult to challenge.

Smugness is based on a self-satisfied or self-righteous attitude. Pride is similar to smugness in that there is self-satisfaction, but generally in a measurable achievement. An entrepreneur, for example, may have pride in building a small business, but "smugness" would be associated with a sense that their achievement made them a superior person because no one else could do it

Arrogance

Smugness is usually implied or hinted at. A smug person's belief in their own superiority is not directly stated or acted on. Those who directly say, "I'm better than you," or do not behave respectfully in ways that treat you as an equal, are demonstrating arrogant behavior. This is the next step up from smugness.

The working hypothesis of an arrogant person is: "I'm superior to most people and therefore much more important, and I can't be bothered pretending that I'm not. Sometimes I have to put them in their place."

In the workplace, arrogant responses may be given to genuine requests for necessary information. For example, Terry, the electrical subcontractor on the site of the new office building, asked the builder, "When can I get access to the building?"

The builder replied without even looking at Terry, "When I tell you that you can have it."

Here are some of the characteristic behaviors of an arrogant person:

- often saying, in different ways, that they are better than you and most others
- being dismissive toward you
- being snobbish
- insisting that only their "expert way" is acceptable
- ignoring you in decision making. The impact of decisions on you will not be a consideration.
- publicly sneering at what is important to you
- being rude and discourteous in the way they speak to you, using a dismissive and bossy tone of voice
- calls are often not returned, or if they are, it takes a long time, as you have low priority on their list
- not apologizing to you after failing to do something or making an error
- they often boast
- they act as know-it-alls, supremely sure that they know everything about an issue or topic and that they couldn't possibly be wrong, ill-informed, out-of-date, or too narrow in how they see things.

Some people show their arrogance by dominating the conversation, cutting across your conversation, implying that your views don't matter. Such conversational "hogs" take up all of the conversational "space" by controlling the topics, often changing the topic abruptly and bringing it back to subjects they want to talk about or in which they have some expertise. They are quite insensitive to the boredom of others, or of their desire to contribute to the conversation in some way.

Superiority by Osmosis

These are people who behave toward others in a way that says, "I am better than you" because they work for or with people who have higher status or more power than the others do. The secretary of the managing director, for example, may behave in a superior way, and keep you waiting, refuse you access, insist that you fill in certain forms beyond what is reasonable before getting equipment.

Why They Do It

- Smug and arrogant people have usually had limited life experiences. Having led narrow lives, their understanding is limited. Lacking the analytical skills to see a bigger picture, they generalize from their own narrow scene.
- They may be envious of your life, so they become smug in the area where they believe they can "best" you.
- The use of black-and-white thinking often produces smugness and arrogance. Those who think this way do not perceive the world as "gray," that is, complex, often ambiguous, and unpredictable in many ways. Those who have learned from life are more humble, irrespective of their achievements.
- Giving themselves undue credit for positives in their lives, they do not acknowledge the role of good and bad fortune or others' contributions.
- They may overcompensate for what they know are areas of "vulnerability" (for example, a person from an impoverished background can become the worst snob of all).
- Limited skills of empathy, which is the ability to understand the world through another's eyes, shows in their lack of respect for another's perspective.
- Smug or arrogant parents may have shown them how to do it, and passed on the attitude.
- They have developed no habits of self-reflection or analysis and thus do not recognize their own imperfection.
- They don't seek other people's opinions, invite feedback, or monitor the reactions of others, so the outcome is no change.

- The "conversation dominators" often have poor social skills and are unable to accurately "read" others' reactions. They really do believe that you think they are wonderful. They fail to understand that socially competent people (who genuinely do impress others) take turns at conversing.

- Some conversation dominators are anxious rather than arrogant. They are worried about the impression they are making on you. Doubting their own worth, they want people to think they are wonderful and be impressed by them. Mistakenly, they believe that the more they talk and show how clever and knowledgeable they are, the more you will be impressed. How do you know the difference? The arrogant person doesn't check with you, but the nervous one will check out your responses, and yet they are so wound up, they will continue talking. They are not game to "give up the floor" until they have made their impression on you.

- Officious people have no reason to feel superior except for some small degree of power from controlling the rules, or from being connected to a powerful person. They wield their pseudo-power by making you jump through hoops to get what you want, and by insisting that you must do things their way. Underneath, they realize their own limited power.

Strategies for Dealing with People with a Superiority Approach

- Recognize the pattern and understand the motive. If these people are important in your life, tolerate as much as you can.

- Model self-reflection. Acknowledge the role of good fortune (for example, "I shudder sometimes when I think how my life might have been different if I hadn't been given assistance in getting out before the collapse of the parent company").

- Be tactful in pointing out the obvious, that it was luck as well, not just skill. Say up front, but inoffensively, how much you have learned about the role of fortune and how you respect people who haven't had it easy.

- Openly debate how much we can feel smug or arrogant about our lives when there are random factors influencing them all the time. This is like, "There but for the grace of God go I."
- For dominators, change the conversation. First ask a lot of questions that require short answers. Then use a linking comment like, "Speaking of new machines…did you hear about…" and change the conversation.
- Ignore them when you can.
- Say, "Really?" in a condescending manner with your eyebrows raised (and say nothing more!).
- Just smile, look at them, and say nothing when they start being smug or arrogant. Occasionally just say, "Mmm."
- Express a contrary opinion without being offensive. Say something like, "Well, you could be right about that in some ways, but. . ."
- Respond assertively if on the receiving end of arrogant behavior.

Strategies for Changing Your Own Superiority Approach

Use more mature and rational thinking. This involves:

- making charitable interpretations of others' circumstances and behavior (that is, think of a kind way to interpret them that doesn't dismiss or totally blame them)
- recognizing that differences are not necessarily defects. There are many equally valid ways.
- accepting that cause and effect cannot be generalized just from your personal, isolated example
- accepting that although we may be better than others in some areas, they surpass us elsewhere. It balances out. This offsets the tendency to be judgmental.
- acknowledging that random good fortune (being born clever and attractive; having a child with an "easy" temperament; being born to wealthy parents; having a timely skill that fast-tracks your career) is often one of the reasons

people have good lives. Credit can be taken for making the most of an opportunity, but similarly, misfortune can mean that some have to work very hard just to stay buoyant. That needs to be recognized and respected, too.

- understanding that random misfortune can befall anyone, at any time, without any contribution from the recipients
- realizing that nobody is perfect, that we all have our imperfections
- seeing that most situations are gray, not black-and-white
- knowing that nothing is permanent
- starting the habit of self-reflection and focusing on your own imperfections to remind you not to judge others
- being open-minded. Other people have equally valid viewpoints and directions.
- not judging until you have been where they have been
- not taking full credit for things that are partly circumstantial (you were in the right place at the right time.)
- realizing that anything can change very quickly, and today's millionaire may be tomorrow's bankrupt in financial or emotional terms.
- recognizing "smugness" retrospectively, even if it's your own; this can increase tolerance.

Lexi and her husband had decided not to have children. As their contemporaries had children or grandchildren, Lexi loudly stressed the advantages of not having dependents and being a couple rather than a family. At first friends were diplomatic, being uncertain whether the child-free existence was voluntary or there were medical problems. They accepted the use of "child-free" rather than "childless" as a legitimate term. But as Lexi and her husband continued to stress, "We don't need to get a babysitter" and "We can afford tickets to the concert because we don't have children to pay for," and criticizing parental decisions with comments such as: "If he were my child, I'd do such and such," friends became annoyed by the assumption of superiority that one lifestyle was better than another.

7

I Have All the Power,
I Know All the Answers

BOSSINESS

KEY WORDS FOR BOSSY PEOPLE
mistrust
criticism
arrogance
power
control

What Is Typical of Most People?

Bossiness is about being in charge, taking over, controlling, dominating, making all the decisions, telling others what to do, insisting, reminding, not trusting, and criticizing.

Everybody is a bit bossy at times, especially when in a position of some power. Power is simply being able to make what you want to happen actually happen. We have power as parents (less and less as children grow into teenagers and young adults), as senior staff, and in certain jobs such as police officer or teacher. But even when we have authority, we find that being bossy is less effective than respecting, requesting, delegating, or negotiating. During emergency conditions we "boss" because there is no time for a more democratic and respectful process. In personal relationships, bossiness can be very damaging if it becomes a chronic pattern.

· · ·

What Is Typical of Bossy People?

"Bossiness" is a balance of what is said, the tone, and whether the person has the right to direct others' behavior. Bossy people act in a parental way as if the person they are bossing is a small child with no knowledge, skills, experiences, or rights. A pattern exists if the bossiness is excessive to the point that others comment and if it occurs in multiple situations in the person's life.

There are two main categories of "bossy" people.

A "Bossy Boss"

A bossy person can be one who does have power or authority over you but handles it disrespectfully. They tell you directly what to do in a pushy way, using an arrogant tone and often in public. The manner in which they exercise their right to direct your behavior is insensitive and dictatorial. They say things like: "you will have to. . . ," or "go and do . . ."

Their message is always, "Do as I say, now!" They direct you to act immediately with no thought of how inconvenient or disruptive that might be for you. They override any reservations you have about the appropriateness of the direction or its timing. They don't listen to you. Lacking manners, they rarely say, "Please," "Thank you," "May I," or "Excuse me." Interrupting or standing alongside, they listen to your conversation until you stop talking to the other person because you feel so uncomfortable. Because they do not trust you to do something, they remind constantly. And you get no choices or opportunities to influence decisions.

Their working hypothesis is: "When I have more power than someone else, I do not need to speak to them respectfully and equally. They are of no importance compared to me. What I want is more important than what they want."

In contrast, good bosses do not boss. Usually they diplomatically direct, lead by example, or suggest. They delegate and trust, allow you to have a say, listen, respect your right to delay a requested action under some circumstances, and answer your questions.

• • •

Those Who Assume Power over You That They Do Not Have

Although not in a position of authority over you, they assume they know best and that you know nothing. They do not trust or respect you to make correct decisions or perform efficiently. They assume overall control without justification. Despite feeling annoyed, because you don't think they have the right, you still find yourself being pushed into doing things their way. And you are annoyed with yourself for not standing up to them.

Their working hypothesis is: "People should pay attention to me and do what I say because I know best and I should be in charge."

Here are some of the behaviors underpinned by a bossy orientation.

Being Overly "Kind and Helpful"

This type of bossy person is overwhelming and offers misguided care. Often decisions are made without your being consulted, and you are expected to be pleased that they have done it for you. Acting as a benign dictator, they undermine your right to make a choice.

They assume command for decisions that should be personal choices or negotiated. This person often acts like a bossy parent and nags. You are not trusted to be competent, so you feel offended rather than grateful for their organizing. An example would be a friend who instructs you on the type of clothes you should wear and even buys expensive personal items that "suit" you without consulting you and expects you to pay for them.

The Officious or "Letter of the Law" Type

Officious people insist on the "letter" rather than the "spirit" of the law. Even when common sense suggests "bending the rules," they insist that the rules under their charge be observed scrupulously. Obviously, it is common sense in some situations, to follow the rules, but at other times it is the person, not the system, that is making you jump through hoops. Minor rules and regulations become more important than the original goals for which they were set up. For example, the cashier who closes up, right on the dot, ignoring the needs of the one remaining customer who has been in line for a long time. "See how powerful I am," this person says by their behavior. "I control rules."

Why They Do It

Anxiety and Lack of Trust Often Contribute to Bossiness

- Some people fear not being respected. This may be linked to a big disappointment or a problem caused by another in the past. Their trust has been challenged. They are fearful of being "let down" again, and their bossiness is a way of offsetting their anxiety over what could happen.
- A tendency to overcontrol and an inability to delegate often accompanies bossiness. Anxious that they will not be able to control outcomes, they may trust only their own decisions and fear allowing others to make critical decisions. Only when they are sure that they can control do they feel less anxious. There are more details on overcontrolling behavior on page 119. Refer also to chapter 11 on "The Inflexible Personality" (page 126), because bossiness can be part of that pattern, too.

Lower Levels of Empathy

Some are more limited in their capacity to stop and think about how another will respond to their actions.

It Is All the Power They Have in Their Life

The little power they do have, they overuse. The "little person" with the "little power" and a "big voice" often confirms that a little power can be a dangerous thing!

Arrogance

Certain people genuinely believe that they are superior, and have the right to tell you what to do with no consideration for your feelings or dignity. They lack social sensitivity and have a low level of empathy. That is, they do not "sense" how people are reacting to their assumed superiority.

Strategies for Dealing with a Bossy Person

Getting a person to do something for you that they don't want to do, or would prefer to do at some other time, is a genuine skill. Staff sometimes confuse management with bossiness. Developing managerial competence takes time, and professional training to develop these skills may be needed.

Do not confuse organizational skills with bossiness. A good organizer may have limited time in which to complete a task on their behalf as well as yours. To get it done on time, they may be less democratic and order you around more than you would like, but they aren't necessarily being bossy unless it is a pervasive pattern (that is, across many situations), which causes people to find them difficult.

Be wary. Bossy people will hassle but not attack or seriously harm you. Nevertheless, they can make a workplace unbearable. They can also damage personal relationships in the long term, as their lack of trust and respect toward their partner takes its toll. No one enjoys being treated like a inexperienced child and spoken to as an inferior. Bossy people need to be kept in check so that they do not see you as someone whom they can continue to "boss." Ultimately, they demoralize you, bringing on feelings of anger and resentment.

Discussion with a bossy person is preferable to divorce, dismissal, desertion, or unemployment. And assertiveness is preferable to running away.

Try to Understand and Be Charitable about Their Behavior

Remind yourself that the bossy colleague or family member may be feeling anxious, and is attempting to control their anxiety by bossing you around. If their bossiness is only a small aspect of the whole person you can live with it by occasionally being assertive. In some cases, people are bossy in one part of their lives but not in others.

Do Not Let It Go Once You Have Identified the Pattern

If people don't know you are upset, they will tend to repeat the bossiness. If you explain your reaction, they are less inclined to be bossy next time. This works best when the person has "assumed" power over you, rather than having official power over you.

Be Assertive (also refer to page 233)

- Tackle bossiness in private, rather than in public.
- Use I-messages, and remember to say both how you feel and what you want. For example: "When you make a request but

speak to me as though I'm a child who can't be trusted, I feel that I am not respected. I consider myself to be a competent person. I would prefer that you speak to me respectfully."

Anticipate and Tolerate Where You Can

- Be a little more tolerant for "bossed" situations when the other person is overtired, stressed, or feeling that things are getting out of control. Make a charitable interpretation such as, "When she is worried about planning a big family function, like now, she tends to feel a bit overwhelmed and then she starts to get bossy. I'll give her a cuddle instead and say, "Honey, it will be okay, honest it will."
- If they are your superior, and more direct approaches have not worked, you may have to tolerate their bossiness. Focus on those aspects of their management that are positive and remind yourself about them often. Stress the positives when you are discussing the issue with colleagues.

Look at Yourself

Ask yourself if you are giving them reasons not to trust you, and hence act in a bossy fashion toward you. Passive-aggressive behavior can elicit bossy behavior (see page 145).

Focus on the Potential Workplace Damage and Confront Gently

- If you are the boss, take the "bossy" person aside and reassure them that their work is valuable and appreciated. Say, however, that you feel they might get a better response from people if they managed rather than directed. Explain about delegation and how it is linked to higher productivity.
- Telling someone who is in a higher position than you that they are bossy is harder, but try, especially if you are not too far below them in status. Explain that some people have asked (don't specify who) for more freedom for independent action. If staff have left the workplace, point out that it could be worth trusting people more with decisions to see if it reduces staff loss. Let the bossy person know that you understand their concerns about productivity and per-

formance, but reassure them that this way of respecting and trusting might be a better way of achieving outcomes.

Consider Discussing the Issue with a Superior

Discuss the issue with someone in an equal-status position to the bossy person whose behavior causes distress. Do not just criticize them. Explain all the positives about the person, and stress your loyalty to them. State your one concern and say how it is causing discomfort and irritation. Ask for direct advice or if there is some way in which they can help to get the message across. Explain that this is not a general complaint about the person, but rather a specific concern which you hope can be addressed. Do not give the bossy person reason to believe that you are an enemy. Do not give the person whose support you seek reason to believe that you are a complainer who undermines your superior.

Don't Respond as the Bossy Person Wants You To

Say a polite "No, I appreciate the thought/idea, but…" if you don't believe the person has the right to direct you.

Rotate Power

"Little dictators" can be found among some voluntary officials of sports clubs, cultural organizations, and any other type of organization. They insist that procedures and meetings have to be run according to their dictates. Other members regard them as "bossy" but are appreciative of the hack work they do. Rotating responsibilities may be a way of lessening opportunities for this kind of behavior.

Use Humor

Say something like, "Okay Fred, I promise to…if you will…" and suggest an exchange that highlights in a nonaggressive way that they are not perfect either. For example, "I promise to keep my statistics up to date if you promise to not fall behind with your coffee money."

Reward Them When They Do the Opposite

On an occasion when they do not boss you, or when they treat you with more respect than they usually do, say: "Thanks for trusting me on that job," or "I always work better when a manager treats me with respect, as you just did when you . . ."

Leave

If other strategies have not produced changes (even small changes can help) then consider asking for a transfer, withdrawing from shared activities where the person has opportunities to inflict their bossy behavior on you, or leaving.

Strategies for Change if You Are Bossy

Recognize that there could be a problem. Directly ask people you trust, "Do I sometimes act too bossily?" If you have been accused of being "bossy" is it when:

- you're tired?
- you feel you have more appropriate skills?
- there is a time pressure?

Hypersensitive people might just be oversensitive to your managerial methods, but it is possible that you need to be more sensitive in the way you speak. Assess whether someone is using the label of "nag" or "bossy" as a way of controlling you or putting you down. If you are a woman, this could be the case when a male colleague refers to you as "bossy." Staff are likely to retaliate against a "bossy" person who gives out the message "you are nothing." They may play practical jokes, make the person look foolish, or simply not cooperate.

Check Constantly

"Is that okay?" Run a few ideas past your friends or colleagues, rather than dictating.

Say:

- How about…?
- What if we…?
- How do you feel about…?
- Any ideas for. . . ?

Objectify the Problem

Rather than ordering others about, make the request less personal. For example, "The lightbulb needs changing," rather than, "you need to fix the light."

Use "We" Instead of "You"

For example, "We need to get the new posters up," rather than, "I want you to put up the new posters." This is a more trusting and delegating message.

Offer Some Leeway with Time

Recognize that the timing of the person who undertakes a task you have requested might not be entirely to your liking. It can help to add a time line, for example, "We need this done within the week," rather than, "This needs to be done now."

Use Courtesy

Are you working on the assumption that although there is no leader, someone has to lead the group, so you take over? If so, have the courtesy to check that it is all right with the others. Ask them, for example, "How about I oversee the big picture?"

"Bossy" probably isn't a strong enough word to describe Sue. She always acted as though she was really important and was the only one among us who had standards. Although she was in a support role and only in charge of a few of the other staff (and not me!) she carried on as though she was God! To give you one example: when I asked her for the key to the room where particular files were kept she insisted that I leave my office keys with her so that if I forgot to return them, I wouldn't be able to lock my own office later that night or get into my car. I just went gaga! How dare she imply that I couldn't be trusted to return the keys and that therefore she had to make sure that I didn't screw up! She had no right to do it but she clearly thought that somehow she was in charge of making sure we behaved as she thought we ought. The clear message was: "You can't be trusted and I can so I'll have to act like your parent and tell you what you can and can't do."

Terri, 33, administrator

Confusing Personality Types

8

The World Is Such a Dangerous Place!

THE ANXIOUS PERSONALITY

KEY WORDS FOR ANXIETY-BASED BEHAVIOR PATTERNS
---

anxiety

worry

avoidant

fear

"flooders"

caution

adrenaline

What Is Typical for Most People?

Essentially, the two things that anxiety reflects are fear of being physically hurt or killed, and encountering psychological harm in the form of shame. The world cannot be completely safe and perfect. None of us can completely avoid criticism or mistakes. Every now and then all of us go through days in which we become excessively preoccupied about being negatively evaluated, rejected, failing, making mistakes, losing things that are important to us, or being alienated from people that we love, and about the pressures of being responsible adults. Eventually, rationally, we acknowledge that we are not perfect, that it is human to make mistakes and there are many parts of the future as well as the present that we can't control. But while dealing with these realities, we all experience anxiety. It is part of a normal and useful alarm system. It lets us know about potential danger, even if it is exaggerated. We need to know when to move fast, get away, or strike out to protect ourselves. Some anxiety is actually a good thing when we are faced with a challenge such as an exam or competitive performance. However, anxiety doesn't overwhelm most people, nor does it occur frequently or in many everyday situations. Most people experience unpleasant but short-lived anxiety when they are in specific stressful or threatening situations, such as being on a plane that hits a turbulent patch, or not knowing whether they are going to be retrenched the next day.

What Is Typical of People with Anxious Personalities?

People with anxious personalities are overreactive to threatening stimuli and are less able to tolerate the normal uncertainties about the future and imperfection because of the "danger" they pose. The reality is that the world is a slightly dangerous place for most, and we need to be reasonably vigilant to protect ourselves. People with anxious personalities, though, tend to develop a general working hypothesis that guides their lives, along the lines of: "The world is a *very* dangerous place and I must always be on my guard to prevent and control any potential threats to my bodily and psychological well-being."

This working hypothesis always operates in the back of their head, but they vary in how much they use and challenge it. The hypothesis develops because so often their bodies are in a state of mild fear even if they don't recognize it as such.

Anxious people have an oversensitive alarm system, which can create problems for them and cause distress to others. They have an anxiety predisposition. We shall use the term "flooders" to describe people with this predisposition, as their bodies are frequently "flooded" with fear hormones, the main two being adrenaline and cortisol.

People with anxious personalities have a heightened fear response and tend to magnify anything potentially threatening so that it seems to be a real and serious danger rather than a possibility. They generalize from one dangerous situation they encounter or read about and see danger everywhere. They are often "scanners" because they constantly scan their situations for potential threat and selectively attend to any signs of danger. Their "fear alarm" is overly sensitive and goes off too quickly and too often. They can cause themselves significant distress and reduce their self-esteem if they do not understand, accept, and manage their anxiety effectively. They can be difficult to work or live with because of some of the ways in which they may express and try to manage their anxiety. They may be difficult in one or more of the following ways. They may:

- home in on every potential problem
- have angry outbursts that hurt others and sometimes damage relationships
- be perfectionists and stress others and themselves by their unrealistic standards
- hoard things and annoy others with their refusal to throw things out
- procrastinate about decisions and actions in case they make a mistake
- be overly cautious and restrict the activities of themselves and others
- sometimes respond hypersensitively and cause conflict by their overreactions
- be overcontrolling as they try to make sure that nothing goes wrong
- be overly dependent on others and thus restrict their actions and exhaust their patience
- be rigidly controlled by routine and annoy others by their inflexibility.

True/False Quiz

1. You can always tell highly anxious people by their nervous mannerisms.

    True   False

2. Anxious people mostly cope by avoiding situations that make them feel anxious.

    True   False

3. People who give public performances as part of their professional role are less anxious than others.

               True   False

4. People with high levels of general anxiety usually had traumatic childhood experiences.

               True   False

5 Highly anxious people are psychologically weaker than others.

               True   False

Answers

1. False. You can't always tell highly anxious people by their mannerisms. Some people with high anxiety do reveal themselves in this way, but many highly anxious people have learned not to show it, except under extreme stress.
2. False. Some anxious people do cope by avoiding situations that make them feel anxious, but most face challenges which elicit anxiety with courage and determination. How much "avoiding" is used to "manage" the anxiety depends upon the severity, the lessons they have learned from life, the situation and how much they understand the process of anxiety.
3. Fear of public speaking is the number one fear for most people. But this statement is false, as people who give public performances as part of their professional role are no more or less anxious than others. Sure, some people are very confident about being publicly "on display" and evaluated (although some anxiety is useful in producing a better performance). But they may also be highly anxious people who have accepted the challenge of public speaking and managing the accompanying anxiety, and then their competence and success reduces ongoing anxiety. Respected stage performers such as Sir Laurence Olivier, Maureen Stapleton, and Carly Simon spoke publicly

about repeated periods in their lives when they were
overwhelmed by anxiety and had to seek support.

4. False. Most people with high levels of anxiety have not had
   traumatic childhood experiences, but some certainly have.
   High anxiety is more likely to start with a biological predisposition to having an adrenaline-releasing brain mechanism that
   is overly sensitive. A predisposition plus early trauma is likely
   to produce high anxiety levels. Many manage those feelings,
   although at times they cope less well than they would like.

5. False. Highly anxious people are not necessarily psychologically weaker than others. Many highly anxious people
   are tough and resilient as a result of the efforts they have
   put into managing their anxiety predisposition, but they
   have to work harder.

What Is Anxiety?

Anxiety is a type of fear. Both fear and anxiety are adaptive reactions to danger. The term "anxiety," rather than "fear," applies
when the danger is not obvious to others, has not yet happened
but is anticipated, or when the apprehension shown by someone
is chronic, that is, present most of the time and across many situations. Anxiety and fear both warn us to be vigilant and make our
bodies physically ready either to run away or defend against the
danger. Hence the term "fight or flight."

How Are Anxiety and Stress Related?

Stress is a form of anxiety, often suppressed and unrecognized for
what it is. The "danger" that occurs when you are feeling stressed is
that you will not have the resources required to meet the demands
being made on you or will be unable to control the situation. You
become scared of being unable to solve the problem, meet the
deadline, resume control that has been upset by others, or meet
the challenges of a task. Stress tends to be restricted to a particular
set of circumstances and hence time-limited. Anxiety, on the other
hand, can be both situation-specific or chronic and pervasive, that

is, affecting many areas of one's life. However, the outcome of a prolonged period of stress may be a longer period of ongoing anxiety and sometimes depression.

Anxiety Hormones Make People More Emotional

If research subjects are given an injection of adrenaline, it tends to intensify their emotional response to almost everything encountered over the next few hours. In one study, people who were injected with adrenaline cried more at sad movies and laughed more at funny ones. So it makes sense to assume that people whose bodies are flooded with adrenaline will have more mood changes and more periods of intense emotion. Those who are flooders tend to be more emotional more often. They tend to feel disappointment more keenly, react with greater distress to rejection or failure, and get more upset over arguments. When criticized, they may become far more distressed than you would expect.

You Can't Always Pick Them

Although flooders are usually more emotional than other people, they do not always show this in the way you would expect or in all areas of their lives. They are likely to be perfectly calm and capable in those areas where they are highly skilled, the situation is clear-cut, they feel competent, or have control. They are not anxious when they do not perceive any danger because things are under their control. Understanding their anxiety, many develop sound coping strategies and learn to keep their emotions and anxiety in check, or talk about this only to people close to them. Others, unfortunately, cope less effectively and become overwhelmed by their anxiety and the emotions generated by it, or behave in alienating ways as they attempt to control it.

Anxiety and Self-Esteem

Chronic anxiety (or chronic stress in certain lifestyles) over a long period causes some people not to cope with events and attacks their confidence. Self-esteem may drop because they perceive themselves as too easily upset, too emotional, out of control, and not coping as well as they would like. We all have self-doubts and learn to ride them out. People with anxious personalities, however, see self-doubts as proof of more danger in their lives.

The Physiology of an Anxiety Predisposition

Three of the most significant neurological factors that are believed to predispose an individual to heightened anxiety are:

- having low or fluctuating levels of serotonin, a neurotransmitting chemical that sends messages to receptors in the brain
- having a "hair-trigger" amygdala (the brain's "fear center")
- having abnormally low concentrations of GABA A-type receptors in certain regions of the brain.

These are all mainly influenced by one's genetic makeup.

Here is how it works: Your brain interprets information received through all of your senses and filters it for danger. It processes threatening sights and sounds in milliseconds, whereas it needs a few full seconds to formulate a thought.

- You smell or taste something and your brain gives meaning to it. What is that smell? Does it mean there is a barbecue or a fire? Why does this dish taste "funny"? Does it mean the food is "off" or just unusual?
- You hear something and your brain identifies it as either "normal" or "threatening." What machine makes a noise like that? Is it relevant to me? Is it dangerous to me?
- You see or touch something and your brain attempts to work out how you should respond to it. Is that someone I know, or are they unknown and perhaps a danger to me? Is that a spider I brushed against or just a cobweb?

In a millisecond, this incoming information is interpreted, that is, given personal meaning. Then these "messages" are passed between brain cells by neurotransmitting chemicals, so called because they transmit messages between nerve cells. The messages are sent to the "correct" neuroreceptor site, according to how we have interpreted them. There are millions of neuroreceptor sites, or reception areas, in the brain. Each has a specific function and "listens" only to messages from a specific neurotransmitting chemical. Each neuroreceptor site is designed like a lock, and the correct neurotransmitting chemical is the key that unlocks it and makes the body respond in a certain way. Although each site responds to a specific neurotransmitting chemical, the same chemical can interact with more than one brain site. In this way, different parts of the brain "talk" to each other and to the rest of the body, and decide what you should do about the messages received.

Serotonin

Serotonin is a naturally occurring neurotransmitting chemical in the brain. It is a chemical messenger that sends messages to the brain that affect sleep, mood, memory, appetite, and fear. Under normal circumstances, your body makes just enough serotonin to function accurately: about 10 mg circulating in your bloodstream. A slight drop in the level can make a crucial difference to your feelings and reactions to threat. If you have less serotonin in your bloodstream than normal over a period of time, these lowered levels can adversely affect how you interpret and deal with fear and mood changes. Fluctuations of serotonin levels are normal and are affected by body rhythms and seasons. The amount of serotonin available at a particular time depends on:

- how much your cells make and excrete
- how quickly it is reabsorbed by the cells
- how active is the monoamine oxidase enzyme (which breaks down serotonin into harmless by-products).

Many factors, both physiological and environmental, can lower the level of serotonin in your brain or disturb its natural process and hence make you react in an anxious way.

The Amygdala ("Fear Center")

There is a thimble-sized piece of tissue in the brain called the amygdala. This is the "fear center." It contains many neuroreceptor sites that respond to "danger" messages from neurotransmitting chemicals. When it interprets something seen, heard, touched, smelled or tasted as meaning "danger," it directs other parts of your brain to immediately release a surge of adrenaline and cortisol into your bloodstream. In some people, this fear center operates on a "hair trigger" and tends to respond quickly and suddenly to all messages that contain even a slight threat. The human memory stores fear experiences very efficiently (for example, being dumped in the surf) and whenever a similar experience or trigger is encountered (for example, having someone try to playfully push you under the water) the fear center responds automatically. We also store memories of things we have been told are to be feared even if we haven't encountered them (for example, being bitten by a snake), and this can set up "anticipatory anxiety."

GABA A Receptor Sites

Studies now suggest that one gene involved in anxiety is the GABA A receptor sub-unit gene. Brain imaging studies of humans with chronic anxiety disorders show that they have abnormally low concentrations of GABA A–type receptors in certain regions of the brain. They concentrate in the hippocampus, the organ that mediates memory, and parts of the cerebral cortex, the "thinking/reasoning" surface of the frontal lobes of the brain. People suffering anxiety disorders can sometimes be treated successfully with benzodiazepine drugs—and benzodiazepines act on GABA receptors.

In detail, here is an outline of how the process of anxiety affects your body, your feelings, and your thinking:

Something happens that you, either consciously or otherwise, interpret as a sign of possible danger. People differ. It could be a barking guard dog, a near-miss in traffic, or a critical comment. It could be a thought that flits across your mind about your partner's behavior toward you ("She seems very cold toward me today"). A simple thing such as a raised eyebrow to something you said could be the sign. Having to face a potentially negative evaluation (for example, a test or an interview), or just being in a place where something bad has happened to you before, starts the process. In a millisecond, this perception sends fear messages to your brain saying, "Watch out, there's danger!"

The neurotransmitting chemical, serotonin, takes this message of "danger" through the bloodstream, via your nerve cells, to the neuroreceptor sites in the amygdala ("fear center") in your brain. These receptor sites deal only with incoming messages about potential danger. They instruct the sympathetic branch of your central nervous system (CNS) to prepare you by initiating the "fight or flight" response. "Energizing" fear hormones (mainly adrenaline and cortisol) are released from the adrenal-pituitary system in your brain into your bloodstream and alert your body for action. These fear hormones help you to focus on survival by responding adaptively to danger. Blood pressure rises, heart rate increases, breathing accelerates, and bodily responses are directed toward self-preservation.

What Happens Next?

Specifically, fear chemicals slow down digestion, so your body can divert blood to the muscles to make them tense enough to get you ready to attack or run faster. They instruct your liver to release glucose into your bloodstream to give you extra energy. Since oxygen is needed to convert this glucose to energy, the lungs have to take in more air and get rid of the carbon dioxide, so breathing becomes faster and hence more shallow. Heart and pulse rates are increased to give you speed and energy, and blood pressure rises as a result. Your salivary glands dry up and sweating occurs to offset the "heating up" of your body as it readies for fighting or running away. Your pupils grow larger to increase the amount of light received and help you to see more accurately. Blood vessels also divert blood to the muscles and constrict, making your face look paler than normal.

At this point you may check to see if there is real danger and decide that it was a false alarm. ("That wasn't my boss coming toward me in the shopping center when I am supposed to be back from my lunch break already, just someone who looked like her from the back.") Then, because you have sent up a "cancel" message to the brain, your fear center tells your parasympathetic nervous system to restore your bodily functions to their normal, more relaxed state. This will slow further surges of fear hormones. Your body may take twenty minutes to physically recover fully from a mild surge of these hormones once you cancel the "danger" signals to your brain.

On the other hand, you may confirm the very real nature of the potential danger ("That really is my boss coming toward me!"), and decide to use a strategy to "talk yourself down" and make yourself less anxious. For example, you say to yourself, "I won't panic. I'll explain to her that I was delayed at the supermarket." If you do this, although some anxiety will remain, there may be no further adrenaline surges because you have taken some control of the main "danger."

If, however, you still perceive danger, the process continues. You become aware that now your stomach is churning or doing "belly flops" and your heart is racing, or you have heart flutters. Your body is full of fear and you start to think, I am feeling so bad that something awful must be happening or is about to happen. If you still can't identify what is frightening you, you panic even more and the message goes up again via the neurotransmitting chemicals to the fear center, where it says, "Quickly send down more fear hormones to help me cope, because there is something about to happen and I can't figure out what it is and that scares me even more."

By now, you feel breathless, because you have started to take quick and shallow breaths. You may have a light-headed feeling because of this fast, shallow breathing, which is called hyperventilation. Hyperventilation quickly reduces the amount of carbon dioxide in your bloodstream and causes your blood to become more alkaline. This alkalinity affects peripheral nerves so fingers and skin may tingle and prickle. Trembling starts and sometimes you experience mild chest pains. You may need to sit down because of weakness at the knees. Palpitations or flutters, chest discomfort, and feelings of unreality may accompany this stage.

Things Get Worse!

When anxiety is intense, due to several surges in a row, you may be convinced that you are about to die. Certainly you are sure that something is very wrong! At this point, if you are able to convince yourself that there is no danger or that you have some control over the danger, the adrenaline surges will stop and your body will take between 30 and 60 minutes to fully recover and return to a relaxed state.

If you are still convinced that there is a danger and you have not been able to identify or control it, the fear sensations may overwhelm you. The more aware you are of what is happening in your body, the more convinced you may be that the danger is actually within. ("These feelings in my body must mean that I am seriously ill, having a heart attack, going mad, or about to lose control of myself.") Because you are so frightened, rational thinking is hard. Either you will withdraw to somewhere safe (for example, a quiet place nearby or your own house or office), become extremely agitated, or go to the doctor to see if you are okay (you always are).

How Anxiety Influences Behavior

After countless mild anxiety episodes, people get more used to the sensations in their body and may become less consciously aware of their fear as fear. But their brain keeps accurately reading their perceptions of possible danger and keeps sending down fear hormones into their bloodstream. They often have many mild adrenaline surges during one day that influence their behavior without their realizing what is happening. An accumulation over time, because you are a flooder or in a prolonged stressful situation, or both, can make you very edgy and tense, and chronically "ready" for withdrawal or attack.

Some People Are More Predisposed to Responding in an Anxious Way Than Others

Only about 5 percent of the population has such severe problems with anxiety that their behavior would meet the criteria for a diagnosis of generalized anxiety disorder, according to the DSM-IV-TR.

However, research suggests that maybe up to 30 percent of the population has an anxiety predisposition, that is, a mild to severe tendency to magnify threat and, too readily, release adrenaline and other fear hormones into their bloodstreams. They often feel stressed all day with no real justification.

Early experiences of fearful situations can then create minds that are biased toward exaggerating the potential for danger. They remember every frightening experience and, on being exposed again to similar situations or reminders of those situations, retreat from the threat or freeze in fear. As mentioned earlier, we have termed these people flooders as they are often flooded with fear hormones.

- Flooders have a hair-trigger response to any situation that they perceive to be threatening, even if sometimes they are not verbalizing to themselves that a situation is actually threatening.
- They experience fear reactions to a great many situations that others would not interpret as threatening. Because their body is often awash with fear, they train their brains to retain fearful memories, to selectively attend to potential threat, and to overinterpret situations as threatening.
- They tend to be less able to "turn off" the fear hormones once they are discharged into the bloodstream. It can take up to 60 minutes for the body to return to normal after a strong adrenaline surge, and flooders have often had several surges in a row without realizing it.

What Causes a Person to Be Overly Anxious?

Genetics

Flooders are very likely to have an inherited biological predisposition to releasing fear chemicals into their bloodstream too quickly and too intensely. As outlined earlier, this tendency appears to be related to lower than desirable levels of the neurotransmitting chemical serotonin, a lower than normal concentration of GABA A receptor sites, and a hair-trigger amygdala. Low levels of serotonin in the body are also related to a tendency to depression, but much is still not known about all the ways in which this influential brain chemical affects our behavior and emotions.

Close family members with a similar anxiety pattern can often be identified, although the expression of anxiety through behavior can take many forms. One person may show anxiety by being a chronic worrier while their mother or uncle may show anxiety by being pessimistic, agoraphobic, or having a nervous breakdown. Undoubtedly there is also some "modeling" of behavior occurring.

In several studies it has been demonstrated that some of this "flooding" tendency can be identified in a significant number of newborn babies. All babies startle when exposed to a sudden, loud noise. They cry loudly, jerk their arms and legs spasmodically, and heart rates increase dramatically, as does the electrical conductivity of their skin. They soon recover once the noise stops and their bodies return to normal levels of functioning. However, a proportion of babies startles more intensely, cries more loudly, has greater changes in heart rates and other physiological measures, and takes much longer to return to normal when the noise ceases. Further studies have shown that a high proportion of those babies are likely to become overly anxious children and then adults with anxious personalities. Social anxiety and shyness (as measured by their responses to people) can also be demonstrated in a significant number of newborns.

We cannot say for sure that behaviors which are present shortly after birth are inherited. They may be due wholly or in part to what happened during the period of the pregnancy or the birth process. However, we can be more confident that there is a strong genetic link when studies demonstrate a high correlation between family members on those behaviors, especially when they are extremely close, such as in identical twins.

Biological predispositions are just one of many factors that influence personality and behavioral style. Some genetic predispositions remain dormant unless certain environmental conditions occur or certain changes occur in your body. For example, it would appear that there are some young people (about 15 percent of the population) with a genetic predisposition toward schizophrenia who may not have actually become schizophrenic. However, when they use marijuana in great enough amounts they trigger the gene and precipitate a psychotic, or "out-of-touch-with-reality," episode. Similarly, the use of marijuana can also trigger anxiety episodes and panic attacks in some susceptible people.

Predispositions, therefore, interact with other inherited biological predispositions and changes that occur in the body, as well as with life experiences. Particularly important factors are the level of intelligence, specific abilities, role models, direct learning, others' expectations, traumatic experiences, and security and consistency of parenting and care.

The degree of severity of an individual's tendency toward anxiety will be determined by the relative intensity and interaction of all of an individual's biological and environmental factors.

Environmental Factors

Trauma

A biological tendency toward flooding with anxiety is worsened by recent or past trauma. A trauma is best defined as an intensely fear-provoking situation outside the range of the normal experience of most people. Trauma is usually about experiences which involve unexpected death or serious injury (or the threat of these) to yourself, loved ones, or people nearby, and is usually accompanied by overwhelming feelings of terror, horror, and helplessness. Because what happens is unpredictable and unable to be personally controlled, a sense of total powerlessness accompanies trauma. Traumatic events could be the sudden death of a loved one; natural disasters such as flood or fire; seeing someone killed or injured; assault, sexual or physical abuse (sudden or long-term); being robbed or hijacked; a serious vehicle accident in which people are maimed or killed; or being attacked by an animal.

After trauma, an intense period of great anxiety is likely to follow which is related to recollection of the traumatic event. Studies suggest that receiving counseling within 48 hours of such an event makes it much less likely that there will be any long-term aftereffects. After trauma, however, most people are likely to be more anxious in most aspects of their lives. Most people appear to recover from this within a few months. For some, though, the anxiety and distress continue past this point. These people may meet the criteria for a diagnosis of post traumatic stress disorder (PTSD), according to the DSM-IV-TR. It is likely that many were already flooders and that this tendency is intensified by their traumatic experience.

For example, while a significant number of war veterans (in both the Second World War and the Vietnam War) developed PTSD, most did not. Studies of identical and fraternal twins have shown that if one twin developed PTSD as a result of a war experience, the other twin was more likely to do so—and the similarity rate was highest in identical twins. The same is true of susceptibility to phobias. These facts suggest further confirmation that some individuals are genetically predisposed to develop anxiety-based conditions such PTSD or phobias.

Identifying the genes involved in anxiety may lead to the possibility that a genetic test can be developed to identify people most likely to suffer from PTSD after some traumatic event. That could allow more effective treatment, or it could allow geneticists to identify individuals who should not be exposed to predictable sources of psychological trauma, such as warfare.

Loss of Self-focused Protective Confidence

To function adequately, we need to positively distort our view of the world in some ways. Most of us tend to distort in the direction of greater safety in our daily activities and say to ourselves, "It can't happen to me." If every time we drove, we reminded ourselves that a crash was possible, because some people do crash, it would be very difficult to contemplate ever going out! So we say to ourselves, "Oh well, it sometimes happens that people have a car crash but it's never happened to me before. Anyway, I'm special because I am me. Those things happen to others I hear about on the TV news and read about in the papers, not me!" This is termed self-focused protective confidence.

If you then do have an accident, or if someone close to you does, that kind of thinking is suspended because you have lost that illusion of special safety. Realistically, you know that the statistical likelihood of a serious car accident occurring to you or someone close is still the same as before, but you have now exaggerated the possibility in your mind because of what has happened, and you now know it can happen to you. Some degree of protective confidence usually returns with time, but in some cases, the loss is permanent and the person never really feels as "safe." This loss can produce or make worse a degree of chronic anxiety.

You can also temporarily lose some of your protective confidence, especially if you have an anxious personality, if someone you cared about dies suddenly or in traumatic circumstances, is severely injured, is diagnosed with a life-threatening illness, or is robbed or assaulted.

Adversity and Grief

Adversity is about loss, disappointments, hardship, setbacks, and reversals of fortune. Adverse events occur in all lives and evoke feelings of grief and periods of anxiety. Retrenchment, separation, hospitalization, the death of a close family member, or major money or health problems may trigger anxiety about repercussions or similar events recurring. There is some loss of protective confidence.

For flooders, such events may trigger an even more intense period of anxiety. It is common for panic attacks to begin after a prolonged period of stress related to adversity.

If such events occur early in life, a child may find it more difficult than an older, more experienced person to cope with the loss of protective confidence. Much will depend on those other factors. A child with an anxiety predisposition (as long as it is not too severe) who experiences a major illness with hospitalization may ultimately use that experience to learn to cope if they are reasonably bright, have optimistic coping adults who reassure and focus on coping, and if they do not experience too many adverse events over a short period.

People handle adversity in various ways, but flooders may become more emotional and distressed than others facing adversity. They may also become more pessimistic and more negatively focused on the future.

A traumatic event or a prolonged period of stress or adversity may permanently change the functioning of the brain, thus creating a "flooding" tendency which may not have been inherited genetically. This is particularly likely if the event occurs early in life when the brain and its neurological networks are not yet fully developed. For example, after early and prolonged periods of hospitalization, especially if there have been medical emergencies, a child may feel fearful so often in a relatively short period that their brain changes and produces a permanent tendency to flooding. However, the research is inconclusive. It is more likely that such tendencies are inherited and then exaggerated by environmental experiences, rather than created by environmental experiences alone. Over time, the brain can become "trained" to release adrenaline in response to very minor triggers. More recent research, however, is suggesting that some changes to the brain can occur after traumatic events.

Role Models

A close family member can share the same biological predisposition toward anxiety. They can also show you how to do it. A highly anxious parent:

- may communicate distorted and anxiety-based perceptions of the world as a very dangerous place where constant vigilance and caution are needed ("You must never travel on public transportation at night, even in a group")
- might model panic behavior when something small goes wrong in their life ("This is terrible. We'll never be able to fix what's wrong with the tent")
- may be observed by their child expressing strong anxiety in situations where only low or no potential for danger existed in the eyes of others (for example, becoming very agitated on a perfectly safe boat)
- may worry excessively and communicate that worry to their child
- may speak and act pessimistically ("I'm not going to spend too much time preparing for this picnic because the forecast said there is a possibility of showers tomorrow so it will probably rain").

If a flooder encounters these "lessons" there will be an increased tendency toward anxiety. But if another, nonflooding parent or significant adult models a more rational view of life as slightly dangerous and where reasonable caution is needed, and provides reassurance coupled with expectations of coping, then a flooder's genetic tendency toward anxiety will be moderated. A child who is not a flooder will probably be less influenced by the behavior of a parent who is.

Other Triggers for Anxiety

Other changes in your body can produce or exaggerate anxiety reactions, especially in flooders.

- As overly vigilant monitors of what is happening in their bodies, anxious personalities can become too focused on every small change that occurs. Their bodies will feel "different" and "funny" when they are coming down with a virus, have a mild asthma attack, or take medicine (for example, an asthma medication) that has stimulant side effects. They will tend to overreact to and overinterpret these small changes.

- Coffee, especially when percolated and strong, can act on the body in a similar way to adrenaline, that is, by making it alert and energized. So can chocolate and cola drinks, which also contain caffeine. That is why we use them as a pick-me-up when our energy and concentration are flagging. So, anxious people may respond as though the feelings in their body that are due to caffeine are in fact signals of danger. They feel distressed, edgy, emotional, and vaguely "threatened" without knowing why.

- Diet pills containing amphetamines can cause direct anxiety reactions coupled with a strong "spaced out" or "unreal" feeling.

- Decongestants and cold and flu tablets containing pseudoephedrine (the part of the medicine that also makes you feel more alert) can cause a pounding heart and other reactions similar to anxiety. Many anxious people cannot tolerate them, especially if they are taken at the same time as coffee.

- Illegal amphetamines ("speed") can also cause anxiety reactions in susceptible people.
- A drop in your blood sugar levels due to a lengthy period between eating or binge eating of sugars and carbohydrates can trigger anxiety reactions.
- Sleep deprivation can cause anxiety reactions because your body will send more adrenaline to keep you alert. The danger is in your vague sense of "not totally under control" and soon your heart pounds loudly, you feel agitated, experience chest discomfort, and so on.
- Overexercising can lead to your body releasing too much lactic acid, which can trigger anxiety reactions.
- Many suffer their first panic attack after using marijuana. These changes in bodily functions can cause some people to feel anxious. When they use "danger self-talk," for example, "What's happening to me?" "Why does my body feel so odd?" "Where is the danger?", they may flood with more fear hormones without realizing why.

Anxious Personalities and the Sleep–Wake Cycle

Anxious people and those undergoing prolonged stress or adversity are more prone to difficulties with their sleep–wake cycle, for many reasons.

- Serotonin, the neurotransmitting chemical that can distort brain-to-body messages about danger, also communicates with the brain about sleep and tells it to release the sleep hormone melatonin several hours before we have trained our bodies to go to bed.
- On going to bed, anxious personalities often worry about the day's events or tomorrow's. This may provoke an adrenaline surge that fights the sleep hormone melatonin, which has been releasing into their bloodstream. This worsens if they have consumed caffeine in the six-hour period before attempting to sleep, as caffeine can also "tell" the brain not to release its usual amounts of melatonin. Anxiety-prone

people and stressed people need to be particularly careful about late consuming of coffee, chocolate, or cola drinks.

- Then, when they realize they feel wide awake, they become anxious that they won't be able to fall asleep. They start to worry, and this produces another adrenaline surge. Long periods of insomnia can result.

- If they go to bed early to prepare for an early commitment, like catching a plane the next day, flooders worry so much about what would happen if they can't fall asleep, and don't get enough sleep, that they produce adrenaline surges that make their worst fears come true.

- If they worry about not getting enough sleep, an internal monitor sometimes wakes them an hour earlier than they had planned. Scientists have recently identified another anxiety and stress-related neurotransmitting chemical called adrenocorticotropin, which is a factor in this process. It appears to be released in the bloodstream just before sleep, during sleep, and then prior to waking in unconscious anticipation of the stress of waking up. The expectation on going to sleep that sleep will end at a certain time triggers the release of more adrenocorticotropin overnight. This then concentrates in the bloodstream and wakes the person up at the feared time (that is, too early).

  This same chemical appears to operate for many people as a natural alarm clock, waking them around about the time they wanted to wake. But it can backfire, too. Anxious people may be overly concerned about the danger of sleeping in and being late. So they release more of this chemical than required and it concentrates too quickly and wakes them up much earlier than they wanted.

- When they are sleeping in motels or others' homes, anxiety-prone people find it harder to control mild surges of adrenaline possibly produced by being in a foreign environment (unknown and therefore possibly containing more potential threat), combined with a previous experience of sleeping difficulties in similar circumstances ("I had trouble sleeping in the last motel I stayed in, so I probably will again. What if that happens and . . .").

The Long-term Impact of Chronic Anxiety or Stress

Long-term chronic releasing of fear hormones, either through a flooding tendency or prolonged stress, has been implicated in both minor and major heath problems. For example, it can:

- make an individual more susceptible to the common cold
- break down bones, causing osteoporosis in women
- allow infections to take hold because the immune system is weakened
- contribute to heart attacks
- trigger various cancers, for the same reason
- destroy appetite
- shut down processes that repair tissue
- create depression, which is also linked to serotonin. Depression and anxiety may be biologically linked, as they frequently occur together. On the other hand, feeling chronically anxious can also make you feel down.

The Severe Version of This Personality Pattern

In its most severe form, anxiety-based behavior meets the criteria for diagnosis of generalized anxiety disorder, according to the DSM-IV-TR. It may also meet the criteria for a number of other anxiety-based disorders. People who believe they may have such a severe pattern should consider consulting a psychologist or a psychiatrist, as their behavior undoubtedly causes them great personal distress, lowers their self-esteem, alienates others, and significantly limits or adversely affects their relationships and aspects of their workplace success. Medication may be appropriate in some cases, as well as counseling.

To make a diagnosis of generalized anxiety disorder, there must be excessive daily worrying about a range of events, which the person finds difficult to control, over the last six months. This must be adversely affecting their work, study, or family relationships and causing personal distress. There must also be at least three of the following six behaviors or symptoms:

- restlessness
- being easily fatigued
- marked irritability
- difficulty concentrating or mind going blank
- muscle tension
- sleep disturbance.

Only an experienced clinician can make a proper diagnosis of generalized anxiety disorder, because the symptoms are easily confused or differently expressed. They may fit another diagnosis just as readily. However, anyone can identify a milder anxious personality pattern that features some of the above symptoms but in milder forms.

The Moderate Anxious Personality Pattern

Here are the kinds of behaviors you would see a lot of:

- frequent episodes of excessive worrying that adversely affect the person's well-being, but the anxiety is controllable with some effort by the person or support from others
- moderate tendency toward perfectionism, pessimism, or overcautious behavior that fluctuates
- tendency to be "volcanic," that is, brief occasional periods of angry attacks in certain situations, often followed by contrition
- tendency to panic, become emotional, or overreact in specific situations where there is a mild threat
- early evidence of some anxiety-based behavior in childhood that has increased in adulthood or with adversity
- moderate sleeping difficulties or periods of sleep problems. They are usually not "good" sleepers. It is useful for people with this pattern to seek help from a qualified psychologist, especially one with a cognitive-behavioral approach.

What about the Kids?

Children with anxious personalities are fairly easily identified. Like adults, they range from mild to severe in their behavioral patterns. An anxious child will typically:

- become tongue-tied in class when put on the spot, fearing they have misinterpreted the question. They get upset when the teacher yells at someone nearby and often report disliking a teacher who is a "yeller."
- may frequent the sick bay or be too unwell to go to school because of effects of adrenaline surges in response to an aspect of their school day, for example, a friendship falling-out, fear of a test, etc.
- sometimes refuse to go to school, especially after an illness, or after vacations. They are anxious about the "known" situation having changed and become "unknown." They are also anxious about being socially "not allowed back in."
- show overconcern for their parents' well-being when separated for even a short period
- resist new experiences until sure of their ability to deal with them. They concentrate on the dangerous aspects of them.
- find staying away overnight at a camp or at friends' houses problematic.
- have specific phobias, that is, intense irrational fear of, for or example, dogs, spiders, or birds
- demonstrates an inability to cope with exams and tests
- be overly concerned about a sporting event in which they will be participating. They then make themselves ill because the adrenaline irritates the lining of the stomach and attempts to expel the contents of the stomach in anticipation of needing the energy that was being used for digestion.
- exhibit perfectionism about school projects and achievement
- be reluctant to participate in discussions or answer questions in class

- feel overwhelmed by the big picture and worry excessively, for example, "I'll never be able to read six books this year" or "What if people don't accept the invitations to my party?"

Other Anxiety-Based Disorders

There are many other types of anxiety-based disorders. It is not within the scope of this book to look at them in detail, but here is a brief summary of the main ones. It is advisable to consult a psychologist or psychiatrist about them.

Phobia

An intense and irrational fear of a specific object, animal, insect, or situation that is out of all proportion to the real danger.

Post-Traumatic Stress Disorder

Intense anxiety and intrusive recollections following a trauma that do not improve after three months.

Panic Attacks

A panic attack is an intense and long-lasting episode of anxiety that is so severe that ultimately the person can pass out from fear. There is a pounding heart, palpitations, flushing, shaking, and a sense of overwhelming terror despite there being no obvious danger.

Agoraphobia

Agoraphobia is a pattern of behavior that involves not being prepared to venture outside a "safe place," usually the home. It is possibly a pattern designed to avoid panic attacks.

There are usually no attacks in the company of people they trust, and the result is often overdependence on certain safe people.

Body Dysmorphia

This is characterized by excessive anxiety and distress over a minor or imagined physical abnormality that the person believes, unshakeably, makes them ugly or misshapen.

Social Anxiety

At first glance, social anxiety seems to be extreme shyness. But unlike ordinary shyness, social anxiety can be so severe that it interferes with daily functioning in the workplace, at school, and in almost all public interpersonal relationships, except with the immediate family and trusted friends. Social anxiety causes the individual to avoid as much social contact as they can because of a persistent fear of being scrutinized by others and of humiliating or embarrassing oneself in public.

Obsessive-Compulsive Disorder

This is characterized by obsessive thinking in which there are recurrent and intrusive thoughts of a distressing nature, for example, believing that you are going to vomit, thinking that food is spoiled, etc. Sometimes there are also compulsions that are rituals, such as excessive handwashing.

In the next chapter we focus on behavioral patterns that are a result of people with anxiety predispositions attempting to bring potential risk and danger under control and hence lower their anxiety. Most people display all of these behaviors at various times when anxious, but some people become difficult to live or work with because they demonstrate one of more of these behaviors relatively frequently and predictably to the point where it could be said to be a pattern.

Over time, George's family learned to accept his "panic" over everything, but it was not easy for them. When one of his children came home with a poor school report he was so upset he couldn't sleep well for a week and had to take a day off work. George was an accounts manager in a large company. He was overly diligent about figures, always checking to avoid mistakes. Once, when a requisition order he was responsible for was unaccountably lost, he became almost hysterical with anxiety to the point where his supervisor told him to go home and calm down. When his sixteen-year-old daughter was half an hour late coming home from a party, George was so sure that something had happened to her that when he didn't get an answer at the phone number she had given him he called the police.

9

Getting on Top of Anxiety

GENERAL STRATEGIES

Not Recommendeded

To feel less anxious, some people, at certain times, use substances such as alcohol or marijuana. These substances reduce unpleasant bodily sensations of anxiety once they have started. Anticipating an anxiety-provoking or stressful situation, such as a social function, we also use them to increase confidence by eliminating anxiety beforehand.

For some highly anxious people, using these substances is their main strategy for coping with an existing or potential anxiety. They use them regularly to deal with daily life, not for the occasional relaxation. This pattern is nearly always dysfunctional and unhelpful in the long run.

Drugs such as marijuana and Ecstasy are often used as an antidote to anxiety, but they can adversely affect brain chemistry.

More Positive Strategies

There are four major types of medication that can be used to help with the management of anxiety. Their use should be discussed with your doctor and counselor.

Symptom Relievers

These are best used symptomatically (that is, only when the person feels particularly uncomfortable, not all the time).

They are usually drugs from the benzodiazepine family, such as Valium. For those whose anxiety expresses itself through insomnia, drugs such as Restoril, also from the benzodiazepine family, can be prescribed. These drugs appear to prevent access of particular neurotransmitting chemicals to its neuroreceptor site in the brain. Xanax is another useful drug for dealing symptomatically with prolonged periods of anxiety in an individual with a long history of pervasive anxiety or social anxiety. However, the medications in this category can be addictive and need to be used sparingly and with caution. They are not a substitute for coping strategies.

Beta Blockers

These drugs (for example, Inderal) are usually taken symptomatically. They prevent the transmission (via beta waves) of anxious messages from the fear center in the brain to other parts of the brain and body. They may be useful occasionally for severe social anxiety or performance anxiety.

Selective Serotonin Re-uptake Inhibitors (SSRIs)

Aropax, Zoloft, and Aurorix are examples of selective serotonin re-uptake inhibitors (SSRIs). They are anti-depressants which also have anti-anxiety properties. They appear to work by increasing the levels of serotonin in the bloodstream by ensuring that the serotonin created in the body is not reabsorbed. This takes about ten to fourteen days to occur, and the medication must be taken continuously for at least several months. Serotonin-norepinephrine re-uptake inhibitors (SNRIs) such as Cymbalta are another similar category of medication used in the treatment of depression and generalized anxiety disorder.

Naturopathic Remedies

St. John's wort is a natural health product that may help with low levels of anxiety and depression by slightly raising serotonin levels, but it cannot be taken in conjunction with an SSRI or SNRI. Melatonin (artificial) can be a useful natural health product which is effective for some people with sleeping difficulties.

Understanding and Dealing with Others Who Are Anxious

Focus on the Positive Aspects of Anxious People

Anxious people are more likely:

- to be moral and break fewer rules of society because anxiety is the raw material of guilt. For example, they are less likely to park illegally, speed, steal, cheat, or lie. Their "anticipatory anxiety" surges and overwhelms them when thinking about how it will feel to break a rule, or when they think about the negative outcomes if they get caught.
- to show greater sensitivity and compassion to others in distress. This is partly because they become skilled readers of others' feelings as a way of picking up potential danger signals and also because their own distress has made them more empathic with the distress of others.
- to be less judgmental because they are more aware of their own complexity, that is, they are often skilled, competent people who are sometimes overwhelmed by feelings and events and have to struggle hard to keep control and manage those feelings.
- to work hard because they have more "nervous energy." This occurs because their bodies are frequently energized by their mild but repeated surges of adrenaline.
- to be eager to please because it makes them feel less anxious. This means they are often easy to get along with when not stressed or affected by anxiety.
- to read signs of potential danger earlier, as they are constantly alert for something bad to happen
- to be well organized and cautious in ways helpful to others.

Understand and Empathize

When dealing with anxious people you need to:

- be compassionate, rather than judgmental
- understand that their behavior is significantly influenced by different biology from yours

- remember that this is only part of who they are, so acknowledge the whole person and give credit to the other strengths and competencies of their life
- make empathic statements which let them know that you understand their concerns, but at the same time, calmly reassure with rational thinking
- share your own experiences and offer details about your own anxiety in a similar circumstance, for example, what you did when you were at the airport ready to leave on a vacation, and thought you had left the iron on.

Reassure

- Instead of becoming involved in escalation of anxiety, reassure the person with a calming touch, if that is appropriate. Don't get sucked in. Reassurance rather than an angry retort will reduce the anxiety. Stay calm. A reassuring hug may defuse a volatile situation in a personal relationship. As you put an arm around their shoulder, say something like: "I can see that this is really worrying you. I'm sorry you are upset but what you are fearing just isn't likely to happen," or "I can see why you're a little anxious, but it isn't as risky as you think."
- Dazzle them with facts and statistics to support your assertion that the risk is lower than they believe. Statistics usually impress.
- When undertaking a new activity, do it together first to reassure the anxious person that it is safe.
- Tolerate some of their safety structures, for example, the occasional extra call to the family member who is cause for concern.

Model Rational Thinking

By what you say you can model more helpful thinking. For example:

- I can understand why you might feel like that, but worrying won't help. It just makes it worse.

- It is upsetting, I agree, but let's concentrate on what we can do about it.

Respect Their Limits

Don't push too hard. Most anxious people can go beyond the limits they have set for themselves, but not necessarily to the level you think is best for them. Take it slowly.

Suggest Cool-Down Periods

Remember, where possible, to allow for a one-hour recovery period after they appear to have "flooded."

You Are Not Perfect, Either

Remember that their imperfections and weaknesses are no worse than yours, just different.

Be More Assertive in Letting Them Know the Impact Their Behavior Is Having on You

Use the format of "When you…I feel…because…" For example, "When you attack me like that, I feel unfairly treated because what I said didn't justify your attack. Could you tell me what you are thinking without attacking me? Or perhaps call 'time out,' and then we can discuss it later."

More details of the skills of assertion can be found on page 232.

Distract Them

Don't say, "You're overreacting." Without being patronizing, refocus their attention away from what is worrying them.

Strategies for Managing Your Own Anxiety-Based Behavior

Understanding and Self-Acceptance

- Become more aware of the fear sensations in your body so that you understand the process and recognize when you have been mildly flooded by adrenaline. Then say, "I'm having an anxiety reaction, so I must not overreact."
- Remind yourself that your biology is different from other

people's, it is not just that you are not coping. However, you can still get better at managing your anxiety.

- Accept the irrationality of your anxiety but also accept the reality of the bodily sensations.
- Accept yourself as an imperfect person and admit to the problem. But remember that it is only part of who you are. Focus on the positives, too.

Release Endorphins to Compete with the Fear Hormones

- Daily exercise causes your body to release endorphins, which are calming or pleasure chemicals and can help off-set mild anxiety and depression.
- Do something pleasurable for yourself.

Reality Checks

Talk to someone you trust to get another's perception. Use this to adjust your perceptions of danger.

Rational Self-Talk

When you talk to yourself in your head, you determine whether or not you will continue to be flooded with anxiety. Rational self-talk reflects reality and is helpful (see page 99). Stand back and see the situation more realistically, and challenge any irrational interpretations, especially those that exaggerate the degree of danger. Exaggeration of these thoughts usually results in more anxiety.

Here are some examples of self-talk to challenge anxiety:

- My anxiety is distorting my thinking.
- If I feel bad, I'll keep busy.
- I am paying too much attention to the bad feelings in my body.
- My body is fooling my brain.
- It is just the anxiety chemicals in my body that are making me think like this.
- I'll try not to think about how uncomfortable it is. The more I think about it, the worse it feels.
- I won't panic at the first sign of anxiety in my body. I can put up with it.

- Biology is not an excuse, but it is a partial explanation.
- Panic means thinking about the worst thing that can happen and assuming it will happen. I won't panic. The worst rarely happens.
- I will be kind to myself because my biology is different from that of many others. I have to wrestle with an anxiety predisposition. But biology is a partial explanation, not an excuse, and I still have to manage it.
- Adrenaline in my body fools my brain into feeling scared and thinking that something bad is going to happen. But it never does.
- I can't totally get rid of my anxiety, but I can get on top of it most of the time.

Facts and Statistics

Focus on facts and statistics to reassure yourself that the likelihood of a particular danger is less than you believe it to be.

Cool-Down Periods

Don't discuss issues when you are flooded with anxiety. Remember that after flooding you will probably need a one-hour recovery and cool-down period before attempting to deal with a situation.

Become More Assertive

Becoming more assertive can offset anxiety. Refer to the section on the skills of assertion on page 232.

Don't Act Precipitously

Don't rush into decisions when you are feeling anxious and emotional. Your emotions (and yours are stronger than most) can distort your thinking. Wait till you have recovered from the flooding before you make decisions about ending relationships, telling people off, resigning, etc. It may be you and not just the situation, and you may regret your actions later.

Use Relaxation Strategies

Use controlled diaphragmatic breathing.

Watch for Other Things That Might Increase Your Flooding
Avoid too much caffeine, pseudoephedrine, and marijuana.

Memory Jogger Card
Make cards for yourself as prompts. Use the rational self-talk statements and select the ones most useful to you to put on your card. Use the P strategy on page 266.

Learn to Live with Ambiguity and the Unknown
Accept that you can't control everything in life that affects you and become comfortable with that fact.

Thought Stopping
Distract yourself when you realize that you have started to worry and agonize or obsess. For example, you can:

- work
- clean out a closet or filing cabinet (this gives an illusion that things are under control)
- try to ignore the thought
- use thought stopping. If the thought keeps messing up your brain, say to yourself: "This is not real. It is just my body fooling my brain. There really isn't any danger." If you can't make the thought fade into the back of your mind, then blink hard to get rid of the worrying image and words in your mind.
- focus on something nice, for example, your favorite TV show, friend, hobby, last vacation or work achievement, or something you are looking forward to. Have it ready to think about.

Admit and Apologize If You Distress Others
Acknowledge and explain that your biology may be different from other people's. But don't be too hard on yourself.

Use Low-Key Language
Put a "stop" to that spiraling, anxious thought by using cooler language. For example, "This is annoying" is more low key than

"This is terrible." Similarly, "This is disappointing" is more helpful than "This is appalling."

Challenge Your Working Hypothesis

Your thinking is guided by this belief: "The world is a very dangerous place. I have to find as many ways as I can to make it less scary."

A more realistic hypothesis would be: "At times, the world is somewhat dangerous and I should be aware and prepared but not unduly anxious."

Become More Optimistic

Refer to the section on page 220.

10

Everything Is Under Control

ANXIETY-BASED BEHAVIOR

THE FOLLOWING BEHAVIORS are most likely to occur in response to anxiety. They are all behaviors that attempt to minimize risk and bring potential threats under control. However, although such behaviors appear to provide control over anxiety by making things more predictable or less threatening, this is usually an illusion. In most cases, a small amount of the behavior, used appropriately, can be adaptive, but when it becomes a pattern, it can cause difficulties.

Excessive Worrying

What Is Typical of Most People?

All of us worry about things that "might" happen and mostly don't! The majority of people have times when they worry more than usual. We all have some anxiety about the possibility of making mistakes, looking stupid, being rejected, or being negatively evaluated. But we don't spend a great deal of time worrying about all those possibilities, and the worry doesn't cripple us. Most people do not worry excessively all the time about most areas of their lives, and with a little effort they can bring worrying under control once it starts.

What Is Typical of Excessive Worriers?

Many spend a lot of time focusing on "what-if" thinking in many areas of their lives. They spend a large part of their time worrying about things beyond their control. They agonize over events that have not yet happened as though this will prevent them from happening or minimize their impact.

Here are some examples. Many will recognize themselves in one or two, but if you are an excessive worrier you may recognize yourself in several. Most are based around the typical excessive worrier's "what-if" thoughts:

- *I have lent my daughter my car; what if she crashes it and kills herself?* (So she lies awake for hours in the middle of night thinking about it.)
- *What if the reason my wife has been quiet over the past weekend is that she is thinking about leaving me?* (So he acts strangely for days as he thinks about separation, or he overdoes his attempts to please her.)
- *What if I'm laid off in the department reorganization and we don't have enough money to live on?* (So she keeps talking to her family about it, becoming more irritating and irritable in the process.)
- *What if my friend doesn't keep my secret even though she said she would?* (So she broods on it for days and never tells the friend another secret even though there is no evidence of disloyalty.)
- *What if I buy the wrong wine to take to the school reunion at the BYO restaurant with my wine-expert friend?* (So he spends hours agonizing and searching for the best one and in the end doesn't take any.)
- *What if no one likes me at my new job?* (So she stays awake worrying for several nights in a row and then approaches her first day at the new job with great trepidation.)
- *What if I say I disagree with the person sitting opposite me at the dinner party and they respond by putting me down?* (So he says nothing but feels resentful.)

How Excessive Worriers Think

Their working hypothesis is: "The world is a very dangerous place so I will focus on identifying any potential threat and agonizing over what it would be like if it actually happened. Then either it will magically go away because I have spent so much time worrying about it, or it won't have so much impact on me if it does actually happen because I am prepared."

Ultimately, most excessive worriers are perceived to be negative and pessimistic people, because they are always looking for potential problems and fail to acknowledge and enjoy the present. Others get sick of their excessive communication of worry.

Bill faces another sleepless night. Again today at work a notice came around advising that the company would be considering major layoffs at the end of the year. Everybody is worried about their jobs, of course, but it is Bill who stays awake night after night agonizing over the possible consequences if he were laid off. All he can think about is how he would not have enough money to pay the mortgage. He focuses on how difficult it would be at his age to get another job. All night he will run those pictures endlessly through his mind until eventually he will fall totally exhausted into a few brief hours of sleep. His wife has tried to reassure him and keeps saying to him, "We don't know yet if you will lose your job. Don't worry about what has not yet happened," but he seems unable to stop worrying about it.

Looking on the Bright Side
- Excessive worriers draw attention to potential difficulties or threats. They act like the canary down the coal mine. Coal miners used to send down a canary ahead of them to check on the air quality. If the bird died, they did not go down! So excessive worriers can be effective warners.
- Excessive worriers are more likely to be sympathetic to others with worries.
- Sometimes when a worry turns out to be genuine, they are better prepared to cope with it.
- They can play the role of devil's advocate by pointing out the alternative views and what could go wrong with a project, which can then be remedied.

The Gender Factor
In our society, women are freer to admit worry and share their thinking. Thus they are more likely to get support, empathy, and reality checks. There is a danger that if encouraged too much, female

excessive worriers will "wallow" and eventually alienate loved ones. Also, certain women are indiscriminate in terms of who they talk to when in excessive-worrying mode, and this can be a mistake.

Men feel more vulnerable if they admit to excessive worrying, so they tend to do it privately or deny that they are worrying. Thus they may miss opportunities to share their worries and get feedback and reality checks in the form of other viewpoints or experiences. In the long term, this denial makes it more likely that they will have health problems.

Strategies for Dealing with an Excessive Worrier

- Understand that their behavior is significantly influenced by different biology from yours.
- Being an excessive worrier is only part of who they are, so acknowledge the whole person and give credit to the other areas and competencies of their life.
- Make empathic statements that let them know you understand their concern, but at the same time, calmly reassure them with rational thinking and, where possible, with facts and statistics. For example: "I can understand why you might feel like that, but worrying won't help. It just makes it worse," or "What is the worst that could happen? Is it likely to? Would it destroy you if it did happen? What can you do that would make you feel better about it?"
- In the workplace, pair them with someone with low anxiety who does not sneer or put down and has abundant patience. Don't pair them with someone who worries as much as they do. Excessive worriers don't like other excessive worriers because they make each other worse.

Strategies for Coping If You Are an Excessive Worrier

Use rational self-talk along the lines of:

- It could happen but is fairly unlikely.
- If it does happen, it is not the end of the world.
- I won't worry till I need to.
- What's done is done. No use worrying about it.

- I can't control everything. I will learn to live with some uncertainty.
- What is the worst that could happen? Would it be the end of the world if that did happen? What can I do that would make me feel better about it?
- It could happen, but it is very unlikely.
- Keep things in perspective.
- Where is the evidence that what I am worrying about is really likely to happen?
- Do what you can about preventing the object of your worrying to happen and then say to yourself, "Worrying won't fix it or change anything."
- Problem-solve instead. Problem solving differs from worrying in that it is action-focused, more rational, and more analytical. Then act where you can.
- Remember that this is only one part of who you are and don't give yourself a hard time. Your biology is different from other people's, but you can still get better at managing your anxiety.
- Distract yourself when you realize that worry has started to gnaw away at you.
- Use thought stopping in which you blink to clear your mind, then focus on a pleasant set of images or ideas that you had already "planted" in your mind for this purpose. For example, rerun your last terrific vacation, think satisfyingly about your last work achievement, or drool over something special coming up.
- Gain an illusion of control by drawing up a "to do" list in relation to the thing you are worried about.

Overdependent Behavior

What Is Typical of Most People?

Relying on emotional support from significant others is something we all do at times. Most people prefer to do certain things, such as vacationing, in the company of others. They like to hear opinions about decisions they have to make from someone they trust. They appreciate and use positive feedback and approval from others. But they expect to make final decisions themselves and can still cope without support, positive feedback, or company, if that is how things turn out. They have a degree of independence and confidence in their own ability to handle their life. They can take care of themselves, initiate projects, and solve their own problems.

What Is Typical of Overdependent People?

People with an overdependent behavior pattern demonstrate an excessive need to be cared for. They rely excessively on the emotional support, strength, company, and ability of others to offset anxiety. Only when they do things with a "safe" person or people do they feel secure and free from anxiety. They need others to help them decide or make decisions for them. They encourage others to take responsibility for most areas of their lives. When they have to rely on themselves or they are alone, they become agitated and less functional. They can become very dependent on others' approval and positive feedback, and need excessive amounts of advice and reassurance. They "cling" and do not dare to disagree with people upon whose support and approval they depend. They are often inappropriately submissive. If they do lose a friend or romantic partner, they will often indiscriminately and quickly attach emotionally to someone else. It is too scary for them to be "on their own." People may only be overdependent in areas where they do not feel competent. In more severe patterns, they are overdependent in all areas of their lives.

Here are some typical overdependent behavior patterns:

Amanda won't attend social functions on her own, and if her partner, Steve, is out of town, she finds it very scary to be in their apartment alone. Steve makes her feel safe.

Terry, 48, has a mild angina condition and has retired on the grounds of ill health. His dependency on the company of his wife is so extreme that she had to give up her part-time job. If she is out of the house even a few minutes longer than she said, he is chasing her on the phone. Without her constant presence, Terry says he feels vulnerable to another angina episode in which he would not be able to get help fast enough.

Pauline is described by her friends as "needy." Whenever she starts a new relationship, she gives up many of her own needs and friends and focuses totally on her new man. In return, she always expects him to "take care of her" with lots of help with decision making, constant compliments and reassurance, financial support, and company whenever possible. She clings so hard that usually he leaves and she starts the process again with someone new. If there is no man around, she continues a milder version of this dependency pattern with her "recovered" friends who cynically recognize what she is doing.

Jack has let his parents make most of his major decisions since he was little. When they changed his school, he didn't object. He gravitated toward only those friends his parents approved of, and he never had unsuitable acquaintances. He rarely misbehaved and was seen as a model child. When he was a senior in high school, his parents decided on the basis of his grades that he should earn a pharmacy degree at the best university, and that is what he did. After graduation, he applied for jobs in the hospitals suggested by his father. Jack never experiences anxiety about making decisions because he doesn't make any. This way, as he sees it, fewer things are likely to go wrong. And if things don't work out, it is not his fault.

How Overdependent People Think

Their working hypothesis is: "The world is a very dangerous place. If I always rely on someone whom I trust or who is stronger or more clever than me, then fewer bad things will happen. If something bad does happen, I am not to blame and they will be able to deal with it. I am not able to cope on my own."

Looking on the Bright Side

- The overdependent person is so reliant on others that they will always compromise, and so the other person will get their own way.

- They value and need others (but can become demanding).
- They are usually available when others need company and will fit in around them.
- They can make some people feel protective or superior.

The Gender Factor

Traditionally, women have been socialized into relying more on men as social partners, financial managers, and protectors. Research suggests that it is marginally more likely that an overdependent person will be female. Men who are overdependent are usually flooders and/or have experienced a major health scare or serious financial disaster. The person on whom they rely is usually their female partner.

Strategies for Dealing with Someone Who Is Overdependent

- Understand that their behavior is significantly influenced by different biology from yours and be compassionate, not judgmental.
- Since being overdependent is only part of who they are, acknowledge the whole person and give credit to the other competencies of their life.
- Make empathic statements that let them know you understand their fears, but at the same time, calmly reassure with reasons and positive expectations: "Yes, it is a little scary being on your own, but I know you will be able to cope."
- Provide smaller security supports—for example, the occasional phone call, rather than a regular one, or the occasional meeting rather than frequent ones.
- Be encouraging when small advances in independence are made.
- In the workplace, give them increasing responsibilities and then provide positive feedback for acting independently.
- Overdependent people can function well if they are assured that someone else is supervising and approving, even from a distance.
- Ask yourself to what extent you have been encouraging their dependency. Although it can be satisfying to have

someone need you, it does not help to make them dependent on you. Sometimes it is a method of control. Be honest with yourself.

Strategies for Coping If You Are Overdependent

- Use rational self-talk along the lines of: I can do this by
  myself. Even if it feels uncomfortable at first, I'll get used
  to it.
- Don't panic and revert to dependency at the first sign of
  anxiety in your body. Put up with it for a while. It is just
  uncomfortable. It will not actually harm you.
- Remind yourself that this is only one part of who you are and
  don't give yourself a hard time. Your biology is different from
  others', but you can improve and become more independent.
  Biology is not an excuse, it is a partial explanation.

Overcaution and Avoidance

What Is Typical of Most People?

Taking reasonable care in planning events, trying to be on time,
and making allowances for contingencies are typical of most people. In a couple of areas, some people are probably more cautious
than necessary because they have had bad experiences in the past.
In areas such as plane crashes, people often exaggerate the risk
factors because of media coverage that makes these events seem
regular rather than rare, which they are. (Your chances of dying
in a commercially scheduled plane crash are about one in two and
a half million.) Everyone calculates the personal risks involved in
activities and situations and plans to minimize risk, but most do
not attempt to cover all eventualities.

What Is Typical of Overly Cautious and Avoidant People?

Overly cautious people exaggerate the statistical probability
of bad things happening. Then they act in ways that minimize or
eliminate that possibility. To some extent their anxiety is about the
unknown, which is therefore less controllable and more dangerous.

Here are some typical situations. Note that many reflect useful strategies when not overdone.

- Always being overly punctual, for example, arriving much too early for a bus or function. Leaving home way too early, and having to "kill time" after arrival. They usually know they are overdoing it. (What if I were late and I missed the bus? What if I upset the people who invited us? What if I missed the start of the meeting?)

- Always packing too much. (What if I needed something I haven't packed? What if it is colder/hotter/more formal than I have planned before leaving?)

- Avoiding physical challenges. (What if I slip? What if the tree falls on me?)

- Overconcern with security, for example, changing locks after a roommate departs even if they have been good roommates; not being prepared to leave your car in a long-term parking lot for fear of vandals; locking all the doors each time you go in and out of the house to your backyard.

- Reluctance to spend money. (What if later I need something urgently and I don't have enough money? What if I don't have enough to live on in my old age?)

- Being overinsured. (What if my house burns down and I have to pay huge bills? What if I lose my luggage and I don't have travel insurance? What if I get an illness which requires countless operations and I can't pay my bills?)

- Overconcern about issues of health and hygiene, for example, excessively disinfecting baby bottles and toys, using bleach with every cleaning, etc. (What if I don't clean them properly and someone gets sick because of my lack of thoroughness?)

How People Who Are Overly Cautious and Avoidant Think

Their working hypothesis is: "The world is a very dangerous place. I need to exaggerate the possibility of disaster so that I will be motivated to take extra precautions to ensure that I am protected from all possibilities, however remote. I don't want to put myself in any position or situation where I might feel anxious."

Looking on the Bright Side

- Like excessive worriers, they anticipate all potential dangers, so they can warn others.
- They are often excellent organizers, although they tend to stress others out at times.
- They are better prepared and hence good to travel with; for example, they will probably have packed an extra toothbrush.
- They are often good project planners because they anticipate and prepare for all contingencies.
- Their caution enables others to take risks or be seen as comparative risk-takers.
- They are often economical in how they go about things.
- If they do have a health problem, their frequent medical visits will pick it up.
- They are usually more law abiding because they think about the consequences of breaking rules and get an adrenaline surge that daunts them (anticipatory anxiety).

Strategies for Dealing with Someone Who Is Overly Cautious

- Be compassionate, not judgmental.
- Understand and empathize but also model rational thinking: I can see why you are a bit anxious, but it isn't as risky as you think. Yes, that could happen, but it is very unlikely. I agree that it is necessary to be prepared, but maybe you could risk packing less in your luggage.
- Share your own experiences of being fearful at first and then overcoming it.
- Dazzle them with facts and statistics to support your assertion that the risk is lower than they believe.
- To reassure them that an activity is reasonably safe, do it with them first.

Strategies for Coping If You Are Overly Cautious or Avoidant

- Feel the fear: do it anyway!
- Analyze. In retrospect, what didn't you need to take with you? Which precautions were unnecessary this time?

- Keep things in perspective. It is not the end of the world if you don't have the correct outfit, enough ice cream for everyone, etc. You cope; nothing disastrous happens. Similarly, it is not the end of the world if you make a social mistake. People usually don't care or remember.
- Use rational self-talk.
- Use a prompting card (see page 265).
- Focus on facts and statistics to reassure yourself.

Perfectionism

What is Typical of Most People?

Most people try to do a good job at work, in relationships, with sports, hobbies, and their community activities. They are motivated by personal satisfaction, group recognition, payment, or the challenge of achieving a good outcome. However, they accept that, due to constraints of money, time, other people's behavior, or mistakes, the result is sometimes less than perfect. They do not necessarily blame themselves or dwell on what did not work. Accepting that making mistakes is part of risk taking, they are prepared to have another go. Others' opinions matter, but if they know they did their best in the circumstances, then this is acceptable. In some areas, people will aim for excellence, but most know that perfection is an impossible goal and it does not enhance satisfaction anyway.

Excellence is objectively doing something as well as possible. Perfectionism relies on others' opinions of the standard reached, and does not tolerate any imperfections.

What Is Typical of Perfectionists?

People who try to deal with their anxiety by becoming "perfectionists" believe that the world is less threatening if they never make a mistake or leave anything undone. If threats are under control, they have less discomfort from anxiety. Being perfect, as they see it, reduces the likelihood that they will miss an important detail, make a mistake, fail, be disapproved of, etc. They are particularly worried about other people's approval and hope that being perfect in some aspects of their lives will protect them from disapproval of other parts of it. A result is unrealistically high expectations of themselves and, unfortunately, of others. They are particularly hard on people who "reflect" on them, such as children, partners, employees, or team members. In the workplace, if they are the type of perfectionist who "overworks," that is, puts in longer hours than everyone else, or voluntarily takes on more tasks, they alienate colleagues. Perfectionists annoy their colleagues because they constantly hint at how good they are and, by implication, are critical of their workmates.

Here are typical examples of people acting like perfectionists:

Jayne always had "perfect parties" with elaborate food, invitations and decorations. She left no detail unattended. Her entertaining cost a fortune and guests always enjoyed the largesse. But the guests rarely invited Jayne and her husband to parties because they felt they could not compete. Jayne's preparations for entertaining caused stress for her family, who didn't enjoy the process, as she insisted that everything had to be color-coordinated, cleaned, and served perfectly. The children had too many jobs, she yelled at them when they didn't get things right, and her husband was on the verge of leaving. Others saw them as "the couple who entertained perfectly."

David put in more hours than everybody in his section and took on most of the tasks that others disliked. He always made it clear to his coworkers and his supervisor that he believed he was the only one who put in a good day's work and that there was a lot of lazy people in the place. Slowly his coworkers detached themselves from him socially. He was rarely invited to go out for a drink after work and increasingly became an outsider in his own workplace.

Denise was the perfect student, or so it seemed. If her teachers specified that they wanted at least two references to be used, Denise used six, even if it meant three round-trips to other libraries. If the word limit was 2,000, she wrote 3,000 words. Even though her teachers specified that over the word limit was unacceptable, they didn't penalize her because the work was of such high quality. She received an A+ in nearly every subject. When she got only an A for one assignment, though, she confronted that teacher, angrily berated her for her unfairness, and then burst into tears.

Jessica was superwoman. As a consultant for a management firm, her full-time work was very demanding, but she also spent "quality time" with her six-year-old twin daughters, made their birthday cakes and cooked monthly dinner parties for her husband's corporate clients. She went to the gym three times a week and shopped only at the organic market to ensure that the vegetables were healthy and fresh. After a near-miss car accident returning from late-night food shopping for her mother-in-law, Jessica realized that fatigue had affected her driving. Although their marriage was seen as "perfect," there was little time or energy for them as a couple. Unless she cut out sleep entirely, Jessica could not see how she could reduce her responsibilities and yet keep to all of the standards that she regarded as important.

Tim is a professional athlete in a team sport. His fellow players hate him, despite his physical skills, because when they lose, he berates them. He trains excessively, piles on the pressure, and criticizes when things go wrong. He wants the others on the team to be perfect. Even when they win easily, he says, "We can do even better."

How Perfectionists Think

Their working hypothesis is: "The world is a very dangerous place and if I make a mistake and people think poorly of me, that will be a disaster. Therefore I will do everything I can perfectly, leaving no stone unturned, so there will be no chance of anything going wrong or of my being criticized or found wanting. Even if I disappoint people in other ways, my perfect record in some chosen area will protect me from their scorn and disapproval. Those who are seen to be part of my life must also be as perfect as possible to protect me from criticism and disapproval."

Looking on the Bright Side

- They are often hardworking and loyal employees, willing to work extra hours or do the additional tasks. They can be highly productive in the amount of work accomplished and are generally very punctual.
- Their household runs like clockwork and their domestic environment is always pleasing (as long as you are allowed to be in it—there is always the downside that you might mess it up!)
- Their work area is mostly clean, tidy, and highly functional. They keep excellent records and can find relevant data that others might have lost or destroyed. Paradoxically, some other parts of their lives may operate at very low standards.

Strategies for Dealing with a Perfectionist

- Appreciate the positive aspects of a focus on excellence, but keep giving the message that while aiming for excellence is good, perfectionism stresses others.
- Understand that their behavior is significantly influenced by different biology from yours and be compassionate, not judgmental.
- Make empathic statements that let them know you understand their desire to do a really good job and have people appreciate them, but at the same time, calmly discourage perfectionism by repeating these rational messages: "Life should be about excellence, not perfection," or "It doesn't matter if it is perfect if everyone hates the process."
- Since being a perfectionist is only part of who they are, acknowledge the whole person and give credit to the other parts of their life.
- Be encouraging when small advances are made, for exam-

ple, when they do not become stressed out about certain less-than-perfect details.

- In the workplace let them know you appreciate their work but point out that over-the-top behavior actually reduces their value to the organization because it alienates colleagues.
- Ask yourself to what extent you have been encouraging their perfectionism. Do you bask in their high achievement or "perfect product"?

Strategies for Coping If You Are a Perfectionist

- Use rational self-talk along the lines of: The goal should be excellence, not perfectionism. It's probably obvious that I am desperately insecure when I try to be perfect, rather than just a human trying hard. It is human to make mistakes. I don't have to be perfect. Nobody is perfect, and if I communicate expectations that another should be perfect, I will harm and alienate them. I don't have to be perfect to be okay.
- Remind yourself that this is only one part of who you are and do not give yourself a hard time if you find it difficult to let go of being "superperson," "superstudent," "superworker" etc. But persevere.
- Delegate more at work. Trust people to do a job well and overcome your perfectionistic expectations. People cannot grow unless they are free to make mistakes and learn from them.
- Aim to do the best job possible within time and budget constraints, but then move on. Sometimes you will need to take shortcuts, and that is all right.

Protective Pessimism

What Is Typical of Most People?

We all protect ourselves by acknowledging what might go wrong or recognizing that there could be negatives in a situation. But most people only do this in small ways, such as allowing for the possibility that you may not get the promotion you want, rather than assuming that you will not. If you are too optimistic and always expect to get what you want, and that nothing will ever go wrong, you can get very badly crushed. Most people work out a balance of optimism (believing it is possible), "realistic hoping," and awareness of the possibility of negative outcomes.

What Is Typical of Protective Pessimists?

Protective pessimists see the worst possible outcomes even for situations that are going well. Their pessimism protects them from feeling anxious from the impact if something bad really does happen. Many people with anxious personalities use protective pessimism to deal with anxiety and miss out on so much joy. If bad things cannot "surprise," they won't be so anxious because they are ready for it. In this way, there is the illusion that the threat of negative outcomes is being kept under control. It is a form of emotional insurance that we all take out, but anxious personalities overinsure.

Protective pessimism can take many forms, but essentially it is about always assuming that the worst will happen and behaving accordingly. Protective pessimists believe that if something can go wrong, it will. If something bad can happen, it will happen, and it will happen to them. Rarely do they expect good outcomes. So they miss out on the joy of anticipation and dwelling pleasurably on the "nice" aspects, in case the gap between pleasurable "dreams" and the reality is too great. They are not game to tempt fate by hoping, dreaming, or wanting, in case they get caught unprepared by negatives. They prepare for disillusionment, sadness and tragedy by protecting their projections with pessimism so they will not get caught by future disappointments. Instead of living up to expectations, they live down, and are often negative in other ways. Other people don't like being around pessimistic people because they can be contagious.

Here are some examples of people using protective pessimism:

When Teresa, 21, got engaged, her mother, Mina, worried. Mina always thought the worst. Her daughter was too young.

She needed to travel or have more relationships first, before settling down. Mina's marriage had ended in divorce, and that would probably happen to Teresa, too. What if she had to bring up her children as a single mother? Would there be enough money? Her fiancé was Italian and she knew the marriage just wouldn't work because Teresa probably wouldn't be able to adjust to another cultural context. When Mina told friends and relatives about the engagement, she always added, "But I don't like its chances."

Annie is tempted to enter her painting in an art competition. She is sure she won't win and says so repeatedly. "Others put in better entries. There are so many entries. Maybe I shouldn't enter. I'm just doing it for fun. I don't expect to win." Another entrant, Sam, knows that his chances of winning are not high but says to others, "You never know. Stranger things have happened. I did put a lot of work into it."

Doug has applied internally for several positions in his company over the last six years. When he submits his application he goes to great pains to explain to everyone that he knows he won't get it and why, usually focusing on things that don't reflect on him, for example, "They usually give it to a woman." He prepares himself and everyone else for his "failure." Eventually it has become a self-fulfilling prophecy because his pessimism and negativity have colored the perceptions others have of him. Many of the people he had spoken to about his negative expectations had been on the next interview panel he faced. In one case, one of the listeners had written his next reference, and his comments about Doug were colored by his awareness of Doug's own low expectations and inability to cope competitively.

Jill has worked in the same company for several years. Her current manager has just called her in to tell her the good news that she is to be given a pay increase. Now she is worried because she is not entirely happy in her current position and if she applies for a job in another company in the future she will find it more difficult to get something because now she is at a higher salary. She fears that they will be less willing to give her a job that can match her new salary.

How Protective Pessimists Think

Their working hypothesis is: "The world is a very dangerous place. Things will always go wrong for me and I will always be disappointed, hurt and let down. So if I expect that these things will happen then I will be protected and they won't take me by surprise. If I expect nothing, I won't be disappointed and anything above that will be a bonus."

Looking on the Bright Side

- They can alert others to possible difficulties.
- Sometimes they can be resilient when disappointed because they expected so little.

Strategies for Dealing with Someone Who Is a Protective Pessimist

- Be compassionate, not judgmental. Make empathic statements, for example: "I know you are worried that you might not get the job, but there is a good chance you will. If you don't, it won't be the end of the world," or "I know how you feel. Not knowing what will happen is a bit nerve-wracking, isn't it?"
- Be assertive. Tell them how hard it is for you to keep listening to their pessimism, how it ultimately makes you perceive them more negatively.
- Use rational argument and positive prompts, for example: "No one ever went blind looking on the bright side," or "Yes, but what are the good things that might happen?"

Strategies for Coping If You Are a Protective Pessimist

- Understand why and when you do it. Accept the irrationality.
- Challenge your pessimistic thoughts with more rational self-talk: I miss out on so much joy. Others don't like being

around me when I adopt an attitude of doom and gloom. I'll become a self-fulfilling prophecy. It doesn't really protect me from anxiety. What good outcomes might happen? I can enjoy thinking about the possibility, even if the chances are low. I won't expect too much but I can still expect.

- Use a prompting card (see page 265).
- Don't catastrophize. Catastrophizing is when you identify the very worst that can happen and then assume that it will happen. Challenge that kind of thinking.

Hypersensitivity

What Is Typical of Most People?

We all have sensitive areas where we perhaps overreact, perceiving others' responses as unpleasant or unfair. Certain people are particularly sensitive to comments about their appearance or presentation, others about their competence. Although no one likes or even welcomes criticism, most learn to handle implied or explicit criticism. Generally, they only respond angrily or by being hurt in response to extreme or unfair examples or outright insults.

What Is Typical of Hypersensitive People?

Some flooders become hypersensitive in that they see criticism, unfairness, rejection, and putdowns in much of what others say and do to them. Expecting to see disapproval, disgust, contempt, and rejection and to deal with the anxiety that these arouse, they attack. Or at the first sign of any of these, they feel slighted and angry— (for example, if someone tries to end a phone call with them they assume this means that they are perceived to be unimportant and say angrily, "I haven't finished yet." Ultimately they develop very low self-esteem.

How Hypersensitive People Think

Their working hypothesis is: "The world is a very dangerous place. People are always trying to be unfair to me, put me down, or make me feel bad. I need to watch for every sign that this might be happening, so I can stop it right away and they won't do it to me again."

Looking on the Bright Side

- They keep you on your toes. You are less likely to take them for granted.
- If they are trained in rational assertiveness, they will stand up for themselves. Here are some examples of people acting in a hypersensitive way:

Jodie made the working environment in her small office very tense because she seemed so intent on taking offense when it wasn't meant. If during a lunchtime discussion, one of the other staff made an offhand remark about the ways in which their husbands engaged in outdoor activities with their sons, Jodie took it personally. She assumed that they were implying that Jodie's sons missed out because she was a single parent. If Jodie made a mistake and it was pointed out, she usually overreacted by saying sarcastic things like, "Oh, and of course you never make any mistakes, do you?"

Michael (mid-twenties) is easily discouraged by anything his friends do that could be interpreted as personal rejection. For example, once they made weekend camping plans that included him but forgot that he didn't have his own transport. Rather than remind them by saying, "Hey, guys, can someone give me a lift?" he personalized the situation as, "They couldn't give a damn about me," and told them he didn't think he would go after all.

Strategies for Dealing with Someone Who Is Hypersensitive

- Be compassionate, not judgmental.
- Make empathic statements in calmer moments. Say, for example, "I realize you have to stand up for yourself and I respect that, but often things that are said are not meant to be critical of you."
- Be assertive. Say, "It really distresses me when you think I am criticizing you and I am not," or "I don't think you are being fair to me in thinking that was what I meant."
- Establish a context of trust and reassure them of your genuine, positive regard.

- Give direct messages of acceptance: "You know how much we appreciate you here."
- Don't get angry. Stay calm. Repeat, "That wasn't what was meant." Or "Yes, you could see it that way, but your interpretation is wrong. I have the greatest respect for your administrative skills."
- Don't patronize by saying, "You're overreacting."

Strategies for Coping If You Are Hypersensitive

- Use rational self-talk: "I wouldn't get upset at a short call. He is busy and between meetings, so he can't talk long. It's not because he doesn't want to talk to me," or "I won't personalize everything."
- Be kind to yourself and self-accepting. This is only part of who you are.
- Remind yourself about how difficult others find being with someone they have to tiptoe around.
- Find ways to feel good about yourself. Highlight your positives. Seek positive feedback.

Hoarding and Procrastinating

What Is Typical of Most People?

All of us keep some stuff we ought to have thrown out or recycled, for example, clothes, documents, files, frozen food, or old tools. Periodically we have a purge and throw out the unnecessary objects that clutter our lives and homes. All of us put off obligations such as tax returns, thank-you letters, visiting relatives, or cleaning out closets for a while, but eventually we do them.

What Is Typical of Hoarders?

Some hoarders are just too lazy to decide what to throw away. Some procrastinators are just too lazy, period. Sometimes the tasks are so overwhelming that they lose heart.

For those who have been through the Great Depression or relocation as refugees, "hoarding" is a form of holding on to the past and a way of securing a future. Relatives who have had to clean out a house after the death of someone who lived during the Depression are conscious of why apparently worthless items have been kept, often in multiples. Hoarding possessions allayed the anxiety of being destitute or without resources if the economy crashed again.

Most hoarders, however, are too nervous to throw things out because they cannot handle the anxiety of coping with their error of judgment if that discarded item was needed later. Or they get the same surge at the thought of how "bad" it is to throw out perfectly good (but useless) stuff.

Many procrastinators put off doing things because they fear doing them poorly or being overwhelmed by them, or they focus too much on the discomfort of the task and not enough on the positive outcomes that can be achieved.

These are typical behaviors:

- Whenever there was a sale on, Carol would stock up on facial cleansers. Her collection of "good" towels grew and grew. But she rarely used any of them.
- Robert kept every flier he had ever gotten and filed them all away in a box. He never used them, but he felt better knowing he had them all just in case some were needed.

How Hoarders and Procrastinators Think

Their working hypothesis is: "It would be absolutely devastating if I made a mistake or an error of judgment and threw out something that I later needed, or that would prove I had wasted money. The best thing is to keep everything. So many things can go wrong that I must keep everything that might possibly be needed."

"If there is something I should do but I am not sure if I can do it well enough, I will keep putting it off and then I will never have to face that anxiety."

Looking on the Bright Side
- Often hoarders have things that do come in handy later, for example, tools or fabric.
- Family historians love hoarders because they usually have kept all the family documents.

Strategies for Dealing with a Hoarder or a Procrastinator

- Understand and accept; this is only part of the person.
- Be compassionate, not judgmental. Be empathic. Say, for example, "It is really hard to throw stuff out, isn't it? I always feel guilty when I clean up but I eventually do it. I feel so good afterward, once the guilty moment has passed!"
- Offer support, for example, by helping them with the filing.
- A major cleanup may be overwhelming. Encourage and praise the tackling of a small section first.
- Offer to help them get started on a task about which they have procrastinated for a long time.

Strategies for Coping If You Are a Hoarder or Procrastinator

- Accept that this is an aspect of yourself, not the whole you.
- Start small. Tackle one area only. For example, always set something aside for donating to charity; always clear out at least one box, closet, or in-box per month. Use the "little by little" method.
- Just do it! Take a deep breath and start.
- Use rational self-talk: "Yes, I might end up throwing out something I need but usually that doesn't happen, and if it does, it is not the end of the world."
- Establish a halfway area that will give you a "second-chance" feeling. Store things in another room, closet, filing cabinet, or the trunk of your car for a month. If not used in that time, throw them out on the deadline.

Overcontrolling Behavior

What Is Typical of Most People?

All of us attempt to alter the behavior of people who have an impact on us. Most settle for influencing and stop short of trying to control others. For example, if you think that a friend might embarrass you by their off-color jokes when you attend a work function together, you might make a semihumorous remark that is intended to discourage their joke telling ("I hope you don't drink so much that you tell those jokes, Sam. I don't think Howard can take them and our jobs might be on the line!"). This is not controlling in that it is neither "heavy" nor "parental." It does not contain a threat of punishment, either.

Most of us keep a reasonable watch on the behavior of people whose performance reflects on us. Now and then, we check with them, occasionally monitor what they have done, and offer advice or direction when required. But we don't keep such a close eye that we intrude. Delegating shows that we trust them to act independently and support experiences that will help them to grow.

What Is Typical of People with Overcontrolling Behavior?

People with an overcontrolling behavior pattern attempt to closely control the behavior of others in a range of contexts. They believe that as long as they control as many of the elements of other people's behavior as possible, less can go wrong and the lower their personal anxiety levels will be. Overcontrolling behavior can produce dependent behavior in others, especially those with high anxiety levels. Other people, however, resist overcontrolling behavior, and the result can be great conflict.

Overcontrolling behavior is a strategy used by some highly anxious people, but you cannot assume that an overcontrolling person is necessarily anxious. Power may be the prevailing motivation rather than protection. The anxious overcontroller is scared underneath, whereas the power seeking overcontroller is insensitive and self-focused.

Typical behavior might be:

- not delegating in the workplace
- supervising staff too closely
- being intrusive with a partner or child, for example, wanting to know too many personal details
- insisting that a child or partner show receipts for items purchased
- insisting that a child or partner ask permission regarding actions and excursions and gives details of time, place, person, etc.

- not allowing independence in one's child, for example; re—stricting freedom inappropriately, refusing certain acquaintances permission to be guests, working too closely with them on homework
- making all the decisions or overriding the decisions of others and refusing to see them as legitimate.

These are some examples of anxiety-based overcontrolling behavior:

Louis, an assistant manager of a small department store, believed that he could not trust others to do things properly and without mistakes, so he rarely delegated. Instead, he would hand out small tasks while retaining overall control. For example, he would give a staff member the job of ordering the Christmas decorations for the store but would not give her the task of organizing the display. Instead, he would tell her how he wanted it done. Then he would continually check to see what she was doing and give advice on improvements and identify mistakes that needed correcting. He believed that his role was to direct, monitor, and give advice, not nurture and encourage. Over time, this became a self-fulfilling prophecy as staff lost confidence in their ability to do their jobs properly. They began to leave because he was on their backs so much. They never felt they were given any chance to learn and grow by taking on tasks independently. One staff member said he made her feel like a child despite her years of experience in the retail industry and the fact that she was five years older than he was.

William, a father of four children aged 8–18, ran the family totally. Rules governed just about everything, and if they were not adhered to, he would be withdrawn or sarcastic for days. He made it clear who the children could have as guests, decided about vacations and outings, and had a major impact on deciding their choice of school subjects. Ages ago, his wife had learned not to disagree with him, and although his rules were strict and he kept tight control over the family, she believed he did so out of love. Occasionally a child would disagree with what he said, but mostly they didn't speak up, because he acted as though they had broken an unspoken rule. Sarah, his third child (16), was the one who rebelled and with whom he had the most conflict. After arguments over her freedom, and her right to alternative viewpoints, she would often "disappear" and end up staying at her aunt's house, because she felt so stifled by her father's overcontrolling behavior.

How Overcontrolling People Think

Their working hypothesis is: "The world is a very dangerous place, so if I control everything that happens, and as much as possible of how other significant people in my life behave, then there is less chance of something going wrong."

Looking on the Bright Side

They usually work very hard and are well prepared.

Strategies for Dealing with Someone Who Is Overcontrolling

- Remind yourself that this is only part of the whole person.
- Offer reassuring comments to encourage them to trust you.
- Be assertive. Say something like, "I realize that you are try-ing to make sure that this works, but I'm finding it very difficult to learn when I'm not given much responsibility. I can see that you want this to go well, but I'm disappointed that I'm not getting much opportunity to try my hand. I would like a chance to try this on my own, if that is okay."

Strategies for Coping If You Are an Overcontroller

- Acknowledge your behavior pattern. Ask someone you trust to be straight with you and tell you if they think you are overcontrolling at times.
- Accept that a good manager delegates and nurtures the growth of junior staff, that no one grows without opportu-nities to be independent, and that most people recognize

that those who overcontrol are scared underneath that you won't respect them for not having the courage to let you try your wings, which will make it harder to fly.

Use more rational self-talk, such as:

- Unless I delegate and allow others to try, they will never learn and I can't do everything. Yes, they may object, but that will be a good learning experience for them. Everyone has to make some mistakes along the way.

Angry Outbursts

What Is Typical of Most People?

At various times, we all act in an irritable and grumpy way, or we get annoyed about nothing. But mostly we keep angry outbursts for serious issues, recognizing how they alienate and damage both ourselves and others.

What Is Typical of People Who Have Angry Outbursts Because They Are Feeling Anxious?

Many anxious personalities spend more of their time primed to "fight" (remember "fight or flight") because the "fear chemicals" are frequently released into their bodies. Their fear (which is not always recognized as such), often makes them act first and ask questions later. Sometimes they are described as "bad-tempered" or on a short fuse. The bodily sensations of anger are almost identical to those of anxiety. They are both produced by adrenaline surges, and it is often hard to tell if you are feeling angry or frightened. To some extent, we differentiate which emotion we are feeling based on how we interpret intention. If a snarling dog is barking at us, we try to get out of the way. But if someone speaks disrespectfully to us (which we interpret as violating our right to be respected) or denies us our rights in another way, such as being uncooperative, we interpret that as something intended to deny us. We see that we need to tackle it, rather than run away from it. But sometimes anxious people attack the wrong target.

How People Who Have Angry Outbursts Think

Their working hypothesis is: "When someone or something threatens me by making me feel anxious, I will immediately attack and defend myself."

Here are some typical cases:

Sylvia has always had a very short fuse. Whenever conflict occurs, she angrily attacks whoever she feels has the most to do with making her angry. She is actually very scared underneath, but attacking is her way of trying to control the situation and reduce her anxiety.

Ken made a passing comment to his wife, Penny, about the stupidity of the morning radio hosts. Penny stared stonily at her breakfast newspaper and didn't reply. She felt Ken was overly critical and was sick of it. Ken's anxiety levels began to increase. He felt ignored and on the receiving end of criticism and contempt. He made an angry retort: "So your newspaper's more interesting than I am?" and then the argument began.

Looking on the Bright Side
- They will defend themselves.
- They are not submissive.
- They can be passionate about issues that concern them.

Strategies for Dealing with Those Who Have Angry Outbursts When Anxious
- One of the difficulties is that people who deal with their anxiety by angry outbursts can't be seen just as "a person who is anxious" because that is not the only thing that motivates them. Sometimes, like all of us, they are also angry and upset about something that has been unfair or harmful to them, or they are just in a bad mood.
- In a personal relationship, give them a hug when you sense they are getting upset, or say, as you put your arm around them, "Let's not let this affect our relationship," or "I can

see that this is really upsetting you. I'm sorry about that but we can deal with it." This may be difficult if *you* feel angry, too.

- Be assertive. Tell them you understand that they are upset but find their way of dealing with a bad situation is distressing to you and you need them to do it differently. Say, for example, "When you attack me like that, I feel unfairly treated because what I said didn't justify your attack. Could you try to tell me what you are thinking without attacking me? Or perhaps call 'time out' and we can discuss it later."

- Be compassionate, not judgmental. Remember that this is only part of the whole person. Focus on their positives.

- Empathize but don't use the terms "scared" or "frightened," especially with men. Use "apprehensive," "troubled," or "upset" instead. For example: "I can see that this is distressing you. You are apprehensive about the idea but can we talk about it calmly, please, without losing our cool?"

Strategies for Coping When You Are the One Who Has Angry Outbursts

- Accept yourself as an imperfect person. But remember that it is only part of who you are. Focus on the positives, too.

- Apologize afterward and ask for support in changing the pattern.

- Remind yourself about the negative impact on your relationships.

- Acknowledge and explain that your biology may be different from theirs.

- Use rational self-talk as a control: "This will work out better if I stay calm. When I attack, I don't like myself later so I'll try not to do it. I may be in the right here but if I attack, I will badly affect my relationship because no one likes being attacked, even when they are in the wrong."

- Practice anger management strategies (see page 239).

11

I'm Always Right

THE INFLEXIBLE PERSONALITY

KEY WORDS FOR THOSE WITH AN INFLEXIBLE PERSONALITY
rigidity
sameness and routine
neatness and small detail
narrowness
inflexibility
self-righteousness
stubbornness
overcontrolling
blaming others

What Is Typical of Most People?

Many of us can be stubborn about issues that are important to us, and don't like to have our views in these areas challenged. We all have our routines because they make our lives flow more smoothly. However, we learn when to be more flexible, when to look inwards at ourselves, and when to negotiate and give ground.

What Is Typical of People with an Inflexible Personality Pattern?

The inflexible personality pattern is a particularly nonadaptive one. It is characterized by excessively rigid and obsessive thinking, an absolute belief in one's own point of view, self-righteousness, stub-

Due: Tuesday, November 02, 2021

Title: Mercy Falls
Due: Tuesday, November 02, 2021

Total items: 2
Account balance: $0.00
10/12/2021 4:45 PM
Checked out: 5
Overdue: 0
Hold requests: 0
Thank you!

Waconia Public Library

Customer ID: **********5253

Items that you checked out

Title: Difficult personalities : a practical guide to
       managing the hurtful behavior of others (and
       maybe your own)
ID: 32086009732851
Due: **Tuesday, November 02, 2021**

Title: Mercy Falls
ID: 32086005020723
Due: Tuesday, November 02, 2021

Total items: 2
Account balance: $0.00
10/12/2021 4:45 PM
Checked out: 5
Overdue: 0
Hold requests: 0
Ready for pickup: 0

Waconia Library hours: Mon & Tue 10am-8pm;
Wed & Thur 10am-6pm; Fri 10am - 5pm;
Sat 10am-3pm; closed Sunday
Renew at www.carverlib.org or 952-856-1250
Thank you!

bornness, pettiness and undue preoccupation with detail, a strong need for routine, and a failure to see the perspective of others. Hence it is also characterized by poor adaptation to life's realities and poor conflict management. People with this pattern can be difficult to work or live with because they make cooperation difficult and they leave others feeling devalued and powerless. They create angry feelings in others because of their inflexibility and stubbornness, and they ignore the feelings of others because of their lack of empathy and inability to express warmth and tender emotions. They often appear cold and controlling, and they demand that everything be done their way. They rarely seek help with their behavior because their complaints are about others and they see little fault in themselves.

Inflexible personalities often become obsessive; that is, they become overfocused on a particular theme in a nonadaptive way. Some engage in a pattern of rigid thinking as a means of controlling anxiety. To understand them, also read chapter 10 on anxiety. Others with this pattern learned early in life through experiences that there is satisfaction in a very controlled and controlling life. By accepting a narrow and egocentric view of things, and by running their life in a very orderly fashion, they feel more sure of what is "right" and get their way more often. Because of their narrow perceptions and their belief that their view is always the right one, they can become obsessive in their determination to enforce their view on others and "win," no matter what it takes. There is a lack of empathy, that is, the ability to see another's perspective and recognize and respond appropriately to their feelings and concerns.

In its more severe form, this pattern is called obsessive-compulsive personality disorder in the DSM-IV-TR. This is different from obsessive-compulsive disorder, but there are some behaviors in common. A diagnosis of obsessive-compulsive personality disorder can be made when at least four of the following eight characteristics are present.

Preoccupation with Details and Routines

The person is preoccupied with details, rules, lists, order, or schedules, sometimes to the extent that the point of the activity is lost. They are often inefficient time managers because they pay attention to the detail at the expense of the overall task.

Perfectionism
They may show perfectionism to the point where the task may not be completed.

Overfocused on Work and Productivity
They may be excessively devoted to work and productivity and not consider leisure time to be valuable. They often inflict this view on others.

Inflexibility and Self-Righteousness
They may be overconscientious and inflexible about matters of morality, ethics, and values. They prefer the moral high ground and like to appear more righteous than others. They will not debate their views and often rigidly hold irrational views on an issue.

Hoarding
They find it difficult to discard worn-out or worthless objects, even when they have no sentimental value.

Overcontrol
They may be reluctant to delegate tasks to others or work closely with others unless they perform exactly as the person wants them to. There is a preoccupation with controlling others' actions so that they do things "correctly."

Miserliness
They may be miserly toward themselves and others. Money is hoarded for future disasters rather than enjoyed.

Stubbornness
They are wrapped up in their own point of view and seem unable to see the big picture or anyone else's point of view. They often can't see the forest for the trees. Even when it is in their own interest to compromise or negotiate, they stick stubbornly to their opinion,

arguing that it is "the principle of the thing." Needless to say, they are prone to blaming others rather than using self-reflection.

Some of these characteristics are difficult to detect because they are subtly expressed. Only experienced clinicians can make a proper diagnosis of this more severe pattern called obsessive-compulsive personality disorder. There are many people, however, who have an inflexible and obsessive personality pattern with some but not all of these characteristics in a milder form, and you can identify these patterns in their behavior. Such people are often described as either controlling, cold, inflexible, selfish, opinionated, rigid, unaffectionate, or self-righteous.

A pattern of rigid thinking, self-righteousness, and inflexibility can be seen in behaviors such as:

- holding a very stubborn and black-and-white view on certain issues. This prevents any debate and the person never shifts their opinions in even the smallest way.
- belonging to the kind of religious or similar group where all the "correct" thoughts are given to you
- having inflexible sequences of behavior and routines, for example, always having to run and then empty the dishwasher before you go to bed; always having a very neat fridge.
- lack of warmth and affection.
- keeping detailed records of things that are not useful, for example, recording every detail of a vacation in terms of costs of meals, what was eaten, airplane seat numbers, and what was packed.
- excessively blaming others and showing no insight into their own behavior.

How People with an Obsessive Personality Pattern Think

Their working hypothesis is: "I will stick to my beliefs, views, and routines, because then I will feel more sure about the world and more likely to get what I want. I will never have to question myself and I will not be forced to deal with the realization that there is a lot of ambiguity, ambivalence, difference, and confusion, all of which are very threatening. I matter more than others."

Looking on the Bright Side

- Their actions are relatively predictable.
- They can be obsessively loyal.

Strategies for Dealing with Someone with a Rigid Personality Pattern

- Be assertive. Let them know in a firm but warm way that what they are doing is distressing you. Say, for example, "I can see that you believe strongly that we can't easily change that system, but we need at least to talk about possibilities because I am not able to work within it as it currently exists."
- Don't bother debating what is not important.
- Use rational statements with respect, for example, "Yes, doing things in the same way feels safer, but you stagnate if that is all you do."

Strategies for Coping If You Have Some Characteristics of an Obsessive Personality Pattern

- Question yourself if you think this pattern may be yours.
- Ask others whether you behave in these ways. If the answer suggests you need to look at yourself more closely, have the courage to do so.
- Be prepared to debate your views. If someone disagrees with you it does not mean that they are correct and you are wrong. If your view is worth holding, you should be able to debate them.
- Work hard to see the other person's perspective. Focus on developing skills of negotiation and rational thinking. See pages 222 and 250. The sections about maintaining a strong personal relationship will also be useful.

Veronica had been very controlling during her marriage to Brad and always got her own way by stubbornly refusing to acknowledge that there was any other way. Brad, although easygoing and more tolerant than most, eventually had enough of Veronica's determination to control all the decisions. There were no problems as long as he went along with what she wanted but he found that any attempt to assert his own rights led to his being "frozen out"—not being spoken to—and no sex for prolonged periods. Her determination to save money at all costs, despite the fact that they were financially quite well off, drove him mad.

When Brad finally left her, Veronica became enraged and utterly convinced of her own justification for doing everything she could to damage him. She told lies about him to his business associates and his family; she raided their joint bank accounts. She mounted ongoing legal actions against the advice of her legal advisers (whom she then fired because they wouldn't agree with her). She was obsessed with destroying him and convincing everyone of her own righteousness in everything. By the time their divorce and financial division were finalized three and a half years and five court cases later, she had cost both herself and Brad most of their communal assets in legal costs, and their two children were alienated from their father. She lost many of her friends as they grew tired of her ongoing self-righteousness coupled with her vicious actions and her total disregard for everyone's well-being. Although no longer financially secure, she was still totally sure of the righteousness of her own actions.

12

Don't Ever Leave Me

THE DEMANDING PERSONALITY

KEY WORDS FOR THOSE WITH A DEMANDING PERSONALITY
demanding
abandonment
disillusionment
fear
rejection
payback
possessiveness
jealously

What Is Typical of Most People?

When someone we care about decides to leave us, it hurts. When a significant person treats us indifferently or is downright neglectful, that hurts, too. Workplace rejection or layoffs cause most workers to feel down, regardless of the reason for the decision. When someone who is special to us gets another friend, most of us initially feel hurt, left out, and less special for a while.

But most of us deal with our initial hurt, anger, or jealousy and eventually adapt to what has happened. Usually we don't attack, lose all sense of self-worth, throw tantrums, rage, threaten, or take revenge when we feel left alone, rejected, or ignored. Probably we share our concerns about not getting enough of their time or attention and tell them about our hurt. But we still accept that we can't have our partner (or friend or colleague) exclusively, and that work demands, colleagues, and other friends and family have priorities, too.

If someone ends a relationship with us, we feel appropriately down and unhappy for a while. We grieve, agonize, reflect, and feel angry, but eventually we adjust and get on with our lives. We often move on to new relationships. If fired, laid off, or dealt with unfairly by coworkers whom we formerly trusted, then we feel upset and angry. It takes some time to recover from the kick in the gut. But we do recover and move on to new colleagues and organizations.

What Is Typical of People with a Demanding Personality?

A person with a demanding personality pattern is absolutely terrified that they are going to be abandoned. If, as they see it, they are abandoned, either they become enraged and take revenge on people for their rejection or sink into despair, often becoming depressed and suicidal. Sometimes they do both. They see potential abandonment everywhere. They can become very demanding and quite manipulative to ensure that they are not left alone and that their needs are met. Relationships and work are difficult with them because of their need for and demands on others, which can be exhausting. A few can also be difficult because of their determination to pay people back for their perceived abandonment.

What Is the Severe Form of This Pattern?

This personality is driven by an intense terror of being abandoned and attempts to stop people from abandoning them. They may take revenge when anything is done that could be perceived as a sign of real or potential abandonment. When this personality pattern is severe enough to become a disorder, it damages oneself and in some cases, others. In the DSM-IV-TR, the disorder is termed borderline personality disorder and is diagnosed in about 2 percent of the population. It causes significant distress and dysfunction, and is diagnosed when five or more of the behaviors listed below are present.

Frantic Efforts to Avoid Real or Imagined Abandonment

When someone significant to them wants time to themselves or spends time with others, they are upset. They may seduce to attract people. Then they will use manipulative behaviors to stop the person from leaving or being more separate than they can handle. They may be vicious toward the people another also cares for, such as a parent's new partner or an adult child's new romantic interest.

Unstable and Intense Interpersonal Relationships

They alternate between idealization and devaluation. They become very easily disenchanted, quickly becoming disappointed and then enraged when the other person does not meet their expectations. They usually have a history of intense, stormy, and conflict-ridden relationships.

An Unstable Self-Image

Uncertainty exists about who they are and want to be. Prone to humiliation, they exaggerate others' reaction to them, so their self-esteem can alternate between arrogance and pathos. They alternate between feeling superior and feeling worthless. It is as if they have no real sense of self without the presence, reassurance, and, sometimes, subservience of others.

Impulsivity

Impulsive behavior is a strong feature. For example, they may engage in impulsive sex with people they hardly know, go on impulsive buying splurges, gamble excessively, binge eat, or take drugs.

Dramatic Recurrent Suicidal Gestures or Threats

These are often made and sometimes acted on to manipulate another from leaving and sometimes out of despair at being abandoned.

Short-Lived Mood Instability

Many experience mood swings over a few hours, ranging from euphoria to anger and then to sadness.

Chronic Feelings of Emptiness and Boredom

There are feelings of being "not really there" when they are by themselves. They may become overwhelmed by terrifying feelings of abandonment if they are left alone, even briefly and for a good reason.

Inappropriate Intense Anger and Frequent Displays of Bad Temper

These occur when their needs are not met, when they are left alone, or when they cannot have something they want from people, such as time, affection, praise, or obedience.

Some of these characteristics are difficult to detect because they are subtly expressed. Only experienced clinicians can make a proper diagnosis of borderline personality disorder. However, there are many people who have a demanding personality pattern with many, but not all, of these characteristics in a milder form, and you can identify these patterns in their behavior.

What is Typical of Behavior Arising from "Terror of Abandonment"?

Terror of abandonment is the fear that someone important to us is going to leave or reject us, and we will be without their support and care. Although we all have some abandonment fear, there are those whose lives can be profoundly affected by the constant and often unrealistic fear that they will be rejected and abandoned. Only when others are fully focused on them do they feel some sense of relief from their terror. Not all show extreme rage. Rather, they become less able to maintain stable relationships because they overreact to any separation or act of neglect that could possibly be interpreted as a bad omen for the relationship. Histories of stormy relationships and fallings out are common. They are often very demanding and controlling in their attempts to tie people to them. Unless able to find a relatively nondemanding partner, friend, or colleague who can tolerate their behavior, they often end up driving away the very people they wanted to keep. Such people are often described as needy, erratic, possessive, demanding, or intense.

When people with this pattern meet a new romantic partner,

friend, or colleague, they work hard to impress and "hook" the person. They can be caring, loving, generous, helpful, supportive, and very available. Often they establish intimacy quickly, and the other person feels like they have known them for a long time. Totally adoring, they become a loud fan of the new person in their life, broadcasting how wonderful they are. They can become good friends, coworkers, and lovers because of superficial nurturing and empathizing skills. But the hidden price is the expectation that the recipient must be available for their needs as demanded.

If the person is *not* available on demand, or perceived as showing signs of possible abandonment, then they can become either depressed or enraged, or both. Possessive, they find it hard to tolerate their partner's having time with friends or family, or spending "too much time" at work. They may resent not having first priority. They simmer when realizing that a liked coworker likes others, too, and occasionally lunches with them. Their self-image is so low, or fluctuating, that they find it hard to believe that a favored person could still want them if there are other people that they also like.

At some point, the idealized person may act in a way that threatens their sense of being cared for and special, and then their feelings take control. Briefly, they may be very depressed and experience intense periods of anxiety. Anger may then take over. They claim that the other person does not care enough, give enough, is not "there" enough. Abandonment is possible, they sense, even if this is inaccurate. ("This person no longer loves me, respects me, or approves of my work, and may abandon me.")

Their anger is intense, often irrational and they are unable to control it. Tantrums, threats, angry recriminations, and sarcasm are common. Most of it is extreme. "Idealizing" has moved quickly to "devaluing." Occasionally, they have some justification for their distress (for example, if someone forgets to invite them to an event), but they overreact. More often than not, the other person simply had a period of temporary and time-limited separation, either physically or psychologically, as in a weekend away with friends, working in the study for several evenings in a row, or spending the evening visiting a relative or a child from an earlier marriage. Even an unavoidable change in plans (for example, canceling a dinner engagement, running very late, missing a plane) can set them off.

After their tantrum or angry outburst, they often feel shame-faced and depressed. However, the pattern recurs when there is another threat of abandonment. Sometimes their anger turns into fury as attempts to control and retain the idealized person don't work. Threats of suicide or physical violence may occur. Sometimes they carry out part of their threats. If the person does reject, leave, or withdraw, they feel justified in avenging in unpleasant ways for a long period.

How Do People with a Demanding Personality Think?

Their working hypothesis is: "The worst thing that could happen to me is to be alone and without care and support, so I will do anything in order to keep people who matter to me. I must constantly make sure they are do not abandon me. If they do, I'll pay them back."

What about the Kids?

Some young children show this pattern early on and find it intolerable to be alone. They often engage in self-defeating behaviors in their inappropriate attempts to get classmates to be "my friend only." They can become very cold, rejecting, and sometimes nasty if a friend, especially a "best friend," enjoys the company of other kids in the class. Similarly, it is not uncommon for kids with this pattern to be overly possessive of a noncustodial parent after a divorce and become very unpleasant toward their parents' potential or permanent new partners.

Why Do They Do It?

- Research suggests that there is a strong familial factor in this pattern, as it is five times more common among first-degree relatives. This suggests either a genetic predisposition or modeling effects of parent behavior, or a combination. The pattern could be easily learned from a parent

or significant adult, but whether there is a genetic predisposition is still unclear. There is weak evidence for some
people with extreme versions of this pattern having lower
brain serotonin activity than normal (especially those who
attempt suicide), or abnormalities in REM sleep and dopamine levels (dopamine is the "pleasure" neurotransmitter).

- Many have a history of parental neglect, parental coldness,
  or rejection, having many parental substitutes, or early experiences of abandonment, separation, and loss. Some may
  have witnessed domestic violence. Any one of these can trigger the preoccupation with trying not to be abandoned.

- Similarly, a parent who leaves the family home after a marital separation and does not maintain reliable and regular
  contact with a child could also have this impact.

- Being emotionally, sexually, or physically abused as a child is a
  reasonably common background factor in the lives of people
  who are diagnosed with a borderline personality disorder.

- Sometimes a young woman develops this pattern when
  she has a father who is emotionally distant in many ways
  and who treats her more like a girlfriend when he does
  find time for her. That is, he inappropriately "sexualizes"
  their relationship, although there is no overt sexual abuse.
  The young woman may then develop an intense jealousy
  toward the mother or any other women whom she sees as
  threatening her relationship with her father. This pattern
  may continue with her romantic relationships; that is, she
  feels constantly threatened by other women. Such inappropriate fathers are often found in the "everyday predator"
  category of personality (see page 172).

- Others with this pattern have a history of overprotective and
  doting parents who made them the center of their world and
  tried to meet their every need. For example, this might happen in some but not all cases: with an only child; when parents
  had difficulty in conceiving; with an earlier serious illness or
  problem; when one parent compensated for an unsatisfying
  marriage by becoming "overinvolved" with a child. In psychological parlance, the two become "enmeshed."

Looking on the Bright Side

- People with this pattern often have superior social skills (as opposed to relationship skills), and can be very appealing.
- They often work very hard to please others.

Strategies for Dealing with People Who Demonstrate Characteristics of a Demanding Personality

- Be aware that they will need much more reassurance, praise, and time from you, although this can become wearying. Convince them that your separateness does not mean that you don't care about them and that they are very special to you.
- Empathize with their distress. Say, for example, "I know you feel lost and down when I have to go away. That's understandable."
- Show compassion without being judgmental. Many have good reasons from the past for their inability to trust and their tendency to see the possibility of "abandonment" everywhere.
- Remind yourself that this is only one aspect of who they are. Accept this as part of their whole person and focus on their other positive parts.
- Allocate them to highly structured jobs in a workplace situation. They have a preference for structured work situations with fewer possibilities for rejection or disapproval. Link them up with a group in the workplace to take the pressure off any individual. Spread them around.
- Don't retaliate with anger. Be assertive instead and use a broken-record statement (see page 236) to help them see the situation more rationally. Say, for example, "No, you are not being left out. We are rotating and you will be on the next rotation. We really value your work," or "I do care about you, but I also want to spend some time with my son, which in no way diminishes my love for you. I really do care for you."

Strategies for Changing Your Own Behavior If You Have Characteristics of a Demanding Personality Pattern

- Avoid interpreting separation as rejection or abandonment. Be kind to yourself. Analyze why you are feeling this way, and then challenge any irrational "abandoned" feelings with more rational self-talk. "Where is the evidence that this person no longer cares for me? All they want to do is have a weekend away with friends. They are entitled to have time on their own. Everyone needs some of that. They are not exceptional in that regard. I'll keep myself busy while they are away rather than dwell on lonely or frightened feelings."

  "She might have had to go away on business unexpectedly and not had time to let me know. Not having called me is not necessarily a sign that she no longer values me. There is no other evidence that she has lost her feelings for me."

  "She can have other friends and still care as much for me as a friend. Just because I am always thinking about her, doesn't mean she's always thinking about me." "He doesn't feel the need to make contact as often as I do. This is my problem, not his."

- Remind yourself that this is only part of who you are. In other ways, you are competent and well liked. Keep the whole picture in perspective.

Erin, 45, worked as an administrative assistant and was especially attentive to her new departmental head, Beth, a 35-year-old MBA graduate who had had a meteoric rise in the company. She did all the jobs no one else wanted to do and loudly praised Beth to anyone who would listen. Erin did a pretty good job of looking after the data for the interstate expansion project, as this was Beth's pet project. But Beth decided that she needed another person on her team and appointed a personal assistant, Jan, with strong qualifications in computer technology. Jan was given responsibility for the project that had formerly been Erin's, and Erin was redeployed in another project of equal importance but requiring fewer computer skills. Erin reacted with jealous outrage. She was furious that this person had taken priority over her in her work status and also, as she saw it, in the relationship with Beth. She fumed and started having tantrums about "small issues" in the office that she saw as her domain. When Beth took Jan with her to a conference, Erin felt slighted and rejected, and started obstructing by losing files or mixing up messages. She did anything that would reflect badly on Jan and help Erin resume her former relationship with Beth, as she perceived it. A month later, when Erin was eventually laid off, she erased all the computer files before leaving the company. She also destroyed the backup disks. This was not the first time Erin had done such things. She had a long history of stormy workplace relationships that started with admiration and closeness but which often culminated in Erin paying back someone who she believed had been disloyal or slighted her. Then she would either resign without notice or be dismissed. When Erin was a child, her mother had engaged in a similar pattern with family members and there had been long periods of feuds and not speaking to each other. Her mother was rather self-absorbed and often obsessed with these family dramas of who had slighted and rejected whom. She had been very limited in her ability to give Erin a secure and stable childhood, one in which she focused on Erin's strengths and gave her unconditional acceptance. Often Erin was treated with the same approach as she treated her family. When she pleased her mother she would receive undiluted praise and time from her. But when she let her mother down in the smallest way, she was punished by being frozen out for long periods of time.

Damaging
Personalities

13

You'll Never Get Me!

THE PASSIVE-AGGRESSIVE PERSONALITY

KEY WORDS FOR A PASSIVE-AGGRESSIVE PATTERN
---

passive resistance

covert

angry

controlling

undermining

manipulation

resistance

stubborn

inertia

What Is Typical of Most People?

At times, all of us feel anger, resentment, hate, or envy toward certain people. Occasionally, we express this in harmful ways and then deny either those feelings or the intent to harm. We do it slyly and cover our tracks. For example, after saying, "I'll do it for you," we then "run out of time" by deliberately making it a low priority. Usually this is done only to workplace superiors or those in authority with whom it might be self-damaging to express negative emotions up front. Ultimately, most learn to deal with negative feelings by expressing them assertively and openly, rationalizing or hiding them.

All of us resent being told what to do or having certain people make requests or demands. Either we just don't want to do it, or we see the demand as unimportant. Our independence is threatened by the other person's power, or so we feel. Resentment of the implication of their subsequent anger or withdrawal if we do not comply may also exist. But most of us learn to adapt by either renegotiating, accepting the need for cooperation (albeit reluctantly), or by asserting ourselves.

What Is Typical for Most People with a Passive-Aggressive Personality?

People with a passive-aggressive behavior pattern have all those negative feelings, too, but are more reluctant to deal with them or be up front. Instead, they passively resist, sabotage, subtly attack, and take revenge or control by insidious and covert behavior that protects them from counterattack. They are not prepared to be assertive about their real feelings and take the consequences.

When this occurs often but in a moderate way in personal relationships and in the workplace, the person could be described as having a passive-aggressive pattern of behavior. Such patterns can be modified if the person tries to change them, or there is ongoing professional support from a psychologist.

If the pattern is excessive, occurs in most areas of their life, and impairs their social and personal relationships as well as their career progress, they may be diagnosed as having the more severe form of this behavior, which is called a passive-aggressive personality disorder, according to the criteria outlined in the DSM-IV-TR. It is unlikely that they can significantly change such a severe pattern without professional help.

Passive-Aggressive Personality Disorder According to the DSM-IV-TR

At least four of the following behaviors must be present to make this diagnosis.

Passively Resist Carrying Out Routine Social and Workplace Tasks

There is passive resistance to reasonable requests by others for adequate performance of social, domestic, and workplace tasks. They fail to do their share of the work, or follow cooperative plans.

They may come up with self-protective explanations as to why the task hasn't been completed, for example, "The file was damaged so I couldn't work on it," or they will blame others.

Complain about Being Unappreciated

They believe that others do not see them for who they are. They feel overlooked, unrecognized for their cleverness, and not known for their good qualities. But instead of trying to let others know who they are, they feel resentful and angry, and either complain bitterly about ingratitude or smolder with feelings of resentment.

Can Be Sullen and Argumentative

They can argue about every little thing, making progress difficult. If they do cooperate they do so in bad grace and let people know that they feel badly treated.

Unreasonably Criticize and Scorn Those with Authority

They consider most of their superiors to be incompetent and express scorn and contempt publicly and privately.

Voice Resentment and Jealousy of Those Perceived as Being Better Off in Different Ways

They express distrust of others' success, imply that others have succeeded only because of cheating or excessively good fortune. Bitterly, they put others down for what they have achieved, but in very subtle ways.

Voice Persistent Complaints of Their Own Misfortune

They believe that they could have achieved so much "if only . . . ," pointing out every way in which they are sabotaged, have been treated unfairly, or are overlooked. They never accept responsibility for their own lack of success in any area.

Alternate between Hostile Defiance and Contrition

Sometimes they are aggressive and nasty, refusing to cooperate. This may be followed by feelings of remorse or distress over the other person's unhappy reaction to their nastiness, and they may try to make up. Scared that they have alienated the other person permanently, they need people more than they are prepared to admit.

Some of these behaviors are expressed in many not-so-obvious ways, and only experienced clinicians can make a proper diagnosis of passive-aggressive personality disorder. However, there are people who have a similar passive-aggressive pattern with many, but not all, of these characteristics in a milder form, and you can identify these patterns in their behavior.

A pattern of this behavior has many of these characteristics:

- harboring anger in a deep and slow simmer toward others who threaten them in some way
- ongoing postponement of decisions that are important to those they resent. For example: "I'll think about it and get back to you [they don't]," "Leave it with me [and I'll make sure that nothing is done]," or "We'll see."
- feelings of being undervalued for their abilities and contributions
- difficulty in expressing disagreement up front, in case they alienate
- conflict between their need for others and their desire for self-assertion, which is resolved by passively resisting and passive hostility. They sometimes actively "plan" this sabotage and resistance. At other times they take advantage of naturally occurring opportunities to frustrate, undermine or sabotage your plans or your reputation.
- lack of courage in dealing with conflict with others, or the inevitable discomfort that follows self-assertion. By avoiding open conflict that might follow their negative expressions, they avoid the repercussions. What if they are "bested" by the other person's counterattack? What if they feel awful afterward? What if the other person punishes them by withdrawing care and approval?
- low self-confidence and low expectations
- envy, jealousy, and resentment of more successful or more fortunate others

- unreasonable and excessive cynicism and scorn toward others
- behavior alternates between stubbornness, hostility and resistance, and contrite feelings
- satisfaction grows, for some, from their ability to control or undermine the responses of others without their realizing how they are being harmed or manipulated.

Examples

- They spread rumors or pass on unflattering and damaging information, but never by gossiping outright.
- They mismanage something important to you or that you have asked them to do, or they "forget" to do it. They then say, "Sorry, I made a mistake," but you suspect they didn't. On pointing this out, you are told that you are the one with the problem because you are too critical and demanding. If you repeat requests they tell you that you are nagging.
- Deliberately procrastinating, they make you wait. They see your requests as demands to be passively resisted, even if they have promised delivery. In some cases, you will never receive whatever was promised.
- They set you up to look foolish by saying one thing in private and another in public.
- Ridiculing or hostile body language, like a smirk, sneer, a raised eyebrow, shrug, or sneering laugh, are weapons of passive aggression. Since you can't judge by one incident, you are unsure. If challenged, they deny your interpretation.
- Instead of openly arguing an issue through to resolution, they will stonewall. They don't hear, don't respond to questions, and go silent. Silence is an extremely effective weapon. This often increases the other person's anger, forcing them to give up on the issue or look out of control.
- Pigheadedness is another difficult behavior in which the person stubbornly refuses to back down from their posi-

tion, concede any point, or negotiate. But they may act as if they are trying to negotiate.

- Humor can be a covert but aggressive behavior. Offensive jokes can be told in front of others who will predictably find them distressing, for example, dirty or sexist jokes, followed by the comment, "It was just a joke, don't you have a sense of humor?" This makes the recipient look prudish or narrow-minded. Putdown humor can be used as a passive-aggressive tactic. For example, "Here comes the overachiever!"

- Recognizing the emotional needs of another person and denying them is a form of passive control. For example, the boss who does not praise the worker who needs it, or the wife who does not make appreciative remarks after her husband's speech at a social function.

How People with a Passive-Aggressive Pattern Think

Their working hypothesis is: "I have to resist anyone's attempt to control or influence my behavior even if they have the right to do so. Others don't see my worth. I could do what they do if I wanted to. Sometimes I may have to take revenge if they threaten me by being too powerful, competent, successful, or popular. But I must be clever and never give them a chance to catch me at it or to counterattack, because then I would be unmasked and it would be to hard to survive an open attack."

Why Do They Do It?

- Some lack assertiveness skills and do not know how to stand up for themselves in situations of conflict.

- Some are not aware of why they do it. All they know is that there is some satisfaction for them in controlling others' behavior and objectives, their crestfallen reaction, or obvious disappointment.

- Some passive-aggressive people had powerful, punishing and/or overly controlling parents, and they didn't succeed in fighting back. They are playing out childhood scenarios, only this time they *are* fighting back, but covertly.

- Often there is a discrepancy between their personal expectations and those that others have of them. Their resistance and aggression toward others may reflect their own negative view of themselves. Their self-esteem is low because they know what they haven't been able to do, but they can't admit that to themselves or others.

- They find satisfaction in having some control over another's life, however covert may be the motivation. This is similar to the satisfaction of anonymous phone callers who know their calls without words are distressing. They are smug about their own cleverness in affecting you without your realizing it.

- Many are eaten up by jealousy and resentment. They have so little belief in their own ability that they feel incapable of trying to compete with the other person. Instead, they attempt to bring that person down but try to avoid retaliation from them.

Looking on the Bright Side

- Their capacity for strategic manipulation can often be put to good use in the workplace.
- They can be highly observant and analytical.
- They often have an ability to recognize vulnerabilities and strengths of others, and this may be used productively if harnessed.

Strategies for Dealing with a Passive-Aggressive Behavior Pattern

These are some of the most slippery behaviors to deal with, rather like boxing with shadows. Often they have a plausible excuse for every default, and you end up feeling paranoid and stupid. As game players, they waste an enormous amount of productive time and emotional energy, especially in the workplace. In personal relationships their behavior eventually creates a distance between those involved.

Here are some suggestions:

- Document the pattern for yourself, and if in the workplace, document for others. Keep accurate records, including other people's reports. Even then it will be hard to substantiate the pattern.
- If a family member or a colleague uses passive-aggressive techniques, don't rely on them.
- Refuse to be caught up in the game. Use rational self-talk (see page 92) such as: "I won't get upset over another instance of noncooperation or sabotage. It's not worth getting agitated over it because I will be the only one distressed and it won't change anything. Either I will let it go, or I will be assertive. But I won't just fume."
- Many will temporarily stop the pattern if you talk to them about it. They respond to a more powerful and assertive approach in the short term, but the pattern will resume.
- In a romantic relationship, if the pattern undermines you, ask your partner to go with you to marital counseling to try to work things out. In the workplace, seek advice from a supportive colleague or superior.
- Where possible, don't work with them. Consider a transfer. Opt to be on other teams. Don't put yourself in the position where you have to collaborate with them or where they can undermine you.
- When officious "small" people try to control you and you are in a higher position, go over their heads. Refuse to play their game. If necessary, make a formal complaint or ask for a change of procedures and responsibilities.
- Assert yourself with them (see page 232). Get your facts right beforehand. Resist attempts to twist things around, claim innocence, or blame someone else. If you have some authority, let them know that what they are doing is unacceptable and you won't tolerate it. Say, for example, "I am very unhappy about those statistics not being compiled. I

can't accept that they haven't been done. We need to identify what you will have to drop in order to finish them.
They must be done by the end of the day or we will need
to talk seriously about what is happening here." Keep using
broken-record statements, for example, "I understand the
problems you are experiencing with this, but they must be
done by the end of the day."

- Keep your cool. If you get aggressive and lose control, you
are playing into their hands. They will feel enormously sat-
isfied if they can produce such out-of-control behavior in
you. They, of course, will remain calm and in control, so
you feel even worse after your outburst.

- In the workplace, if the person has power or is in a position
to influence your reputation for future work or promotion,
confronting is an option but a difficult one. You may need
to talk to them with a mediator present. This might be a
mutual superior, a senior person outside your section but
within the organization, or an external, professional mediator. Contracts and agreements may need to be drawn up
along with review processes.

Strategies to Use If You Have a Passive-Aggressive Behavior Pattern

- Be truthful with yourself. Acknowledge that you will lose
work and personal relationships unless you change your
pattern. A passive-aggressive pattern damages relationships
in the long term and you will end up with major losses and
disappointments.

- Changing relies upon acknowledging why these passive-aggressive behaviors are used. Understand your own process.
Talk to someone you can trust.

- Are there other sources of influence or power available to
you? Can you influence people in more productive ways?
Use your analytical skills to boost your own self-esteem.

- Learn the skills of conflict resolution and anger management (see pages 248 and 239).

- Above all, have the courage to be more assertive (see page 233) and up front. Start small and notice the difference. Monitor the more positive reactions you get.
- Become more positive and less defeatist about yourself. Stop thinking about how successful and clever you could be, and just do it. Have the courage to find ways in which to test out exactly what you are capable of. You will probably be pleasantly surprised.

Don drove his family mad because he never delivered on his promises. His children were always disappointed after long discussions about vacations, because he would either procrastinate for so long about organizing them that the vacations never happened, or he'd book an alternative vacation in which they were not particularly interested (but he was). Often his excuses were transparent. For example, he would say, "The real estate agent said houses at the beach were impossible to get unless you booked them a year ahead, so I've reserved a campsite instead" (which was his original plan anyway).

Although his wife held down a full-time job and took care of most domestic and parenting responsibilities, she was continually frustrated in attempts to get Don to take care of the garden, or the cars. This had been the agreed-upon division of labor early in their marriage. Sometimes, he would spontaneously tackle these tasks but only the ones he chose, not the ones his wife knew needed to be done. At work, things were not much better. His position involved being in charge of payroll functions. Colleagues found him unhelpful and slow to process workplace requests. He was, in fact, very competent, as was evidenced by the times when he made the decision to help a friend and carried it out immediately. However, he would choose when *not* to act competently or in a timely way.

14

A Silent Nightmare

THE BULLYING PERSONALITY

KEY WORDS FOR THOSE WITH A BULLYING PERSONALITY
need for dominance
humiliation
intimidation
power imbalance
unempathic

What Is Typical of Most People?

As children, most of us occasionally tease others. Often this is done as part of a group. It is developmental. We are learning about the rights and feelings of others. Just as many of us try lying, stealing from our parents, or shoplifting, some also try bullying. If we don't *initiate* the bullying, we take part in smaller ways by laughing, hanging around, participating, watching or by doing nothing about stopping it. Because we are also developing our skills of empathy and our moral reasoning, though, few of us continue for very long, and nearly everyone will have stopped completely after a certain age.

Most adults do not bully. At worst, we might occasionally overuse power, or respond insensitively. Bullying, however, is a systematic attempt to humiliate and disempower another, and few adults do that. But some people do engage in a pattern of bullying, and they are highly toxic in their impact. For the target of their bullying, it becomes a silent nightmare of pain, shame, humiliation, and fear. Victims stop trusting others and their self-esteem declines.

Again, most of us sometimes, and temporarily, experienced a hard time at school. But some were bullied for long periods without respite and without anyone to support them, and they felt the effects right into adulthood. Some adults are bullied, although it happens to fewer adults than kids. But in many ways it feels worse, especially if you were also bullied as a child or adolescent.

What Is Bullying?

Bullying is a pattern of aggressive or humiliating behavior arising from deliberate attempts to cause physical or psychological distress to others. Recent studies suggest that it occurs in the workplace more than we have realized in the past. It also occurs in personal relationships.

Bullying is similar to other behaviors based on a power imbalance, such as child sexual abuse, gangsterism, and rape. The features that these have in common are:

- each is done where people who could stop it are unaware that it is happening
- the perpetrator has the power advantage in some way
- there are direct or implied threats of retaliation if the target seeks help
- the perpetrator makes it clear that they or their supporters are prepared to go "further" than you are in this behavior
- the perpetrator (and sometimes others) implies that the target "brought it upon themselves" in some way.

What Is Typical of Bullies?

A bully wants to enjoy the privileges of living and working in an adult world while not being prepared or able to take on adult responsibility.

At work, a bully may assert power (with pleasure) and control resources. A company where bullying is rife is characterized by high staff turnover, excessive sick leave or stress-related disability leave, a high grievance rate (often with legal consequences), and a large number of ill-health retirements. At home, a bully uses physical or verbal abuse to intimidate and control.

Bullying is perpetuated by a climate of fear, silence, tolerance of and reward for antisocial behavior, and ignorance. Bullies create an environment of alienation, psychological danger, inefficiency (everyone is too focused on protecting themselves to work well), demoralization, and demotivation. Attitudes toward victims become less supportive with age, as people believe you should deal with harassment yourself: you are a grown-up. This shows a failure to realize that bullying is partly a group dynamics issue to which you may be a contributor. And it is difficult to deal with it by yourself.

A bullying pattern of behavior is similar in many ways to a sociopathic pattern (see page 172) because of the preparedness to sacrifice another's well-being for one's own ends. If a bullying pattern coexists with other kinds of antisocial and deceitful behavior, then you are dealing with a sociopathic pattern with bullying as one of the included behaviors. However, if the behavior is only exploitive and antisocial, then, although there are sociopathic aspects to the pattern, it can also be identified separately as bullying.

Bullies are prepared to intimidate, humiliate, or destroy another in order to get what they want. They want you to do what they say, and they also want power, recognition, popularity, or status in the eyes of others. Bullying is a repeated pattern of negative actions toward a targeted individual, which is intended to intimidate and demoralize. It:

- causes hurt, discomfort, embarrassment, or distress for the recipient
- occurs more than once
- is intentional, and makes the recipient look foolish personally, socially or in the workplace. It may involve physical abuse.
- is carried out by someone who is more powerful, in that they may be:
  - supported in the behavior by others (whom they influence

by creating a reputation for the targeted person which isolates them and makes others think they deserve what happens)

- more articulate
- physically larger and stronger
- in a superior position (for example, being able to fire or reprimand)
- prepared to go further in their attempts to harm than is the recipient in responding.

Forms of Bullying

The bullying can take many forms, such as:

Reputation Damage

By, for example:

- finding a mistake and exaggerating it in public, conferring reputations that discourage support from others. For example, by saying, "He's a wimp, or "He sucks up to everyone."
- ridiculing
- publicly questioning competence
- spreading rumors
- retelling something that was told in confidence.

Demoralization

By, for example:

- being highly critical of another's work
- character attacks (especially domestically). For example, "What would they expect from someone like you!"
- oversupervising a coworker, for example, noting down starting and leaving times, or checking their work unnecessarily
- setting someone up to fail, for example, by not giving them the information they need to complete a task well.

Causing Inconvenience

For example:

- blocking their vacation dates so that they can only take inconvenient times
- transferring someone to a less desirable department or shift.

Name-Calling and Insults or Verbal Put-Downs

Saying, for example:

- That's stupid (ridiculous, absurd, dumb)
- What would you know! (in domestic bullying especially)
- You're such an idiot (in domestic bullying especially)
- Any fool can see that the only way to...

Nonverbal Expressions of Contempt

Typical examples are:

- smirking and smiling at someone else to give the message "Both of us agree that you're stupid/unlikeable, etc."
- eye rolling
- snorting in derision
- laughing at what you say
- deliberately looking bored or doing something else when you speak.

So-Called Practical Jokes or Initiations

For example:

- writing crude messages on T-shirts that are visible only under ultraviolet light such as is found in nightclubs
- sending offensive phony e-mails
- sending the new apprentice out to buy striped paint, or a cordless screwdriver, etc.

• • •

Nuisance Behavior
For example:

- hiding personal property or completed work
- altering answering machine messages
- altering computer settings.

Damage to Property
For example:

- erasing computer files
- breaking power tools.

Physical Intimidation or Attacks
By, for example:

- blocking the way and making the other person walk around them
- tripping
- elbowing
- all forms of domestic violence.

Threatening Behavior
Through, for instance:

- subtle threats about "concrete shoes"
- making "noose" or "shooting" gestures
- saying, "Don't turn your back on me."

Social Exclusion
This is when someone is, for example:

- not invited to post-game or workplace functions
- deliberately sent to the wrong address
- not told about meetings
- ignored when they speak in the staff room.

• • •

The Impact of Bullying on the Targeted Person

- The targeted person suffers a loss of self-esteem and might be angry at the failure of senior staff and the company to protect them. They can experience a drop in productivity and competence, thus making the bully's achievements look even better. This may further reinforce the bully's sense of superiority.
- It often adversely affects health.
- Often a poor health record makes getting another job less likely.
- Depression adversely affects their intimate relationships because there is a loss of trust.
- They can be bullied out of the job because they become so desperate to get away from the harassment.
- Those who let someone in authority know what is happening may be called whistleblowers and may pay a high price.
- If legal action is taken, the person can be seen as a troublemaker.
- A bullying boss may be able to withhold a reference or, when phoned by a prospective employer, make sure the person doesn't get the job.
- When someone is bullied by their partner they lose confidence and self-esteem. This often makes it almost impossible to leave the relationship.

Characteristics of a Bully

Mistakenly, bullies are often perceived as poor souls with a marked inferiority complex and low self-esteem who bully others because of inadequacy. Research, however, suggests that few playground or workplace bullies are like this, although domestic bullies may be. Bullies were once believed to be socially inept oafs, but research now confirms that they are more likely to be highly skilled people capable of sophisticated interpersonal manipulation of others. They can send a victim over the edge without anyone seeing the "pushes" they use. The profile below is particularly true of the serial bully. This type of bully has done it before, is doing it now, and will do it again.

Difficult Personalities

On the whole, your typical workplace or playground bully:

- does not have low self-esteem and is usually confident but with an inflated view of their own worth
- is not anxious
- usually has average to good popularity
- has a stronger than normal desire to dominate
- believes that attaining popularity, status, and admiration, through dominance of someone less powerful, is acceptable
- lacks the ability to empathize with the feelings of another or turns their empathy off when it suits them.

Whom Do They Target?

Bullies choose a range of people as targets for harassment. But they are most likely to select someone who has some of these characteristics. They:

- tend to be anxious (especially socially anxious)
- may not be as assertive as some
- may be less articulate
- may be smaller or physically weaker
- find themselves temporarily without support (e.g., a close colleague may have left the workplace)
- tend to be less powerful—for example, younger or newer staff, people who work by themselves, or who are from a minority cultural group
- may be of a different religion
- may have an obvious aspect of facial appearance about which they can be teased (for example, freckles, red hair) although this is only the focus of the bullying, not the reason for it
- may be overweight
- may lack social skills
- may occasionally have demonstrated that they can be be hot-tempered and/or hypersensitive
- have the lowest level of education
- may be women who have never married or are divorced.

The adults that bullies select as targets for harassment are more likely to have had some of the following characteristics when they were children:

- showed patterns of anxiety (this is the most likely characteristic)
- relatively passive and submissive
- may have been provocative and short-tempered, and so easily baited
- didn't smile much
- seemed depressed
- were socially uncomfortable
- avoided eye contact
- became upset easily
- had an exaggerated fear of getting hurt
- were clingy
- became jumpy or distressed when separated from a parent
- were inflexible and rigid in their views and in following rules.

How Do People with a Bullying Pattern Think?

Their working hypothesis is: "I must impress myself and others with my power, so I will do whatever is required to coerce, intimidate and humiliate someone I think is vulnerable and not likely to retaliate or seek help to let everyone here know how powerful I am."

- Persistent bullies have limited capacity to empathize, and believe that a display of power over others is an acceptable way to achieve status. Empathy is the ability to recognize and respond appropriately to another's feelings. Bullies either lack this or choose to turn it off in some situations when it suits them to do so. They are more likely to come from homes where aggression is accepted as a social tactic and where there is low parental involvement, but this isn't always the case.
- Some people bully to break the monotony, and most have

poor impulse control. At work, the greedy may bully to control resources or use aggression to further their progress. When in a more senior position, they may bully to cover up their own incompetence.

- The person with an ongoing bullying pattern may be sociopathic or may have used the behavior many times in a successful way with no consequences to themselves (see page 172).

How Do They Get Away with It?

Bullies may be tolerated because they "get things done" and further the achievements of the organization. Often when they are removed, it is because of the economic and legal outcomes; bullying is not always seen for what it is: a moral issue. Others fear being the next victim, so they pretend it is not happening and no one informs senior people. Some people indirectly encourage the bullying by finding what they do to others amusing. They are often backed up by the "hangers-on," those people who go along with it but don't initiate.

- Certain attitudes (including those by senior staff) dominate, which allow them to turn a blind eye to it. For example, if someone is getting a hard time from another, they must have done something to deserve it. This is called the "just world" view, whereby they naively believe that good things happen to good people and bad things to bad people.
- Some believe that it is part of being accepted. It's not. Occasionally being teased is part of being accepted, but being bullied and harassed isn't.
- Companies may say "But what can we do?" or incorrectly reframe what is happening as a "personality clash." Management or those in authority can do the most to stop bullying.
- "I haven't seen it, so I'm not convinced it's happening," may be the cry. Bullying is a covert behavior—you wouldn't expect much to occur in the presence of a supervisor.
- Many believe that the target provokes it. Sometimes the target *is* difficult to deal with, but this is no justification for nasty and systematic harassment.

- Many believe that "sticks and stones will break their bones, but names will never hurt them." But the damage from name-calling is very serious in terms of the harm to a person's well-being, self-esteem, productivity, and performance.

Is Gender a Factor?

Men bully more than women and their targets are more likely to be other men. Females, especially girls, tend to suffer more indirect bullying (e.g., rumors, lies, attacks on their reputation) while male bullying tends to be more direct. Male bullies are more likely to use physical attack and ridicule, but they often use indirect bullying tactics as well. Females are more likely to use verbal abuse and social ostracism because they are after social power and popularity.

Women tend to be more supportive of the targets of bullying because of their socialization, which stresses empathy.

What about the Kids?

- When parents of students who had been bullied were surveyed, 75 percent said that it had been the worst problem their child ever had to face.
- One in seven students are severely bullied, while 7 to 10 percent are bullies.

Strategies You Can Use with a Bullying Behavior Pattern

If You Are the Target of the Bullying

- Do not let bullies win; have the courage to report it to management or the authorities.
- Tell somebody. Keeping it quiet is more harmful to your mental health. Telling puts the bullying in context. You realize that it is the bully who should feel ashamed, not you.
- Change your usual response to the bullying. For example, with a smile say, "Thank you for telling me," "Gee, thanks," "Good one!" or "It's going to be one of *those* days, is it?" Then walk away and don't make eye contact.

- In a group, ignore what they say and talk to the person nearby.
- Just agree with them. For example, say, "Yeah, right." But it is the tone in which this is said that is important.
- Sound confident, not frightened.
- Naturally you will feel angry and initially say to yourself, "They can't do this to me! I want to get back at them." Remind yourself of the possible negative consequences of retaliating without support and make a more cold-blooded plan to stop it by collecting your evidence and speaking calmly and logically to the appropriate senior person who has some power and authority to do something about it.
- Decide to take action, but remember that the real problem belongs to the bully, not you.
- Bullying is ambiguous and slippery. It can be difficult for management and others to clearly identify who did what. Be systematic. It will keep your mind off how the bullying is affecting you. Keep records noting the time, place, and date. List witnesses. Report every event and keep a record of when, where, and to whom it was reported. Collect evidence of the experiences suffered by others at this person's hands. Use a recording device to record their nastiness. (This is also a good deterrent.) Print offensive emails and use the screen-capture tool on your computer to make a copy of anything that may be uploaded about you to the Internet.
- Go to the "top" if the bully is protected.
- Learned helplessness fuels bullies. So ask them to stop. Say, "I want you to know that I find your behavior unpleasant and childish. I don't know why you need to do it and I don't really care. But if you do it again, I will take action with senior staff here. This company has integrity." The message here is: "Your behavior stinks and something is wrong with you. I will take action. This workplace doesn't like people like you."
- Give them a summary of their comments and reflect back to them what they said. This can make them realize how

ridiculous they sound. For example, "So you think I am an inefficient and stupid person and that I should be on a diet. Not only that, but I need cosmetic surgery on my ears. Is that correct?" Try to say it in a calm, not angry voice. It sometimes has an impact, but not always.

- Use a broken-record statement such as: "I can see you feel strongly about this. Can you tell me why? I am sorry that you feel the need to try to demean me in public. I have no idea why you need to do that, but it's not acceptable to me. I will not put up with this and it has no place in this organization. If it continues, I will report it." (Keep repeating the last phrase.)
- Use "standing up for yourself" body language. This won't necessarily stop the bullying, but you'll feel better. For example, throw your shoulders back, make firm eye contact, use a firm but not aggressive tone of voice and, no matter what, when you are giving a *firm* message, DON'T SMILE!
- Don't use the term "bully" to them. Instead say, "Please don't make public criticism of my work. If you need to comment on my performance, tell me privately."
- Don't speculate on their motives. They enjoy your doing this. It doesn't matter.
- Recognize that it is more difficult to deal with a bullying situation if several people are doing it to you. Ask coworkers to support you. Say, "This is really hard for me to ask, but I need some support. So-and-so appears to be attempting to harass and intimidate me and I cannot deal with it by myself."
- Use positive self-talk like this: "Bullying is wrong but often it's hard for those in authority to deal with it and stop it. It's not my fault and it is not going to continue forever. But I will have to report it if simple measures don't stop it."

If You Are a Coworker of a Target or Bully

- Accept that people who are being bullied don't deserve what is happening to them.

- Let them know that you understand and support them.
- If you are present when bullying occurs, act. Otherwise, by watching and doing nothing about it, you are offering support to the bully, and this implies a tacit acceptance. Say, "Your behavior is making all of us uncomfortable. Please stop so that we are not placed in a position of having to report it." Or use firm eye contact and look surprised when you say, "Pardon me?"
- Say something like, "Several of us have noticed that Gina is very demoralized right now. One of the reasons is the way you raise your voice to her and speak disrespectfully to her in front of all of us. Please don't continue doing that. It distresses all of us."
- Bullies enjoy an audience. So, all leave and say, "We don't want to watch or take part in this." Take the targeted person with you.
- Appeal to whatever "good nature" the bully or their hangers-on might have. Say, "You have not always been like this. I remember when you were very supportive of . . ."

If You Are the Boss of a Target or Bully

Acknowledge that when management does not deal effectively with bullying, workers perceive that there is tacit acceptance of it in their workplace. Providing a safe, supportive environment for workers, in which bullying is recognized as totally unacceptable, should be the aim of the organization. Once workers feel free to support others who receive harassment, to report it, and do not provide encouragement for bullies, your workplace will be more productive.

Management should:

- commit in writing to eradicating workplace bullying
- raise awareness of the issue of workplace bullying and produce a policy outlining what people who are bullied should do, whom they should tell, and what action will follow
- clearly identify what bullying is and what behaviors are typical

- protect people who come forward
- dismiss anyone involved in bullying after they have been given a warning to stop it
- create teams and build morale so that people support each other and no one is isolated
- assume that bullying could exist and keep an eye out for it. Don't just wait to hear about bullying behavior.
- show respect to everyone from the top down. Lower-level bullies may be taking their lead from senior staff who bully.
- communicate to the bully's target that: "You are important. I believe that this is a serious problem for you." Then act to stop it.
- move the bully (*not* the victim) to another department or give the bully instructions to keep away from staff who have been victimized by them
- report (for example, to the relevant Occupational Health and Safety personnel in your workplace) every suspected bullying incident, however small, and keep ongoing records. Break down the code of secrecy and silence.
- develop friendly, conscientious supervision and remove opportunities for bullying to occur. For example, actively supervise high-risk areas such as storerooms and other isolated areas.
- take steps to ensure that retaliation doesn't occur. When people report being bullied, it sometimes gets worse because of retaliation.
- implement strategically placed suggestion boxes for anonymous reporting
- take action with those who overtly or tacitly support a bully. All staff who participate in a bullying situation are part of the problem, as are bystanders who watch and take no action.
- recognize that workplace absenteeism may be related to bullying.

Many people who do not have a pro-victim attitude tend to believe in a "just world" view whereby "Bad things don't happen to good people." That is, they believe that if the person is being treated badly they must deserve it. They find it hard to accept the randomness of misfortune. You should model this understanding of "injustice."

People who merely observe or are aware of bullying taking place in the workplace feel unsafe and anxious.

Remember that low-bullying and high-bullying organizations differ mainly in terms of the level of commitment of the senior staff to reduce bullying.

If You Are a Bully
- Be aware that your bullying behavior may have legal consequences.
- Ask for feedback from people who know you well.

Audrey, who is 47, worked in the accounts section of a large machinery repair company. The job was important to her, as her husband was in rehabilitation after a major car accident, and she needed the income as well as a distraction from caring for him at home. Unfortunately she didn't get along very well with some of the male technicians. On several occasions she had asked them to watch their language, as a few of them were very foul-mouthed. She had also taken one of them to task over his sloppy paperwork on several jobs. She was usually in the right, but she had put them off by her slightly condescending manner. When she arrived at work one morning, her ergodynamic chair was at the wrong height so that when she sat down, she miscalculated the height and sat down awkwardly with a "whoosh," injuring her back. The next morning she discovered that her computer keyboard had been disconnected and her mouse was nowhere to be found. It took ages to locate another one. This pattern continued for weeks. Every day something else in her office had been interfered with. The senior managers were concerned but were unable to find a way to stop it. Even when she locked her office, it still happened. She dreaded coming to work and hated facing the man she believed to be the leader of the bullying. Eventually it got too much for her and she went on disability leave due to stress.

Dee pressured her retired mother-in-law, Ginny, to buy expensive presents for the five grandchildren, and to babysit regularly. When her fashionable friends were around, Dee would put down her mother-in-law's accent and background, and ridicule her dress sense. Not wishing to lose touch with the grandchildren, and trying to help her son, who was working an extra job to pay debts run up by Dee, Ginny persisted. Widowed, she had moved from a suburb in another state mainly to be near her only son and her grandchildren. Dee insisted that Ginny catch the bus to come and babysit even though Dee had a car. But when Dee returned late from a day out with the girls at the casino, criticized what Ginny had cooked for the children's dinner, and complained that the ironing hadn't been done, Ginny decided she'd had enough.

15

Everyday Predators Among Us

THE SOCIOPATHIC PERSONALITY

KEY WORDS FOR SOCIOPATHIC BEHAVIOR
cold-blooded
amoral
exploitive
remorseless
lack of guilt
unprincipled
deceiving
antisocial
dishonest

True/False Quiz

Before you begin this chapter, take this quick test.

1. It is unlikely that I have personally come into contact with a sociopath.

          True   False

2. All sociopaths are serial killers or potential killers.

          True   False

3. Sociopaths are mentally ill.

          True   False

4. It is easy to identify sociopaths because of their behavior.

    True   False

5. The best word to describe a typical sociopath is "violent."

    True   False

Answers

1. False. Most of us come into contact with a few sociopaths in our lifetime. However, we rarely recognize them as such, because we lack understanding of how sociopathic individuals behave.
2. False. Only a very small number of sociopaths are involved with serial killing.
3. False. Sociopaths are not mentally ill. They can see the world realistically and they can clearly differentiate right from wrong. They have a personality disorder and choose to behave in an antisocial manner that is condemned by society.
4. False. Sociopathic behavior is usually complex and difficult to identify. It takes a long time to work out the pattern in many cases.
5. False. Not all sociopaths are violent. A lot are, but there are also many who focus their unprincipled, dishonest, manipulative and exploitive behavior on obtaining money, sexual favors, affection, and power from others.

All of the quiz statements are false and represent misconceptions about sociopaths. These myths have been created by the worlds of film and literature, which have commonly oversimplified the concept. Sociopaths are complex and varied.

You may have as friends, coworkers, or lovers people who show sociopathic patterns of behavior. They can be so charming, convincing, and confident initially that you do not recognize the dangers. When, too late, you realize that they are frauds, you have been hurt emotionally, betrayed, sexually exploited, financially "conned," or your business ruined. They are predators.

What Is Typical of Most People?

Sociopathic behavior is unprincipled, exploitive behavior that harms others, and is carried out with little or no concern for others' rights and feelings. Little guilt or remorse occurs, even when the person is found out. They don't suffer; they make others suffer. Antisocial (sociopathic) behavior is a continuum, not a simple category. Those who are on the upper end of the continuum demonstrate a strongly immoral, antisocial, and exploitive pattern of behavior. Some are in the middle of the continuum. They have a sociopathic pattern, but not to such a severe degree. Most of us are on the lower end of the continuum.

All of us have some antisocial impulses. Which of us hasn't come close to cheating on our partner, lying, stealing when the opportunity arises, or catching a train without buying a ticket? But mostly we curb these impulses and don't act on them. The capacity *not* to act on negative and destructive impulses is critical to a happy life, good relationships, and self-respect. Occasionally, we do act on our antisocial impulses. We do cheat on a partner, make overtures to a friend's girlfriend when he is away, "borrow" some company stationery, make personal long distance calls from the work phone, fudge on our taxes, or tell the occasional lie to cover our tracks or avoid hurting someone. But we don't do much of it, or do it often. Our conscience makes us too uncomfortable to continue lying, betraying, cheating, or stealing from others. Our moral alarm goes off loudly. We recognize the need for a community to operate on the basis of trust, and we fear getting caught.

Above all, we recognize that our action is wrong, as it harms others. Our conscience is based on our ability to care about the feelings and rights of others as well as our own. That is why it is easier to fudge on income tax than to steal from a friend. In stealing from a friend, our conscience and empathy make us feel uncomfortable because we wouldn't want it done to us. We imagine how it would damage them financially and how hurt they would be. But the income tax rules are less absolute and keep changing. Also, we don't feel any personal concern for another human if a few more deductions are claimed than we are entitled to.

So someone is not necessarily sociopathic if they have an affair, cheat a little on their expense reports, or tell the occasional lie to protect themselves. Certainly these are antisocial and deceitful practices that have the potential to hurt others, but they are within the normal range of behavior. But if a person has many affairs, cheats frequently on their expense reports, tells a lot of lies to many people to get what they want, and never feels guilt about any of it, then they may be higher up on the continuum of sociopathic behavior.

The Severe Form of This Behavior Pattern: Antisocial Personality Disorder

The technical term for a sociopath is a person with an antisocial personality disorder, as outlined in the DSM-IV-TR. The term "sociopath" replaces the older term "psychopath," with which most people are more familiar. The term "sociopath" recognizes that their behavior causes distress to others (hence the prefix "socio"), rather than causing psychological anguish, distortion, or confusion to themselves (implied by the prefix "psycho"). antisocial personality disorder is the term used to describe a reasonably predictable syndrome of behaviors. It isn't a physical illness like diabetes, or a mental illness like schizophrenia. It certainly isn't a defense in law. People with this disorder are neither mentally ill nor insane.

People with an antisocial personality disorder are possibly the closest there is to the concept of "evil" people. They are deceitful, exploitive, callous, cynical, and contemptuous of the rights and feelings of others. But their pattern of behavior can be so subtle and so hard to piece together that you can miss it. There is almost total ignorance in our community about sociopathic behavior. Even after reading this chapter, you may find such behavior too hard to believe, because it is so remote from how you can imagine yourself behaving. But it exists, and it is more common than most of us would like. With today's emphasis on "greed is good," "looking after number one," and a greater tolerance of corruption, it is perhaps becoming a more common behavior pattern. In many political, business, sporting, and entertainment contexts, it is approved, covered, and sometimes actively encouraged.

Sensationalized in movies and novels, the stereotypical socio-path is a clever person plotting to take over the world, or under-taking a serial killing spree. This is only fiction; most sociopaths are not like that. They are infinitely more banal. But they *can* be violent, some do murder, they are greedy and desirous of power, and they often think themselves more clever than the rest of the world. It has been estimated that 3 to 4 percent of men and 1 per-cent of women are sociopathic, but many psychiatrists believe these are underestimates. There are many "successful" sociopaths who blend in and pass for normal and who are adept at avoiding detection. They don't necessarily come to police attention. Possibly these constitute another 5 percent of the population. Estimating is hard when so many go undetected and few present for treatment because they see themselves as "winners" rather than antisocial or disturbed.

These are the features of an antisocial personality disorder, based on the diagnostic criteria from the DSM-IV-TR. The individual has to show only three of these characteristics for a diagnosis to be made. Overall, their pattern is one of contempt for and violation of the rights of others. They:

- break the law, even if they have not been found out or pun-ished
- are deceitful in that they either repeatedly lie, use aliases, or con others for personal profit or pleasure (for example, for sex, affection, money, or power)
- are impulsive
- can be irritable or aggressive and may frequently be involved in physical fights or assaults
- show a reckless disregard for the safety of others, and some-times of themselves
- may demonstrate ongoing irresponsibility, for example, be out of work a lot when they could find jobs, not honor their financial responsibilities, etc.
- lack remorse, and are indifferent to or rationalize having hurt, lied to, mistreated, or stolen from another. They feel no (or very little) guilt or shame about their actions.

What Is Typical of People with an Identifiable Sociopathic Pattern of Behavior?

People with an ongoing moderate to severe antisocial pattern are cold-bloodedly amoral and act on their impulses without regard for the devastating consequences their actions bring to others. They lack remorse or concern for others. They have little or no conscience. But they can often appear to be perfectly normal, and, in many ways, they are. Keep in mind that even the most severe sociopaths will still have many areas of their lives in which they behave quite normally, and sometimes act kindly and generously. This seeming contradiction is often what confuses when you are trying to work out why they are causing you such distress.

Typical Behaviors
The male pronoun has been used because research suggests that most are male.

- He commits antisocial acts, behaviors that the society in which he lives condemns. These could be any or many of the following:
    - directly unlawful behavior such as theft. The thefts can either be subtle, such as fraud or financially routing a system, or more obvious, such as armed robbery or embezzlement.
    - chronic lying to a range of people
    - acting dishonestly within a "system" in ways that are less obviously unlawful but that gain them advantage, for example, claiming bogus experience in an interview, using contacts to gain university entry for one's child without the necessary prerequisites
    - forging signatures on memos
    - lying to and using people dishonestly in relationships
    - serial infidelity
    - assault, which can range from bullying and intimidation to grievous bodily harm or murder with torture (but only some sociopaths are violent or sadistic, not all).

- He is prepared to sacrifice others to get what he wants. Ruthlessly, he uses others for his own ends.
- He demonstrates very little empathy, that is, recognition and concern for the rights and feelings of others. He "de—personalizes" those he hurts, unable to feel genuine distress or concern for them as people. After the event, he rationalizes his dishonesty and the harm he has inflicted on others ("They asked for it," "Why didn't they see what was in front of their noses?" or "It was their own fault. They were greedy." "They threw themselves at me" and "Everyone else does it. I'm just better at it than most people.")
- He does not experience much guilt, shame, or remorse (unless it will be useful to him to claim that he does feel them). He has a very underdeveloped conscience or set of moral principles to live by. He could best be described as amoral.
- He is quick to blame others, rather than accept responsibility. When caught out, he is likely to turn the blame on the people who have caught him. ("What did you expect when you showed me so little trust.")
- With poor impulse control, he never denies himself, no matter who gets conned, harmed, or used.
- He likes to live on the "edge" and has a thrill-seeking orientation to life. Unlike others who are "sensation seekers" in acceptable ways (for example, explorers, adventurers, entrepreneurs, stunt pilots), his thrills always involve some element of antisocial behavior and exploitation of others.
- He is not insane. Fully aware that what he does is condemned by his society and viewed as wrong, he chooses to do it anyway. The hardest idea for the lay person to accept is that someone who commits horrible crimes, or who uses and exploits others, can be quite sane. It would make most of us feel better if sociopaths were mentally ill, because otherwise we have to accept that this awful, threatening, and antisocial behavior pattern is "normal" for some people.
- Often irritable, he is inclined to throw temper tantrums when thwarted.
- Many have described the unnerving "visual stare" of those

with a severe sociopathic pattern. This is an unbroken and (sometimes) intimidating gaze that can be taken as exuding confidence and self-assurance or hostility and contempt.

How People with a Sociopathic Pattern Think

Their working hypothesis is: "I am a clever and superior person. I am entitled to use people to get what I want and get my kicks out of the game of exploitation."

The Gender Factor

More males than females have been identified as having sociopathic patterns. This could be due to a number of reasons:

- In general, women are physically weaker and have less testosterone, so it may be less likely that they will engage in violent actions. However, violence is not necessarily present in the pattern.
- Women are more likely to be socialized in the direction of care and concern for others, so there is a greater likelihood that they develop empathy and moral principles regarding their treatment of others.
- Women are more heavily punished for antisocial or aggressive acts as children than boys are.
- Women tend to have a more well-developed area of the brain for empathy and social behavior.
- Women are less likely to be in positions of power that might enable them to act in a self-rewarding way (again there are some notable exceptions). However, you may still encounter women who display a sociopathic behavior pattern.

The Two Types of Sociopathic Behavior Patterns: Unsuccessful and Successful Sociopaths

A lot of media and cinematic attention has been given to the kinds of sociopaths who physically hurt, torture, and murder others, especially serial killers. However, mental health professionals have stressed that there are two kinds of sociopathic behavior patterns. Although both are characterized by ruthless and unprincipled use of other people for their own ends without remorse or guilt, one pattern has been described by many experts as "unsuccessful" and the other as "successful."

"Unsuccessful" Sociopaths

"Unsuccessful" sociopaths are people who have very few skills or attitudes that would allow them to become successful in society on their own merit and hard work. They are unsuccessful in two ways. First, they lack the skills and adaptive characteristics to enable them to become successful in society through honest effort. Second, they mostly get caught.

The "unsuccessful" sociopath is one of two types. They are either an irresponsible lawbreaker or someone who is sadistic and violent.

The Irresponsible Lawbreaker

This sociopath is a low-life. Little charm or ability is present. He may destroy property, harass, set fires, steal, or deal in drugs. He often uses aliases and lies about everything in his life. He is very irresponsible. Unexplained absences from work are common. He may leave jobs without warning, move out of shared apartments without paying rent, sneak away, or suddenly leave a partner or children without support. Recurrent speeding fines, repeated drunk-driving offenses, harmful sexual behavior, or putting himself or others at high risk of infection with HIV would be characteristic. Neglecting or failing to care for a child, or defaulting on child support would be indicative of the irresponsibility of this type of "social loser" sociopath. Often there are significant periods of unemployment despite available job opportunities. There are often many appearances in court and periods in jail. A female "social loser" may also act irresponsibly with her children and jobs, shoplift, be sexually promiscuous or prostitute herself, use drugs and alcohol irresponsibly, or become welfare cheats. She often has several children at a very young age, and many are removed from her home.

There is often a history of neglect or abuse from their own parents, low levels of education, and a family background of law breaking and irresponsibility.

Obviously, some people, because of extreme poverty or tragic backgrounds, find themselves in very difficult financial and social circumstances and with a sense of "helplessness." Despite such circumstances most people do not show a pervasive antisocial pattern, although they may occasionally default on payments, attempt to cheat the system in a minor way, leave a job without obvious reason, or neglect a child temporarily. They can still feel genuine remorse about the effect of their behavior on others, and this motivates them to improve.

> Casey (33) has a very erratic work history. Often stoned, he doesn't turn up for work or is late and ineffectual. He was fired from his last job for dealing drugs to coworkers. He doesn't pay the required child support and frequently will forget or break appointments on "his" weekends. His children sit waiting, but he doesn't turn up. He has stolen tools and equipment from his employers (when he is working), and he "borrows" money from friends that he rarely repays. He cons others into paying for most of his drinks and currently is driving without a valid license, after losing it for drunk driving. He boasts about how he gets away with it all.

The Sadist/Killer

These sociopaths hurt others physically, often enjoying the process of torturing and humiliating their victims. They are bullies, gangsters, murderers, serial killers, or individuals who have a history of physical assault. They are remarkable for their sadism, total lack of remorse, and their depersonalization of their victims. You would be awfully unlucky to encounter one of this type in your everyday life. They usually get caught and most end up in prison, but it may take some time if they have the cover of associates.

- They do not have much power in their daily lives through their own skills.

- They are "small" people in that they have few character-istics and skills that would impress others. Violence can intimidate in the absence of any positive impression.
- There is often a history of abandonment or neglect, failure to bond with a parent, abuse from parents or care-givers, witnessing of violent acts, approval of criminal behavior, etc. However, not all people who experience these events become sadists or killers, and not all sadists/killers experi-ence these events.
- They usually function poorly in society and have lower lev-els of education and intelligence.
- A small number can be charming in a superficial way, espe-cially if it enables them to "position" their victims.
- Females sadists or killers more typically harm or murder members of their own families or children. Female serial killers are more likely to work in tandem with a partner, or murder several of their husbands or children. But there are exceptions.

Unfortunately, newspapers are full of reports of this kind of sociopath, for example, Al Capone, the well-known American gangster who ran a crime syndicate that engaged in illegal activities such as bootlegging, robbery, smuggling, and murder during the Prohibition era (1920s and 1930s); Frederick and Rosemary West, who are infamous for their "house of horrors" and their sexual tor-ture and murder of children in the UK; Myra Hindley ("The Moors Killer"), who murdered several children for fun; David Berkowitz ("Son of Sam"), the serial killer who killed six people and wounded seven others in a murder spree in New York in 1976 and '77 and wrote letters to the police and the media during his killing spree); Dr. Harold Shipman, perhaps the most appalling serial killer of all time, convicted in 2003 of murdering fifteen of his patients in the UK and suspected of murdering possibly another 150; and Gary Ridgway (The "Green River Killer") who confessed to strangling forty-eight women between 1982 and 1998. They fascinate us because we find it so hard to believe what they have done. But if you have no conscience, no capacity for empathy, don't experience guilt after hurting someone, and you are a "small" person looking for power and thrills, this is an easy way to get it. The media, by giving them so much coverage and a glamorous title, feed their egos. They often enjoy the notoriety.

Ted Bundy was an American serial killer who raped, bludgeoned, and strangled to death more than thirty women between 1973 and 1978. Police estimate that the number of victims may have been even higher. Bundy has been described by those who knew him as a clever, well-mannered, well-dressed, good-looking, and charming man. He was a good student in high school and was actively involved in his local Methodist Youth Fellowship and Boy Scouts troop. But at the same time there is some evidence that he was also actively involved in auto theft, shoplifting, and forgery. At college he studied psychology, and as part of his studies, he worked as a volunteer night-shift counselor at a suicide crisis center in Seattle. In 1968 he managed the Seattle office of Nelson Rockefeller's presidential campaign and went on to become involved in further work supporting politicians.

His first murder was probably committed in 1974. His predatory pattern appears to have been similar in most of the murders. He would play on the sympathies of the young women he planned to abduct and murder by wearing a fake sling or arm or leg cast and ask them to help him carry some things to his car. Sometimes he pretended to be a police officer. In this way he gained their trust and was able to lure them into his car or get them to open their door to him. Bundy was executed in Florida in 1989.

"Successful" Sociopaths

The widely held notion that sociopaths are always social losers, cold-blooded murderers, low-lifes, hardened criminals, or serial killers is wrong. Many psychiatrists have argued that there is a second category, termed the "successful" sociopath. They are not "social losers" and usually do not have a pattern of physical assault or committing obvious or violent crimes. But they still harm and use others without remorse. Like all sociopaths, they are cunning, clever, and have no moral principles.

This group is described as "successful" sociopaths for two reasons. First, they could be reasonably successful without being dishonest and exploitive, but prefer the thrill of deceit and want the bigger rewards that come more readily through dishonesty. Second, they get away with their dishonesty and exploitation more often than the "unsuccessful" type, although they may be found out later in life.

These sociopaths are no less sociopathic than the "unsuccessful" type, they just do it differently. There is often no violence involved, although some pay others to be violent on their behalf. They differ from the "unsuccessful" category in that they are adaptive, that is, they have enough skills and advantages to be successful by honest effort if they choose. But they don't. Out of greed, an overwhelming drive for power, and a thrill-seeking orientation, they choose deceit and dishonesty instead. They are more likely to get away with their sociopathic behavior for a long period, as they are often charming, well-networked, and know how to exploit the system. Their associates often cover for them, not realizing the extent of their antisocial and exploitive orientation. Very few of those who deal with sociopaths have the whole picture, so the pattern isn't obvious for a long time. Some become "high fliers" as a result of talent coupled with this pattern of unprincipled and exploitive behavior. Sociopathic patterns of behavior are found in many powerful individuals who achieve political, entrepreneurial, sports, and business success. But their behavior threatens the safety, well-being, and security of individuals, businesses, and our overall society.

Blending in, they pass for normal. Many lead seemingly normal lives, and in many areas of their lives they appear to behave in normal ways. They are capable of superficial kindness, generosity, and "good" behavior when they choose. The German-Jewish political philopher Hannah Arendt coined the term "banality of evil," noting that some of the extreme sociopaths of history, such as the Nazi Adolf Eichmann, still played happily with their children, remembered their wedding anniversaries, were generous to their friends, and cried when their parents died.

There are two main kinds of individuals in this category:

- "the con artist" and
- "the chameleon."

The Con Artist

A con artist successfully pretends for a short time to be what they are not, and then usually "hits and runs." They generally do not sustain their "pretence" over a long period.

After scamming their victims, the con artist usually disappears, sometimes to find new victims elsewhere for the same scam, occasionally to find a new scam. Scams may include:

- claiming bogus qualifications and credentials
- convincing the old or gullible to spend outrageous amounts on unnecessary house repairs
- selling products or services that either don't exist or are not what they appear to be, for example, offering fraudulent medicines and medical services with "miracle cure" claims
- encouraging investment in get-rich-quick schemes that turn out to be fraudulent
- borrowing money or items or that they have no intention of repaying or returning
- romancing lonely or vulnerable people with lies in order to get them to hand over money and valuables, and then disappearing
- stealing roommates' property and disappearing without paying back rent
- embezzling or stealing from employers shortly after working hard to gain their trust, which enables them to have access to money they can slowly siphon off. It is a well-planned scheme, not an impulse to steal.

Bernard Madoff, a financier and former chairman of NASDAQ, was sentenced to 150 years in jail in June 2009 after being found guilty of what has been described as the largest investor fraud ever committed by a single individual. Madoff defrauded thousands of investors (including many of his lifelong friends) of an estimated $22 billion by operating a Ponzi scheme. Madoff admitted that all of the money he was supposed to invest for his clients went straight into his own business account. Like many "successful" sociopaths, Madoff created a phony persona to hide his intentions. He presented an image of a warm, charming, charismatic, and honorable family man. However, he was serially unfaithful to his wife throughout their marriage. He served on the boards of many not-for-profit institutions, many of which invested in his scheme and have now been ruined. Some investors who lost everything they owned in Madoff's swindle have since committed suicide. The judge who sentenced Madoff described his fraud as "extraordinarily evil" and noted that he had received no letters from Madoff's friends or family testifying to any good deeds, and that the absence of such support was "telling."

Gregg O. McCray, a former special agent with the FBI, stated that Madoff appears to share many of the destructive traits typically seen in a sociopath (such as deceiving for the fun if it, manipulation, feelings of grandiosity, and callousness toward their victims) and that explains why so many people who came into contact with him have been left dumbfounded and confused. According to McCray, they become "like chameleons. They are very good at impression management. They manage the impression you receive of them. They know what people want, and they give it to them."

Female con artists often entice people they wish to con by using sex and/or the promise of love and affection. They may also be involved in stealing from their employers after convincing them of their "impeccable" reputation.

"Marilyn" (50) was supposedly a "respectable" mother and grandmother who obtained work as a nurse or housekeeper to wealthy but lonely elderly widowers with the aim of blackmailing them on sexual harassment charges. A lawyer's letter, outlining a list of alleged offenses under the Equal Opportunity Act of 1995, would be sent. An amount was suggested as compensation and the case would be taken no further. Usually the man paid up so his adult children would not be embarrassed and to avoid scandal. Her "sting" was successful.

Con artists are likely to be:
- superficially glib, charming, and persuasive. They are very convincing at seeming not to be conning you.
- adept at creating a single temporary false image that impresses you

- apparently socially relaxed and confident
- able to read other people's needs, wants, and vanities, but at a superficial level only. They can become whoever you want them to be and whoever will convince you.
- completely duplicitous, since they expect to move on to their next victim soon and do not have to be "real." Because they are so exaggerated, they convince, and then leave.

The Chameleon

Chameleons can change to fit the background they are in. They blend in and have interchangeable masks. These individuals may be just sociopathic or, more commonly, have a combination of an antisocial personality disorder (that is, they are sociopaths) and a narcissistic personality disorder. They may have all the symptoms of both or some from both.

There are some similarities between people with the two disorders. Both are self-absorbed, unempathic, and interpersonally manipulative and exploitive. According to the DSM-IV-TR, an individual with a narcissistic behavior disorder (who is more often male) can be described as:

- arrogant and shows a need for ongoing admiration and adoration
- has fragile self-esteem and deep feelings of inadequacy, although this is not always apparent to others
- has a grandiose sense of self-importance (for example, exaggerates achievements and talents, expects to be recognized as superior)
- is preoccupied with fantasies of unlimited success, power, brilliance, beauty, or ideal love
- believes that he or she is "special" or unique and can only be understood by, or should associate with, other special high-status people
- has a special sense of entitlement, that is, unreasonable expectations of particularly favorable treatment or automatic compliance with his or her expectations

- is interpersonally manipulative and exploitive, that is, takes advantage of others to achieve their own ends
- lacks empathy: is unwilling to recognize or identify with feelings and needs of others
- is often envious of others or believes others are envious of them.

Narcissists have unrealistic expectations of superior outcomes in their lives and are prepared to use people to get them. However, they are not necessarily deceitful, dishonest, or law-breaking in all areas of their lives, and they are capable of some degree of remorse and guilt. So, although some chameleons are just plain sociopathic, it is possible for an individual to have both patterns of behavior. Thus, a narcissistic sociopath needs admiration and adoration because of deep feelings of inadequacy, which they cover up, regarding their real worth. They go after this, as well as what they perceive to be their "rightful" amount of power, fame, and money, in an exploitive, dishonest, unprincipled way, without conscience or remorse. They feel entitled to whatever they want because of what they believe are their exceptional skills, status, talents, looks, etc.

Chameleons create ongoing lifestyles based on deceit, pretense, and using others. They are referred to as chameleons because they have a great capacity to blend in and change according to their surroundings. You rarely see them as they really are, because they take off one mask and put on another. Usually bright, competent, and hardworking, they function successfully in society. They may be professional people, highly successful investors, performers, athletes, celebrities, entrepreneurs, or people who own their own companies. They are "real" people, not bogus in terms of their name, qualifications, or credentials. But they cheat, lie, steal, break the law, care about nobody very deeply except themselves, have very little conscience, and feel little guilt after using or harming others. They behave ruthlessly, sure in the knowledge that they are winners, surviving in a vicious world. Chameleons are so much harder to pick up on until after they have made you suffer, because they are more clever than the "unsuccessful" sociopaths. They are also more clever than the other type of "successful" sociopaths, the con artist, because they can sustain their deceit and pretence over a lifetime, not just a short period. Sadly, without this antisocial and exploitive view of people, they could do well in society anyway, as they often have many talents. Instead, they choose to run their lives dishonestly because of their greed, belief in their own superiority, and the need to live on the edge and take chances because it is more exciting. At times when close to exposure, they are saved from disrepute by their social status and connections, charm, influence, and sheer force of wit. Many do get caught eventually, and some decide that suicide is the only way to handle their exposure.

Typical Characteristics and Behaviors of Chameleons

They Are Completely Egocentric

Most chameleons are remorseless egocentrics who want, want, want, and see people as objects to be manipulated. They regard life as an exciting game in which other people are pieces to be controlled and used. Their key characteristics are interpersonal ruthlessness, inability to genuinely empathize with others, and a complete lack of moral principles and hence no shame or remorse for their exploitive behavior. Totally self-centered, they often have an inflated view of their own worth, ability, and importance. With a minimal interest in others as people, their conversation is usually egocentric.

They have only superficial relationships characterized by repeated disloyalty. Capable of lustful sex but no real emotional intimacy or commitment, sociopaths are incapable of really falling in love or being loyal in romantic relationships. People are like tissues to be used and discarded. Although unable to experience genuine deep love for another, they can form sexual or superficial emotional attachments, and feel sentimental and warm toward some people. Many form romantic attachments, pretending genuine loyalty and love but using and deceiving the lover. They are unable to handle real intimacy because they cannot afford to let someone know them well and because intimacy requires truth, loyalty, and commitment. They see intimacy as causing them to be powerless, and above all they want control over others.

Emotionally immature, they are more like an early adolescent. They have very limited relationship skills and are usually repeatedly unfaithful to their partner(s), sometimes with more than one extra-marital relationship at a time. Their open philandering is often known to others but not necessarily to their partner. They usually have an acknowledged partner who feels as if they are "going mad" during suspected repeated betrayals, as the sociopath lies with such sincerity. They often see long-term partners as useful in having their children and with offering them "cover," status, or respectability. Sociopaths give the impression of experiencing genuine emotions, convince their current companion that he or she is the one they like most, trust, are close to, or love. Multiple partners are often romanced concurrently, and all are convinced that the relationship is permanent and exclusive (or potentially so) by what is said or promised. Finally, when they decide to move on, sociopaths are often cold and emotionally detached. The smarter ones try not to alienate abandoned partners and may in some way do them favors or become a friend to avoid exposure. Slowly, they weave a web of deceit around associates, friends, and romantic partners, and exploit them for personal profit or pleasure (for example, for money, sex, affection, adoration, power, or fame). Their process of lying and strategic manipulation gives them enjoyment and a sense of power. There can be real satisfaction in their own cleverness at lying and conning. They feel impervious to discovery. Besotted with their own "cleverness," they sometimes act inappropriately in that they have "odd" emotional responses to events, or boast of their antisocial and dishonest deeds, without recognizing that others are horrified. Some sociopaths control this "leakage" more successfully than others.

A Chameleon Male "Preys" on Women

He selects a vulnerable woman and targets her for exploitation. He goes after a woman whom he sees as more controllable, in that she has one or more of these features:

- is nurturing and "soft"
- may have just come out of a troubled relationship and is "needy"
- may have low self-esteem
- may be less assertive than some.

If she is also a "prize catch" as he sees it, she becomes an exciting challenge to win over. He "reads" what the woman wants and soon becomes the "perfect potential partner." He makes her feel special and adored, ringing constantly and expressing his amazement that someone like her would bother with someone like him. Few conflicts exist because he doesn't expect to be around for long and therefore has no interest in dealing with ongoing relationship concerns. He then starts the process of mistreating them but enticing them to come back for more. On one occasion he will be so loving, thoughtful, and enamored that she will think she is the luckiest woman alive. The next time, however, he will be cold and distant or will criticize her in an offhand way so that she wonders, agonized and fearful, what she has done wrong, and whether he going to leave her. It doesn't take long before she is "broken in" and demoralized, and he can do almost anything he wants. She becomes well controlled. She puts up with neglect and signs of lying, infidelity, and anything he dishes out. As long as he occasionally returns to the "I love you" treatment, she is "hooked" and investigates no further.

They Are Ineffective Parents

Too egocentric to parent well, the growing maturity of their adolescent children is a threat. Unable to have a parental relationship with daughters, they often have a sexualized one instead. They usually (but not always) stop short of actual outright sexual contact, but they may treat their daughter more like a romantic partner than a child. They often neglect or bully their children. Sometimes their children are "useful" to them in maintaining an image, and at those times they suddenly become "doting parents."

They Are Capable of Gross Hypocrisy

They can be quite hypocritical, telling others off for their unacceptable behavior while behaving in appalling ways. The more "socially blended" and high-profile chameleons can appear to be pillars of respectability, publicly holding views that condemn the behavior of others. They do not see an inconsistency between their speeches and their own actions. They may complain about those who manipulate the system, don't look after the elderly, or who drink and drive, while personally avoiding paying taxes, financially conning old people, or being serially unfaithful. They may be obsessive about some public issue for the "good" of society, or full of moral outrage about some group who is "destroying the country" by their actions.

They Can Be Quite Bright

Often they have above-average intelligence, with a good educational background. However, they can appear more clever than they really are because of their charm and their ability to bluff.

They Are Superficially Very Socially Skilled

Cunningly persuasive, sociopaths read people very well at the superficial level of: What does this person want? What are their needs? Their weaknesses? Their vanities? What do they need to hear? What aspect of their ego can I massage? How can I gain their trust? Who do they want me to be?

They have an uncanny ability to identify vulnerable people, especially those with low self-esteem, and figure out how to control them. They make them feel very special. Chameleonlike, they become whatever the other wants them to be so that they can take advantage later on. Cheats are very good at creating a trusting bond very quickly. Displaying confident eye contact, lots of smiles, confident body language, and an adeptness at managing groups as well as one-to-one situations, the sociopath is superficially very socially skilled. Good listening skills encourage the target to think the sociopath is interested and interesting, but there is no genuine depth.

They Are Excellent Liars

Dedicated liars, they often appear to enjoy the thrill and power of lying to others. They lie not only to get what they want, but because they can, and because they are good at it. Lying is a pleasure, because they love getting away with it. Even if there is nothing to be obviously gained from it, they will lie, with apparent sincerity, often prefacing the lie with convincing and dramatic phrases such as:

- Honest to God
- Believe me
- I wouldn't lie to you
- I swear to you.

Their memory is good because they are able to remember the lies they have told to different people and keep them going. Their nonverbal body movements are controlled, so they appear genuine. They look intently into the other's eyes, lean forward, and appear very interested. On a polygraph test to see if they are telling the truth, some can do well, even when lying.

They lie well by telling nearly the whole story so it sounds more convincing because it is mostly true (except for one or two crucial details). They lie well by making a few self-deprecating and negative comments about themselves that convince the listener that they are telling the "raw" truth. They turn it back on you if you question their lies ("What is this, the third degree?").

They Engage in Dishonest Financial Dealings

Some embezzle outright, but chameleons are more inclined to evade taxes, use shady tax shelters, have dubious money transfers, or claim in major ways for things to which they weren't entitled, like medical rebates, expenses, concessions, or discounts. They easily cheat business associates.

They Often Bully Less Powerful People

Often they bully family members or people in lower positions, while pretending not to. Use of intimidation, humiliation, overcontrol, or put-downs to reduce the target's self-confidence are common. However, the more skilled also "play" and "stroke" the less powerful people when it suits them, in case they can use them later to provide cover. They like to control partners and children through intimidation coupled with charm and reward.

• • •

They Act Like Chameleons in Positioning Themselves Well in Their Business and Social Network

This is a deliberate strategy and they are good at knowing how to play the game and working the rules. They use charm to target significant people and manipulate publicity to ingratiate themselves. They can wisely be "nice" and attentive to the smaller and less powerful people in an organization, too, when it suits them. Highly skilled at covering their tracks, they are also persuasive in convincing others to cover for them. They are skilled at making alliances, so that if they go down, their allies will be dragged down with them, thus there is an incentive to cover for the sociopath. Blustering, they may accuse the accuser of lying with such passion that others believe them. Therefore, it takes time before a pattern emerges, because few people have the whole picture, and fewer still are willing to speak out against such a skilled tactician (who is often vengeful as well).

They May Be Ambivalent about Their Own Amoral Behavior

Sometimes they speak of the "good self" and their "bad self." They recognize that others would disapprove of their antisocial behavior if it were made public and therefore acknowledge the unworthiness of what they do. But they are also excited by their own cleverness in getting away with it, and continue to seek self-gratification at the expense of others. Some, especially those who may have had an upbringing that did stress empathy and concern for others, may have occasional bursts of self-loathing because of what they do. These pass quickly, however, and they return to their normal pattern.

They Have Tantrums When They Don't Get What They Want

They can be moody, vacillating from pleasantness to anger and violence.

They Are Very Vengeful

They always take revenge, ruthlessly and cold-bloodedly, even if they were the main offender. They are determined to "win" at all costs.

Why Do They Do It?

Are "sociopathic tendencies" due to genes or environment? Research is inconclusive, but the most plausible explanation for sociopathic behavior involves the interaction of genetic, developmental, and environmental factors. There are one or two identifiable biological factors. However, where people are protected by their companies, families, or colleagues, or are in an environment where corruption and ruthlessness are permitted, there is a greater likelihood of sociopathic tendencies being acted on if they are already present. The more they get away with, the more likely they are to keep doing it.

Genetics

We have only weak trends in the research about how the brains of sociopaths function. It is difficult to get sociopaths to voluntarily participate in research studies. The evidence is fairly weak for a biological predisposition toward sociopathic behavior, but there is some.

A familial trend exists with sociopathic behavior patterns in that one is more likely to behave that way if a first-degree relative also behaved that way. But that may be more due to environment than genes, and many sociopaths do not have a family history, especially the "successful" types.

Some sociopaths appear to have little capacity to empathize and show impaired moral development from an early age. This may be due to an impairment in the functioning of the parts of the brain that handle empathic and moral thinking.

Sociopaths appear to have lower levels of "anticipatory anxiety," that is, the anxiety felt when we are about to do something wrong according to our principles or when we might get punished. They are very "cool" people, who have lower levels of anxiety and hence don't learn as readily not to behave badly or in ways that may attract punishment. This is a reason that many can lie successfully on a lie detector test. The test assumes that people will show by changes in their body when they are not telling the truth, and that these changes are assumed to reflect anxiety about lying.

- They show a greater than normal preponderance of EEG slow-waves in their brain and, consequently, emotional situations may have less impact on them.
- Many sociopaths seem to have higher levels of the "thrill-seeking" gene D4DR-7, which influences how nerve cells respond to the neurotransmitting chemical dopamine in the brain. They are sometimes lower in dopamine, which affects the control of movement and impulses and which, in too low levels, can produce understimulation and boredom and hence a need for constant stimulation. (Dopamine is also involved in pleasure.) Many are chronically under-aroused. Many have a history of attention deficit hyperactivity disorder or have a family member with this problem.
- Sociopaths tend to have a higher rate of alcoholism than the rest of the population, or have family members with this problem. If there are factors that for some lead to a sociopathic predisposition, then a combination of thrill seeking, boredom, lower levels of anxiety, reduced ability to respond to others' feelings, and impaired moral development may lead certain individuals to be attracted to particular kinds of power-oriented and corrupt environments. There they thrive and are often protected by similar kinds of people or those who benefit from them in certain ways.

Environment

For the "unsuccessful sociopath" there is often a history of abandonment or neglect, inconsistent parental discipline, failure to bond with a parent, abuse from parents or caregivers, witnessing of violent acts, approval of criminal behavior, etc. Some chameleons (i.e., "successful" sociopaths) experience parents behaving in a similar way, but most don't.

Certain situations encourage the acting out of sociopathic tendencies which are already present. A postwar study of Nazi SS officers demonstrated that most had already displayed such antisocial tendencies before the war. The researchers theorized that these sociopathic tendencies, already present at an early age, allowed them easily to commit murders in the concentration camps, and their behavior was sanctioned and encouraged by their training and the command structure. Similar contexts can be created in the business, entertainment, and sports worlds, where the emphasis is less on physical harm and more on control, financial gain, and status. Chameleons, in particular, find the environment of wealth and fame very seductive, as it offers them the chance to be "superior" to others and behave as though the normal rules of society do not apply to them.

The "greed is good" philosophy has led us to privately and publicly admire the ruthless pursuit of personal goals. "Ruthless" is defined as "lacking in compassion, merciless, cruel, and single-minded." In applauding the "single-minded" aspect of ruthlessness, we ignore the aspect that stresses "at any cost and with no consideration for the rights and feelings of other people." The sociopath may get so hooked on being a "winner" that he continues to behave amorally, believing that his ends justify his means and that people admire him for what he does.

Usually the sociopath gets away with his behavior far more than he gets caught. The normal process of being punished for antisocial behavior does not occur and so he is not deterred. Because it is so difficult to identify sociopaths, especially the chameleons, their victims don't see the behavior pattern until too late. Even then, many don't tell others, or don't bring charges for fear of looking gullible or being seen as "fools." As children, sociopaths often receive support and concern when they mistreat or exploit others, because the school system is set up to help and modify, rather than judge or severely punish. So the sociopath repeats the patterns of behavior that appear to be working, and if there are few deterrents like being caught, told off, punishments, prison, or fines, they continue. The one thing that stands out in research on sociopathic behavior is that one of the main reasons it develops and increases is the lack of consequences for antisocial behavior. Some "successful chameleons" may *never* be identified and forced to face the consequences of their actions.

Trisha has a confident and outgoing manner, and those who meet her are initially attracted. However, she has no lasting friendships because when people find out about her cold-blooded selfishness and complete disregard for others, they withdraw quickly.

Trisha's husband is a high-earning professional who seems unaware of his wife's activities. Trisha borrows things from family members and acquaintances but rarely returns them. It's not that she wants to keep them necessarily, she just can't be bothered returning them. When bored, she likes to shoplift. Acquaintances have been uncomfortable when, after knowing them for a while, she has told them, laughing, of her shoplifting adventures in a large store where she has also "fooled them" by changing price stickers or placing small items inside larger ones. She points out that those stores make a huge profit out of overcharging anyway, so "they deserve it." Trisha has a great variety of sexual partners, enjoying the thrill of attracting a man and lying to her husband and children about her movements. She has sex once or twice with the men and then moves on. She particularly likes to take as lovers the husbands of women she socializes with. She had one sexual relationship with her next-door neighbor, despite the fact that Trisha and her husband were friends with the neighboring couple. She liked to snicker about how stupid her husband was in not figuring it out. Trisha had moved into a house three doors up from her parents for babysitting convenience. One big thrill, when her husband was away on business, was to send her children to her parents' house for the night and invite the next-door neighbor over for a wild night. She got off on the danger of having her family nearby and her lover's wife 100 yards away while she was having illicit sex.

Jason was only 26 when he died in a car crash. His live-in lover, Adrian, was shattered. They had lived together in a relationship for six years and had started a business together that had just begun to be successful. Gail, a friend of Jason's and Adrian's, was one of the mourners at the funeral. Adrian was puzzled because Gail appeared completely devastated by Jason's death. Adrian knew that Gail and Jason had been close but hadn't realized the depth of their friendship. But it wasn't friendship that had been between Gail and Jason. During four of the six years of Jason's relationship with Adrian, he had also been having a heterosexual affair with Gail. She was in love with him, and over the years Jason had gained total control over her life.

Gail was vulnerable and had low self-esteem. She was easily

manipulated by Jason, putting up with all the conditions that he imposed on their relationship and forgiving him for outrageous acts of thoughtlessness and exploitation. She lent him money, much of which was never returned. If he had arranged to come to her house for dinner, there was a very strong likelihood that he simply wouldn't show up. When she would angrily call him the next morning he would berate her for her possessiveness or insist that he hadn't actually agreed to come.

Jason had told Gail of his sadness over the death of his parents and only sister in an accident when he was sixteen. So it was with some surprise that she was introduced to his mother, father, and two sisters at the funeral. He had woven an elaborate tapestry of lies to make her feel sorry for him and make her more likely to put up with his behavior.

Adrian, too, was in for more surprises. Although he never found out about Jason's real relationship with Gail, he was shocked to discover, while going through Jason's letters and diaries, that during their six years of living together, Jason had had at least fifty casual homosexual affairs, usually lasting from a week to several months, as well as three or four serious love affairs. He had obviously been living several secret lives, and everyone involved with him had been very badly betrayed and hurt. There was more to come. Discussions with the bank manager over the next few weeks revealed that Jason had lied about his financial dealings as well. Their company and Adrian's finances were now seriously at risk because of Jason's lies about loans that had been taken out and for which Adrian had signed in good faith without really understanding what the paperwork meant.

How Do Successful Sociopaths (Con Artists and Chameleons) Get Away with It?

Most people who hear about the victims of successful sociopaths, smugly believe it could never happen to them. Most of us, however, can be easily conned by a practiced sociopath, especially one of the "successful" types. A chameleon sociopath has made a career of deceit and charm, and can quickly identify how to manipulate and charm even the best business mind or a resistant potential sexual partner. Here are reasons why they manage to get away with it for so long.

People Are More Trusting Than They Realize

In order for society to function, we have to assume that most people are telling the truth and will not cheat or use us. Imagine the trouble for our community if we had to assume that everyone we met was out to deceive or exploit us! Those in respected roles such as doctor, bank manager, or lawyer tend to be trusted in our society, but sociopaths operate even in these occupations, as the case below illustrates.

A psychiatrist had sexual relationships with at least five of his patients and also charged for consultations wholly or partly used for those sexual activities. At his hearing by the medical board, evidence was given that he had also beaten one patient until she lost consciousness, kicked her, and thrown her out of his moving car because she was being "difficult." The board heard that he had put on a charade of being caring and prepared to listen to these emotionally troubled patients, but used these tactics to systematically win trust and exploit them. The board banned him from practicing as a doctor and described him as "evil," "predatory," "amoral in the extreme," and "lacking any conscience," a man who had almost destroyed the lives of the five women in his care. They recommended that he never be allowed to resume his medical career. However, one newspaper reported that he had already started to drum up business among former patients as a therapist on a cash-only basis. Only some states require a license to practice as a therapist, but all states require licenses for medical doctors and psychologists.

People Don't Believe It Even When They See It!

It is hard to convince people that this pattern of behavior exists. Most recognize sociopaths only as serial killers, not as regular people who seem to behave normally in many ways. Also, this kind of sociopath takes great pains to appear more trustworthy and more "together" than the average person.

You Lower Your Guard

A sociopath who presents confidently or who has been successful in the world of sports, media, business, or finance is better able to deceive and use people. What could they gain by being deceitful? They already have everything! Why should an apparently handsome, confident, and wealthy professional with many possessions and a caring partner need to steal, make things up, or have countless exploitive affairs? So you lower your guard and let them into your life. Sociopaths behave in whatever way will take you in. Because we have limited experience in dealing with this kind of pattern, we are not well protected.

Many People Don't Realize What Has Happened to Them

Those who have been used, betrayed, or deceived by a chameleon or con artist don't realize what they have been trying to deal with and blame themselves instead. Embarrassed victims don't advertise how they were taken in. They see themselves as inadequate. "If only I had been more loving/trusting/attractive/astute, etc., this wouldn't have happened," they say to themselves. When the dishonesty involves financial dealings, this is less likely to happen. However, self-blame is especially likely in romantic relationships and friendships. Sociopaths usually get away with it many times before someone figures out the pattern, and the pattern is not well known to most people for what it is.

No One Person Has the Full Picture

Everybody has one part of the overall picture but the parts don't get put together. Usually, each piece of this evil jigsaw is not shared with others because a single hurt doesn't add up to a pattern. Exposure occurs when several people in the sociopath's life get together and share their observations or when the pattern occurs repeatedly and in a range of areas.

Others Cover for Them

Because of embarrassment, misplaced loyalty, self-protection, or difficulties in accepting that someone could really be behaving as they suspect, others cover for them. Thus sociopaths, especially chameleons, often don't face the consequences of their actions. Sometimes an organization is sociopathic in its orientation, and actively encourages dishonest and exploitive behavior.

Strategies

16

Strategies for Coping with Sociopaths

Can Someone with a Sociopathic Pattern Be "Cured"?

The simple answer is no. Usually a sociopath seeks treatment only in the middle of a legal crisis and then pressures the therapist to help him get the legal outcomes he wants, not modify his behavior. Sociopaths are poor candidates for counseling and therapy because they:

- fear intimacy
- want control. They cannot accept criticism or authority figures. They often try to charm or outwit the counselor.
- believe (mostly) that there is nothing wrong with what they do and that the problem belongs to others. On the surface, they take all the right actions to suggest remorse and willingness to change. They rarely follow through, though. If forgiven, there is a honeymoon period for a few weeks and then they are back on the same path.

A chameleon male who also has narcissistic tendencies may have a small chance of reducing his pattern with the right relationship. A supportive and ongoing relationship with a woman who sees him realistically and keeps him in line by standing up for herself means he feels safer and more in control. Then he knows that he is loved as he really is, not as a sham. Such a stable relationship may moderate his behavior if the sociopathic pattern is not severe.

As they get older, sociopaths' antisocial actions taper off, perhaps because of loss of power or being found out. But their basic self-absorbed, dishonest, guilt-free, and exploitive orientation and attitudes don't change much.

Those who are mildly sociopathic may have some chance of changing if they voluntarily seek counseling for their behavior pattern. Preparedness to seek help (and genuine follow-up) because of expressed remorse about harming others may be a positive sign.

Strategies for Handling Moderate to Severe Sociopathic Behavior Patterns

Sociopathic behavior patterns are found in ordinary people and also in powerful individuals who have achieved political, entrepreneurial, sports, media, or business success. Your partner, friend, or coworker may have a sociopathic pattern. Here are some guidelines for dealing with that possibility. This is an extremely toxic category, where it may be impossible to change the behavior pattern. To protect yourself, the only change possible may be in your attitude and actions.

The capacity for and preparedness to extend empathy to others is what makes us human. These people lack empathy. Be on your guard! When confronted, people with this pattern are usually very calm and controlled, and seemingly low in anxiety. They don't operate under any feelings of guilt for what they are doing, so their stress levels are low.

Don't Fool Yourself That the Sociopath Will Change

Lower your expectations if you decide to continue to live or work with a person who has a sociopathic behavior pattern. Don't trust them. Don't make yourself vulnerable. Don't expect loyalty or honesty. Be much more on your guard than with other people. Protect yourself. Change is unlikely, and if it does occur, it is limited.

Check If You Suspect

Once you begin to identify a possible pattern, check out as many facts as you can regarding their behavior. Collect facts and keep records. It may take a while for the pattern to emerge because they are masters of deceit and the cover-up, and are often able to convince you that what you know is happening actually isn't.

Sharing information with others may be the only way for you to confirm the patterns of sociopathic behavior and enable you to plan how to react. If you don't identify their behavior patterns, you will be miserable and not know why. Many people (especially women) who are in a relationship with someone like this, spend years depressed and worried, knowing something is wrong but not verifying suspicions. Similarly, many people who suspect that a business partner or coworker is like this wish they had followed their suspicions earlier. Only later do they realize that some checking might have prevented personal theft, fraud, being set up, or lied about in court.

Don't Be Hard on Yourself

Don't be hard on yourself if you get used or conned by someone who turns out to be a fake. Few people see through a sociopath. But be more vigilant from now on.

Consider Leaving

Most people do not stay with a lover, coworker, friend, or boss with a moderate to severe pattern of sociopathic behavior. However, human beings are full of hope and it may take a while to reach this conclusion. Hannah Arendt's phrase "the banality of evil" has been used in several descriptions of sociopaths to indicate the "ordinariness" of parts of their lives that makes it so hard for colleagues, relatives, and friends to recognize and accept the evil they do in other parts of their lives.

Don't Stop Trusting People

If you have had a bad experience with someone like this, inevitably you will be less trusting. Try to put things into perspective. Most people do not have sociopathic patterns of behavior and can be trusted. But it may take you awhile to trust again.

In the Workplace

If there is a sociopath in your company, it may cost money, require legal action, or cause public embarrassment. Valued staff may be lost due to the actions of a sociopath within your company, which may be held responsible for the actions of a sociopathic employee or associate. If one of your employees is sociopathic, the company may end up being exploited or defrauded. You may be personally defrauded. Small businesses that tend to take people "on trust" and believe they are what they profess to be can be caught by skillful "high-flying" sociopaths and face financial ruin.

The corporate world needs to be able to identify sociopathic behavior and to prevent sociopaths from being in a position to make crucial decisions that may damage the company and its employees. Sociopaths may also be making crucial but immoral decisions that can affect the entire community.

Acknowledge the Possibility that Your Partner, Coworker, or Boss May Be Sociopathic

They may not just "have a problem" or just be "making a mistake." Remember, it is the pattern that is important, not one behavior. Anyone can be guilty of one extremely selfish or immoral act, but most don't adopt it as a way of operating in most aspects of their life. Unfortunately, you may not know enough about their past or any "hidden" life to detect the pattern. Be alert for the possibility and check if you are suspicious.

Observe and Identify the Patterns of Behavior

Look for unprincipled patterns. Ambition may in fact be ruthlessness and a lack of ethical behavior. Flirtatiousness may be harassment and exploitation. Shortcutting or creative accounting may be theft. Keep in mind that one unprincipled action does not make someone a sociopath; none of us is so perfect that we don't make mistakes or act in ways that we later regret. But a pervasive pattern of immorality and exploitation coupled with a lack of remorse may indicate a sociopathic behavior pattern.

Check

Don't cover for a colleague, boss, or partner who you believe is behaving in unprincipled ways, such as lying, cheating, stealing, or harassing and harming others. Lack of consequences is part of what keeps a sociopath operating. If possible, let them take the consequences of their actions, even if there is no remorse.

Keep Records and Copy Documents

Document your concerns regarding an individual's behavior even if you initially feel you may be overreacting. Talk to a senior person about your reservations and show them written evidence. Document your own part in decisions about which you are uncomfortable. Learn meeting procedures so you can officially abstain or have your objections noted in the minutes if you feel something is being forced through or is suspect. Warn staff that if they continue to cover for a colleague and close ranks, they may also be liable. Since the sociopath is unlikely to change, others, including yourself, need to identify the patterns of behavior, collect evidence, warn each other, and be prepared.

Be Wary

Be wary of anyone asking you to provide money or resources up front, without a similar commitment on their behalf. Develop a healthy mistrust if you find a number of troubling inconsistencies in someone's story, résumé or track record, especially if they appear to change jobs frequently.

In Romantic Relationships

If you are in love with someone who continuously devalues and demoralizes you and you feel like the inadequate person in the relationship ("I have failed him as a partner"), think again. It may be that you have a lover who is chronically unfaithful with many different partners. By constantly lying, deceiving you about joint finances, and using psychological abuse (a form of bullying), he keeps you under control. If it is a woman who has a sociopathic pattern, she will be adoring and aim to please you as a form of control. But she may also constantly threaten to leave, as she deceives and uses you, always with a good story to cover her tracks.

You may think, "I am the only one who can endure this person's abuse and still love and stay, and that makes me special to them." In fact, though, you are probably one of the few who hasn't seen their pattern or is in denial about what you really "know," even if your don't have any hard facts.

Identify Possible Indicators That You Are Being Deceived

If you always feel insecure with your romantic partner/husband/wife and can't identify why, it is possible that you are regularly being deceived by a very effective liar. Your stomach will be knotted; you will feel alternately good and bad about yourself depending on their mood toward you; and you may be chronically depressed and not know why.

If you are very sure that the problem isn't just your own anxiety or feelings of low self-worth, trust your intuition and check out the situation thoroughly. Don't be put off by dramatic assurances about how they could never do such a thing to you. Sociopaths know how to use drama to con. They don't feel much real emotion themselves, but they know how to fake it to persuade and convince. Here are some possible indicators:

- Have they set up a "smokescreen" life? For example, away a lot, erratic work times, lots of uncontactable time, lots of "cover"?
- Do they have a second cell phone, phone line, post office box, voice mailbox, e-mail, or credit card?
- Do they discourage you from calling them on their cell? (They might have someone else with them who doesn't know about you!)
- Are they good liars? For example, they dramatically assure you that they are telling the truth, but you still have doubts; they attack as a defense; they tell 95 percent of the truth, but a significant but minor detail is wrong (such as who they were with); they make you feel guilty (your gut instinct tells you that there is something wrong but it all seems to add up).
- Do they call you at a time when they know you will be there so that you are less likely to take the initiative and call them later and find out they are not where they are supposed to be?

- Do they "accidentally" leave the phone off the hook/have a phone breakdown/fall asleep early a lot so they have an explanation for why they seemed not to be home when you called?
- Are they very romantic and dramatic when you spot a "suspicious sign" so that you are readily convinced once more of their feelings for you?
- Do they regularly use "darling" or another endearment to save using the wrong name?
- Do you hear negative reports about their past that they deny?
- Are they charming and seem to know what you want (but only at a superficial level)? For example, do they listen well, share feelings, call you all the time, say the words you want to hear? Are they too good to be true in some ways? This makes it harder to believe that they are using or deceiving you and sucks you back in after you are suspicious.
- At some point do they say to you, "I don't know if I can love"?

Be on the Lookout for Attempts to Emotionally Manipulate You on a Regular Basis

Be especially aware of a pattern whereby someone harms or deceives you and then attempts to manipulate you into forgiveness. They appear to be genuinely remorseful and there are dramatic reassurances, tears, and promises. They open themselves up to you for a time, and intimacy is rediscovered. You forgive them (yet again) but they don't change their deceitful and disloyal behavior, and a few weeks or months later the pattern resumes.

Be Wary

Develop a healthy mistrust if a potential partner seems charming and almost too good to be true. They may be genuine, but check out their stories.

• • •

What about the Kids?

An antisocial behavior pattern can show up early in life with "unsuccessful" sociopaths. The DSM-IV-TR categorizes a tendency toward antsocial behavior in a child a conduct disorder. Technically, the diagnosis of antisocial personality disorder can only be made if there has been a history of conduct disorder as a child. However, many psychiatrists and psychologists dispute that this is a precursor to all sociopathic behavior patterns.

A conduct disorder is described in the DSM-IV-TR as a repetitive and persistent pattern of behavior in which the basic rights of others are violated or major age-appropriate societal norms or rules are violated. The behavior pattern must cause significant impairment in social life or school achievement and have been apparent for at least 12 months (to rule out the possibility that the pattern is reactive to a major trauma or adverse event and hence temporary). There have to be at least three of the following:

- aggression or cruelty to people and animals. For example, the individual bullies, threatens or intimidates others, initiates physical fights, uses a weapon, steals while confronting a victim, rapes, or sexually assaults.
- destruction of property (such as arson, vandalism)
- deceitfulness or theft (such as breaking into someone's property, lying to obtain goods or favors or to avoid obligations, lying to con others, shoplifting, or forgery)
- serious violation of rules (for example, the individual often stays out at night despite parental prohibitions, runs away from home overnight or for a period of time, is a truant).

It may be less likely that such a pattern is apparent in the childhoods of "successful" sociopathic con artists or chameleons. These two types (especially the chameleon) are likely to have been liars and bullies at school, thus showing signs of psychological aggression and deceitfulness. Or they may have been arch manipulators and users, because they can be very popular due to their charm and ability to superficially read others. They recognize the need to work from within the system to avoid punishment and to "hide," so they are less likely to blatantly flout the rules. They are more subtle. In early adulthood, they may show the full extent of their ruthlessness and lack of remorse if they find the right environment in which they can get away with it and cover their tracks.

Andrew works in the world of sports and displays sociopathic behaviors that have put his organization at risk of legal action and have cost them valued staff. Despite his achievements, he appears to have a strong need to lie and cheat. He is attractive, charming, physically fit, and very well known in the sports world for being a man with a problem when it comes to women. His capacity for deceit and exploitation is hidden behind the facade of a charming, decent man who seems to adore women. Because he reads people and situations well, and his organization has covered for him, he has been able to project a public image of a hardworking man of integrity. Knowingly carrying a sexually transmitted disease, he has nonetheless sexually harassed and pursued female colleagues and contacts for years. Some of his targets have been the partners of colleagues, who, on realizing, often confront, resulting in ongoing organizational tension, or leave, taking their skills with them. Fearing a lack of organizational support, many of the women have learned to keep out of his way rather than make a formal complaint. He refers to women as "prey" and deliberately selects those who are vulnerable—widows, recently separated or needy women. He has maintained at least three, sometimes more, casual but concurrent sexual relationships, in addition to his marriage and a long-term mistress, for many years. Each sexual partner was encouraged to believe that she was the only one with whom he was involved or that he would leave his wife for her. There have also been hundreds of brief sexual encounters. Some of his dealings, financial and otherwise, have also been suspect, but people have covered for him.

How Can Someone Be So Good and So Bad at the Same Time?

This is the question everyone asks themselves when they come into contact with the chameleon style of sociopath. How can they be so contradictory? On the surface, they are not monsters. In many ways, they are perfectly normal and reasonable. They are capable of sentiment, attachment, and some genuine feelings for others. But their attachments are superficial and the emotions do not run very deep. The concern and sentiment dry up quickly when they want something else and you get in the way.

17

Making Decisions About Difficult Situations and Relationships

IN JUST ABOUT every distressing situation encountered, there are four behavioral options. These can be summarized as CAST, which is an acronym for:

- Change: change what you can and improve the situation
- Accept: accept that the situation can't be changed and learn to live with it
- Stay and suffer: stay in the situation as it is and continue to feel distressed
- Take off: admit defeat and walk away from the situation entirely.

Change What You Can

You cannot directly change anyone else's behavior, only your own. In changing your own, you sometimes act as a catalyst for change in another, but not always. So accept that if you stay in the situation on the assumption that you can change another person's behavior, you may be disappointed.

If you aim to change how you think and what you do, however, then that is more achievable. The best sequence is this: first change how you are thinking, then change what you are doing.

Change Your Thinking

Sometimes, just changing how you think is enough, but not always. Changing your thinking can be done in two ways:

- by challenging your irrational or unreasonable ideas or interpretations of a situation. (See the chapter on pages 222–232 on rational thinking.)
- by continually reminding yourself of what is really important to you. You may find optimism and empathic thinking useful here (see pages 218–221).

Change Your Own Behavior

Target one small behavior at a time. Select the one that will make the most difference to the other person or to your own peace of mind.

Keep a journal of how you are doing. Then reward yourself when you are able to do what you have decided on. Here are some possibilities:

- stand up for yourself more. (Use rational self-talk first, for example, "It's reasonable to insist on people being on time for appointments.")
- ask more often for what you want
- manage conflict better
- get your anger under control
- focus on other parts of your life, not just the part that causes you distress
- improve your relationship skills.

Change What You Can in the Situation

There may be factors in the situation that you can change, such as living arrangements, schedules, outside support or advice, financial reworking, or changing plans. Talk things over with a friend. They can help you brainstorm the alternatives.

Accept What You Can't Change and Learn to Live with It

If you make this choice, you are not attempting to change things, you are deciding to live with things as they are. This may mean putting up with an incompetent coworker who doesn't do their fair share, or living with a partner who gets upset when you have to go away on business.

The secret to doing this successfully (and it can be done!) is to give up any belief that the other person will change.

Accept that:

- difference isn't defect
- nobody is perfect
- some problems can't be solved
- life isn't fair sometimes.

Remind yourself of what damage will be done to your own emotional health, when things are unchangeable, by not accepting how things are. You can:

- lower your expectations
- reduce the number of distressing situations in which you are involved
- distract yourself and refocus on the positives.

You need to accept that what you recognize cannot be easily changed without resentment. If you accept with resentment, then you are really staying and suffering.

Stay in the Situation and Suffer

This is a sad choice but one which many feel they have to make. They can't change their own thinking and they don't have enough power to alter key factors in the situation. They can't learn to accept things as they are because certain things are unacceptable. They feel that leaving (a job, partner, etc.) will be too damaging to others or themselves in terms of financial loss, guilt, loneliness, loss of status, etc., so they stay and suffer.

Take Off, Admit Defeat, and Leave the Situation

This tactic may be appropriate if you are dealing with particularly damaging behavior. It may, in fact, be dangerous for you to stay. It may also be the best solution if, having tried all other options, you feel you can't psychologically survive any longer and that your mental health will be damaged.

Understanding: Using Empathic Thinking

Empathy involves detecting and responding compassionately to the feelings of others. Some can do this more readily than others, but we can all make a choice to do more of it. Being able to think from the emotional viewpoint of another in this way is a skill that can be learned. Do you have to have an identical experience before you can truly understand how another person feels or why they behave as they do? This is the most reliable way to understand another. The person who has lost a child can know that experience when it happens to someone else and understand the feelings associated with it in a way that no one else can. But in one short life we cannot experience everything firsthand. Fortunately there are other resources available to us in our attempts to understand another's feelings and behavior.

Here are some ways to access empathy, in order of effectiveness.

- We can tap into personal experiences that are either very similar or that have similar themes, such as rejection, anxiety, embarrassment, and so on. For instance, we can understand how someone might feel after a marital break up in which one partner leaves for someone else by recalling our own feelings of rejection and jealousy in other situations. A parent who has experienced fear at the swimming pool when a child under their care disappeared momentarily has not suffered the same intensity as the parent who has lost a child by drowning, but there is a common fear as a starting point.
- We can recall what others have told us about similar situations and how they felt or reacted. Family members and friends help us to have a fuller understanding by what they tell us about their own feelings in certain circumstances. Those who listen well gather more secondhand emotional

experiences to compare or draw on. This should not degenerate into a "top this story" contest but may provide useful data to enable us to understand what another is going through or feeling.

- We can read about the way others reported feeling in certain situations from newspapers, books or magazines. For example, we may not have had a car accident but we can learn how traumatized people feel after such an event by reading their firsthand accounts of the after effects. Those who read widely about behavior and people, and think about the implications or discuss them with others, are likely to have more emotional resources as well as access to research facts and theories.

- At the very least, we can imagine how a person feels by projecting ourselves into their situation. We can walk ourselves through how we might feel and respond in those circumstances. The ability to project oneself into another's situation requires thoughtful visualization. What if this had happened to me? How would I feel? How would I react? Have I had any similar experiences I can draw on to help me imagine what this would be like? Would I consider suicide if I had a debilitating terminal disease? Would my view on euthanasia change?

- Obviously, those with wide or deep life experiences have more deposits in their Empathy Bank than those who have led relatively narrow lives. Realistically, we need to be empathic about negative feelings more than positive ones. People with sheltered lives or those who have taken fewer risks (and therefore fallen down less often but also achieved and perhaps grown less) may find it more difficult to empathize.

- Whatever your life experiences, you will have more successful relationships with others if you try to see the world through their eyes and understand how they might be feeling and hence why they behave as they do. In particular, empathy is a powerful tool when you are trying to maintain a good working or personal relationship with incompatible people or someone who is in the Confusing and Troubling Personality category, that is, anxious or demanding people.

Optimistic Thinking

Optimistic thinking is based on looking on the bright side. Psychologists such as Martin Seligman, the author of *Learned Optimism*, have identified the kind of thinking that enables us to stay optimistic in difficult or emotionally challenging situations. Here are the kinds of self-talk that lead to optimism:

- When one bad thing happens it doesn't mean other bad things will follow. Bad occurrences are specific, not general.
- When one bad thing happens it doesn't mean that it was all your fault or because of who you are. There are many factors outside your control, such as other people's behavior, global events, and bad luck, which may have contributed to a negative outcome in your life.
- "It will pass." When something bad happens, it might only be bad for a brief time. Most bad times or bad occurrences are temporary and time-limited.
- When a bad event does happen, try to find the small positives within it to hang on to for a while. For example, you may have crashed the car, but no one was injured. Or you have lost your wallet, but your credit card was in the other bag.
- When good things are happening for you, tell yourself they probably will go on being good for a long time. It is highly likely that they will lead to other good things. For example, your sales figures are up this month. No reason why they can't improve next month, too.
- When good things happen, focus on the positive things you did that contributed to them. You have a lot to do with making good things happen. You can make a difference.

For example, the monthly sales figures went up because you did 10 percent more cold-calling and followed through on expressions of interest. You decided to call back later in the day and not just give up after the first voice mail response.

18

Rational and Irrational Thinking

RATIONAL THINKING IS a useful strategy when dealing with difficult personalities. It is also a good strategy for making your own behavior less difficult. It allows a considered response rather than just a knee-jerk emotional reaction.

Rational thinking is logical and reflects reality, that is, how things are rather than how you imagine them to be. It calms you down and helps you to get what you really want. It makes you feel better and helps you achieve what is really important to you. You can read more about Albert Ellis's theory of rational thinking; see the "Rational Thinking" section in the list of Books You Might Want to Read, on page 273.

Keys to Rational Thinking

- Look for the truth of the situation. It may not always be obvious but you need to try. Remember, an interpretation is not a fact. Interpretations need to be checked.
- Do a reality check by asking others what they know about the situation and how they see things. They may not be right, but at least you rethink by going back and questioning your perceptions.
- Look for evidence rather than making assumptions. For example, if you believe that someone is avoiding you, look for other supporting evidence that stands up to challenge: Are they also not returning your calls? Have they criticized you to others?
- Look for evidence for an alternative way of seeing things.

For example, maybe they are dealing with a crisis at the moment and you are the last thing on their mind. Do others report similar treatment, or are you the only one?

- Don't "imagine" what might be happening and don't try to mind-read how people are thinking and feeling. Check for evidence instead.
- If in doubt, be assertive and ask directly how people are thinking and feeling.

Rational Thinking Is Helpful

If someone criticizes the way you managed a situation, it is understandable that your first response might be, "How dare they criticize me!" and you feel angry. However, it is not helpful if you snap angrily at them, then try to avoid them for several weeks. If you do that, you get upset and feel bad afterward because of the alienation between you and them. It is more helpful to you to remain calm and maintain a good relationship with them if you think in a way that helps you achieve these two goals. For example, "I don't like being criticized, but they don't see it my way and I will just have to accept it. I think my way was equally valid. But I'll also say, 'We will just have to agree to disagree' to let them know I think their criticism was unnecessary."

Self-Soothing Thoughts

These are more helpful than distress-maintaining thoughts.

Rational thinking is about "talking yourself down" and using thoughts that calm rather than further distress you. For example, when you are frightened because you are in turbulent air space in a plane, it is understandable that you might respond initially with emotional distress, thinking, "We are going to die. This is so terrible I can't stand it. The storm will never end." However, it is more useful to use self-calming thoughts such as, "Planes rarely crash. I've been in turbulence before and everything was okay."

Here the truth cannot be identified because at this point you don't know if it is serious or not. Also, there is nothing you can do about it anyway. So you might as well use self-soothing thoughts rather than distress-maintaining thoughts, because they help you cope.

Timing is a factor. At the time an incident happens you may be tired, highly emotional, irrational, and think in ways that are neither accurate nor helpful. However, after you have calmed down you may be better able to think more realistically and usefully. Don't be too hard on yourself if you need time to get on top of it.

Typical Irrational Assumptions (Beliefs) That Need to Be Challenged

IRRATIONAL ASSUMPTION	EXAMPLE OF THIS IRRATIONAL THINKING	RATIONAL VERSION
Everyone I meet must like me or it means I am an awful person.	I had an argument last week with the receptionist over a mistake she made. Now she is making it clear that she doesn't like me. I must be an awful person.	It is unreasonable to expect that everyone I meet will like me. Sometimes things will happen that make others feel negative about me. That's just the way it is. Encountering someone who doesn't like me doesn't make me unlikeable.
Everyone must think I am correct, or else I am worthless.	People were critical of the way I priced the goods at the booth I ran at the bazaar last year and were not enthusiastic about my doing it again next year. This means I am incompetent and hopeless. I'll never volunteer again.	The fact that another doesn't agree with the way I do things doesn't mean that I am wrong or incompetent. It does mean that I should consider their criticisms but not necessarily agree with them.

IRRATIONAL ASSUMPTION	EXAMPLE OF THIS IRRATIONAL THINKING	RATIONAL VERSION
I must do everything perfectly and never make a mistake or it means I am incompetent.	I left out a vital piece of information in the report. I am incompetent and I can't be trusted. This is a disaster.	It is human to make an occasional mistake or error of judgment. It is not a disaster, just a nuisance.
People should always be fair and reasonable.	My elderly father made what I think are unfair comments to me about what he saw as my neglect of him. I visit him as much as possible. He should be fair to me.	There is no guarantee that I will always be treated fairly or reasonably. Sometimes you don't get the good things you deserve and bad things happen to people who don't deserve it. All I can do is try to change injustice. That's just the way it is.
People must always do the right thing, and if they don't, I should punish them.	My nextdoor neighbor parked in a way that boxed me in. I will let her know she did the wrong thing.	People sometimes do things incompetently or thoughtlessly. I can just let it go and not attack them. I'll reserve that for people who do it deliberately or all the time.
I must have everything I want or else my life is meaningless.	My fiancée called off our wedding and I am destroyed because having her as a partner was the thing I most wanted in the world.	There is no guarantee that I can always have what I want. I can try to be persistent. But sometimes I have to live with the fact that there is something I want that I can't have. It is not a catastrophe. I will recover.

IRRATIONAL ASSUMPTION	EXAMPLE OF THIS IRRATIONAL THINKING	RATIONAL VERSION
I must be able to fix every problem that arises for me or the people I care about, or disaster will occur.	I couldn't convince my brother to get counseling for his problem with alcohol. I have failed. There will be a disaster. This is awful.	I don't have total control over the world and other people. Sometimes there is no answer and sometimes I can't fix things. Disaster may happen but I can do nothing about it.
Feelings just happen and you can't help having them. You can't have any influence on them.	I get upset when my partner drinks too much at parties and I can't help feeling angry and worried and making sarcastic comments to him.	It is understandable that I feel worried and angry but what I am doing is not helping the situation.
Because something bad happened to me at an earlier stage, I will be haunted and affected by it forever.	My parents favored my sister over me and I will never feel confident or good about myself because of it.	Something bad that happened to me at an earlier time does not have to continue affecting me adversely for the rest of my life.

Challenging Irrational Thinking

The best way to manage strong feelings is to debate and dispute any irrational thinking that underlie them. Here are some of the ways in which people think irrationally.

All-or-Nothing Thinking

This involves thinking in a black-and-white way with no allowance for gray. To challenge this irrational thinking:

- change your thinking to "No one is completely good or bad" and "No situation is completely bad"
- stop using "always" and "never" about your own behavior as well as that of others
- avoid labeling your own or others' behavior in a permanent way. For example, say "Sometimes I get angry and upset" rather than "I am a bad-tempered person."

Awfulizing

Awfulizing involves believing that something bad is "really, really terrible," not just bad. The "awful" language makes people more upset than is necessary. To challenge this irrational thinking:

- change your thinking to "I don't like it but it's not the end of the world," instead of "this is absolutely terrible"
- identify things that truly are awful to get things in perspective. For example, is it as awful as a child having been killed? Useful phrases here are:
  - Don't sweat the small stuff.
  - This is a pain, not a disaster.
  - This is no big deal.
  - The world isn't going to come to an end.

Catastrophizing

Imagining the worst possible outcome and assuming it will happen is termed "catastrophizing." To challenge this irrational thinking:

- change your thinking to "that could happen but it probably won't"
- point out that worrying about something that has not actually happened and probably won't happen is a waste of energy and time
- use estimates of probability to demonstrate the low likelihood of the "worst case scenario" actually happening.

• • •

"I-can't-stand-it-itis"

This irrational thinking focuses on the belief that you will not be able to deal with something and that you will "go under." To challenge this, change your thinking to:

"I don't like it, but I can bear it."

Trying To Live Up to Your Own or Others' Unrealistic Expectations

We all make unrealistic assumptions about how we should behave. Obviously, there are some nonnegotiable rules, such as not lying, cheating, stealing from, or harming others. But there are no rules about the rest, just expectations that we have absorbed. And they can be challenged. Ask yourself, "What page was that rule written on?" because there is no rulebook for much of our lives. Just because someone else believes that you should do something doesn't make it right or sensible. Keep saying to yourself, "No one is perfect. I'm human and imperfect, and I just do the best I can."

Using "Musts, Shoulds, and Oughts"

Challenge the "musts, shoulds, and oughts" in your life. Replace them with preferences or eliminate them all together.

IRRATIONAL THINKING	MORE RATIONAL THINKING
She should have been fair about it.	It would have been better if she had been fair, but she wasn't. Either I can do something about it or just live with it.
I should have known that and done something about it (irrational guilt).	It would have been better if I had known that but I simply didn't and what is done is done.

Assuming Too Much Control Over Events and People

This involves believing that your actions can surmount impossible obstacles and that you are the one who must be able to fix things. Change your thinking to, I'll change what I can and accept what I can't.

Making Demands of Life Instead of Having Preferences

Be a "wanter" instead of a "demander." If you "demand," you expect and insist that things must be as you want them, and that your wants must be fulfilled or life will be unbearable. This is a recipe for misery and discourages you from accepting things the way they are. If you "want" rather than demand, then you prefer that things will be as you want them and you act to make that happen as far as you can. If it doesn't happen that way, however, you don't get overly distressed. This encourages you to accept things as they really are rather than as you unrealistically demand they should be.

Use Low-Key Language to Keep Your Thoughts More Rational

The kind of language you use makes a difference in how rationally you think.

LOW-KEY WORDS AND PHRASES THAT KEEP YOU CALM AND CAN HELP REDUCE DISTRESS	WORDS AND PHRASES THAT REV YOU UP AND CAUSE DISTRESS
annoyed/irritated	angry/furious
apprehensive/nervous	anxious
uncomfortable	upset/angry
concerned/I have concerns about	worried/distraught/frantic
sad	depressed
serious	traumatic
disappointed	devastated/angry
regrettable	terrible/disastrous
embarrassed	humiliated

Rational Self-Management of Emotions

All these hints start with the letter "P" to make it easier to remember and apply rational self-management strategies to handle your own emotional reactions to difficult situations and to others' behavior.

Proof

Is there any proof that what I am worrying about or thinking is true?

Can I do a reality check with a friend or someone I trust? For example, I am worried that my friend is angry with me because I couldn't do the favor she requested. I could ask her if she is upset with me. I could ask a mutual friend for her opinion.

Possibilities

Is it possible that I am misinterpreting this situation? Are there any other ways of viewing this situation that are equally valid and more helpful in terms of coping, at least in the short term? For example, perhaps she was upset over not getting the promotion she expected.

Positive Aspects

Is there any positive aspect of this situation that can give me some comfort, even if it is only small? Is there more than one? For example, she has agreed to meet for lunch next week. She can't be too upset with me.

Perspective

Do I have this in perspective? Is it as disastrous as it first seemed? Is this really going to destroy my whole life or is it just one not-so-good thing I have to come to terms with? It probably won't last very long, and even if it does, it is still only a part of my life. For example, this is only a small aspect of my life. Even if she is upset with me, it is not a disaster. I would prefer that she weren't, but if she is, I can deal with it.

Plainer Language

Am I using "catastrophic" and exaggerated language that is making me feel worse than I need to? For example, "furious" instead of "annoyed"; "humiliated" instead of "embarrassed"; " depressed" instead of "sad"; "frantic" instead of "concerned." I'm concerned, not distraught.

Personalizing

Am I taking this too personally? If I personalize situations and the behavior of another I am making the assumption that it means something about me. Often situations and responses are normal under the circumstances, or are the result of factors which I may not have anything to do with. I won't personalize. I'll normalize instead.

Panic Paralyzes

Panicking won't help. Panic just paralyzes and I need to remind myself of that. I'm less likely to cope and get what I want if I panic. Can I get a grip so I can think about what to do rather than going out of control?

Problem Solving

What options do I have for doing something about this, instead of panicking and worrying? Is there something I haven't thought of? For example, perhaps I can bring up the subject at lunch next week.

Persistence

Have I given up too soon on the strategy I was using to change or manage the situation? Do I need to grit my teeth and try again?

Put It Aside for a While

Can I stop thinking about this for a while, so that I return to it later, in a calmer way, and deal with it?

Physiology

Is something happening in my body that might be making me feel less able to cope than normal, such as tiredness, not eating, illness, or hormones? For example, I think I am coming down with a cold.

Problem Ownership

Is this really my problem or is some or all of it, in fact, a reflection of a problem someone else has? For example, she can be hypersensitive. Perhaps it is her problem as much as mine.

• • •

Rational Thinking to Manage Specific Kinds of Feelings

To Manage Anger

I can expect to feel angry in this situation because I have been hurt or treated badly, but I can cope with feeling angry even if I don't like it. I won't deny my feelings, but I won't exaggerate them either. Is there something constructive I can do to improve my situation? If there is, I'll do it. If there isn't, I'm not going to make myself feel worse than is reasonable. I know that I won't be angry forever, and I will come to terms with what has happened. I can cope till things get better.

To Manage Anxiety

I have had this uncomfortable feeling in my body before. Last time it didn't mean anything, even though it felt like something bad was going to happen. It went away and nothing bad happened. It will go away again just like last time. It is only my body fooling my brain. I have to relax until it disappears. I can live with it until it goes away

To Manage Worry over Conflict

It is not the end of the world if someone is annoyed at me. I can stand it, even if I would rather they weren't annoyed. They may be the one with the problem. It is not possible to go through life without upsetting people some of the time. My rights are just as important as theirs. Conflict is not always a bad thing.

To Manage Sadness

I can expect to feel sad and upset in this situation because I have lost someone or something that was important to me. But I can cope with feeling sad even if it feels bad. I won't deny my feelings, but I won't exaggerate them either. I know I will have to learn to come to terms with this loss. I'm not going to make myself feel worse than is reasonable. I'll try to find ways to get through this. I know that things will probably be better in a while and I can cope till they are. Although this is bad, it is not the end of the world, even though at times it may feel like it.

19

Healthy Self-Assertion

MANY PEOPLE ARE frustrated because they feel used or pushed around, or are not achieving the things they want. Healthy assertive behavior in place of passive behavior can reduce this frustration. Some people believe that because they do stand up for themselves or stand up to other people, they are being assertive. Mistakenly, many people are being aggressive and hostile, not assertive.

Passive Behavior

Characteristics of passive behavior include ignoring your own rights; allowing others to violate your rights; not expressing your own needs, feelings, and ideas; and allowing others to choose or make decisions for you. After being passive, you often feel resentful or angry with yourself. A delayed reaction might be, for example, "Why didn't I say what I really felt? Why did I say I would do it when I'm too busy? Why didn't I ask for what I really wanted? Why am I avoiding making that phone call of complaint?"

Passive behavior reduces self-esteem and may invite others to exploit or bully you. It is less likely to earn you the respect of others.

Aggressive Behavior

Aggressive behavior may be triggered by extreme anger or anxiety. You may be standing up for your rights, but in doing so you have attacked others and violated their rights, or forced your views or decisions on them. So you have achieved your rights, but at their expense. After behaving aggressively, you may feel guilty about dominating or humiliating the other person, and your self-respect diminishes. Constant aggressive behavior will distance you from other people and lead to ineffective relationships.

Assertive Behavior

Being assertive means standing up for your rights without attacking or violating those of others. You make your own choices and decisions, and give others the same right. You do not force your opinions or decisions on other people, and you do not let them do so to you either. After you have been assertive, you feel calm, and your self-respect and confidence grow.

Good Reasons for Using Healthy Assertion

By speaking up about your own views and needs you gain self-respect, and respect from others, too.

When you stand up for yourself in an assertive, direct, and honest way, the other person usually benefits in the long run. You don't hurt others by trying to control them through hostility, intimidation, or guilt.

- Not letting others know what you think or feel is just as selfish as not attending to other people's thoughts and feelings. How can they respond appropriately to what they don't know?
- If you continue to be unassertive and sacrifice your own rights, you train other people to take advantage of you and treat you with disdain.
- When you are assertive and tell another how their behavior affects you, you are giving them an opportunity to change and you are respecting their right to know where they stand with you. They don't have to become mind readers.

• • •

Here are some of the fears that can prevent you from being assertive.

FEAR	REALITY
The other person will become angry with me if I'm assertive.	If I assert myself, the effects may be positive, neutral, or negative. No one is thrilled when you act assertively with them. But they will respect you more and they will be less likely to behave that way again. And it isn't the end of the world if they are initially upset with you. You can stand it even if you don't like it.
The other person will reject me if I am assertive.	This is unlikely. They are likely to respect you more if you speak up, as long as you do it without attacking them. If standing up for yourself causes them to leave you, what sort of relationship is it anyway? One where you have no rights.

The Steps of Healthy Assertion

Identify Your Rights

Identify your rights and those of the others. But remember that rights aren't rules or laws. They are just beliefs about what is fair and reasonable that motivate you to act on them.

Change Your Thinking

- What irrational fears are stopping you from being assertive? "What if he's annoyed when I say I can't lend him my car?"
- Exaggerate these fears by extreme "catastrophizing." "What if he gets so annoyed that he doesn't want to be my friend anymore?
- Evaluate whether or not the "catastrophe" would destroy you. "I want him to continue being my friend, but if he

chooses not to, that wouldn't be the end of the world."

- Assess the probability of the "catastrophe" actually occurring. "He'll be a little bit upset, but he's been a good friend and is unlikely to end the a friendship just because I'm uncomfortable about lending him my car."

Use the Nonverbal Skills of Assertion

You can, for example:

- stand comfortably close
- use eye contact—constant, not glaring
- "stand tall"; adopt an erect, relaxed posture
- face the other person
- use relaxed gestures and control aggressive or anxious mannerisms
- look serious and don't smile unnecessarily
- speak firmly and fluently.

Use I-Messages Instead of You-Messages

An I-message allows you to "own" the feelings being expressed rather than offloading them onto another. Here are some examples of how they differ.

YOU-MESSAGE	I-MESSAGE
That joke you made about me at the meeting was offensive. You are such a nasty person.	I dislike rude jokes aimed at me, like the one you told this morning. It's embarrassing for both of us. Please don't do it again.
How the hell are we ever going to afford an overseas vacation. You're being ridiculous!	I think an overseas vacation would be too expensive for us right now. I don't want to do it.

Use the "Broken-Record" Technique

Calmly repeating an "I" statement of what you want is the "broken-record" technique. This technique allows you to feel comfortable and avoid manipulation in the form of verbal sidetracks, counterarguments, insults, and implications. Note the "fudging," or ignoring an argument, which allows the person to avoid the trap of being sidetracked or manipulated.

Sue: *I know that you need someone to make a speech but I don't want to do it because it isn't something I do well.* (I-message)
Andrea: *But no one else wants to do it either and someone has to do it.*
Sue: *I realize that* (fudging) *but I don't want to be the one to do it.*
(I-message)
Andrea: *But who else can we get?*
Sue: *That's going to be difficult* (fudging), *but I really don't want to do it.*
(I-message)

Use Protective Assertion in Personal Relationships of Importance

Protective Assertion is a style of assertiveness that is gentler and less confronting than what is sometimes used in other situations. It involves:

- making a statement of the problem in a way that allows the other to save face. This is best achieved by accepting that the problem is a mutual one. For example, "We seem to have had a misunderstanding here."
- using very low-key language. For example, "I am uncomfortable about …" rather than, "I am angry about …"
- using Goodwill Retracking (see page 253).

Making a Complaint and/or a Request

Objectively describe the behavior that troubles you and how it makes you feel. Use the structure of "When you … I feel … because …" For example, "When you don't remember to lock the door at night I feel angry because I feel unsafe."

- Avoid exaggerating.
- Check with the person you are talking to and invite their response to what you have said.
- Listen and respond.

- Don't apologize for your complaint or your request.
- You will get nowhere if you talk in generalities. Work out what you want to happen and state your preference clearly and specifically. For example, "Could you make a point of remembering to lock the door last thing at night?" is better than "I want you to be more considerate."
- Request agreement from them about your preferences. For example, "Is that possible?"

Saying "No" When Someone Asks You to Do Something You Don't Want to Do

- Take time to consider before you answer. You can contact them again later. You can also change a "yes" to a "no."
- Listen for alternatives or compromises.
- Explain briefly without giving an excuse.
- Say "no" seriously. Shake your head.
- Repeat it in a slightly different tone and give the same explanation.
- Finish the conversation.
- Don't feel guilty.

Warning!

When being assertive or resolving conflict, you need to proceed more carefully with someone who is hypersensitive. Obviously, you will be using protective assertion wherein you state your feelings in a way that protects the relationship from fallout. But you will be more effective if you "overdo" comments that stress how much you care about them. Also stress that you are trying to solve a problem, not attack them. You may need to keep repeating these two kinds of statements.

20

Managing Your Own Anger and the Anger of Others

"LAST STRAW SYNDROME" is a condition in which so much stress and anxiety is being experienced that even quite minor upsets can feel like one thing too many. People who are suffering from this syndrome are often puzzled by their own outbreaks of anger. They often make complaints about issues that formerly they would have let go. Also, they can be unreasonably cranky and irritable in the street and in stores. Their emotional resources are being depleted by the tasks of dealing with major stress and so they are increasingly intolerant of minor stressors.

What Does an Angry Person Want?

An angry person wants these things from you:

- acknowledgment
- validation of their feelings even if you do not agree with how they are seeing things
- empathy and understanding
- respect
- a solution
- a commitment from you for follow-up action.

Responding to an Angry Person

Remember these key facts:

- The perceptions by an angry person of what you say or do will be temporarily distorted.

- It is not about winning the encounter, no matter how determined the other person is to see it that way.
- The most effective way to deal with other people's anger is to respond thoughtfully rather than react in a knee-jerk fashion. But this is hard to do if your emotions get out of control.
- You need to keep reminding yourself of your objectives, for example, protecting a relationship or keeping a client.
- It is not about venting your own angry feelings, no matter how justified they are.
- It is about solving the problem in a way that protects relationships.

Keep Things Calm, Including Yourself
- Take a deep breath and use self-soothing thoughts to keep your own anger and anxiety under control.
- Relax the other person by your calm tone of voice and by focusing on being ordinary. For example, "Let's go and get ourselves some coffee and talk this through."
- Calmly assert your wish to listen and help solve the problem. For example, "Tell me what the problem is so that we can work together to find a solution."
- Don't become sidetracked into defending yourself.
- Don't take the anger personally, even if it seems personal.

Fully Attend and Listen until They Are Calmer
- Pay full attention.
- Listen carefully.
- Don't interrupt.
- Seek information.
- Check your understanding.

Use Empathy and Respect the Other Person
Share perceived differences by making a "respectful disagreeing" statement where you focus on areas of agreement first and then state where you stand on the issue. For example, "I know that it

seems like an unfair situation but we are not in a position to change it at this time." "I agree with you that there may be too much money going out of our bank accounts on unnecessary things but I don't accept that I'm spending all of it."

Empathize with the other person's position. For example, "It isn't going to be easy for you, I realize that."

Use a Broken-Record Statement If Appropriate

Use a broken-record statement in a calm and friendly tone of voice to restate your position and communicate a desire to resolve the situation.

Stay Problem-Focused

- Keep your focus firmly on the issue.
- Don't be sidetracked into trying to defend yourself.
- Don't try to change the other person's mind by arguing or debating. An angry person doesn't respond well to logic or explanation until they have calmed down.

Negotiate Solutions

- Don't smooth over or minimize a problem without addressing it.
- Negotiate a solution where possible (win–win).

Commit to Following Up Where Appropriate

Take action and follow up.

If the Other Person Remains Angry

Make it clear that you are willing to discuss the problem but not to engage in a fight or be intimidated. Use a broken-record statement in a calm voice. For example, "I am prepared to work with you to find a way to figure this out, but I am not prepared to trade insults and be yelled at."

Terminate the discussion if the other person remains angry. For example, "We don't seem to be getting anywhere at the moment because the issue is making us both emotional. Let's make an appointment to tackle the issue later." Don't blame them for this. It is a mutual problem.

Make a commitment to follow up when they feel calmer.

How to Make Things Worse!
- Criticize or insult them by giving negative you-messages. "You are being stupid…"
- Try to make them feel guilty. "You're not the only person who has rights here."
- Insisting on the supremacy of logical argument. "Don't you realize that…?"
- Interrogation. "Did that really happen? Are you sure?"
- Empty reassurance. "I'm sure it's not as bad as you think."
- Inappropriate humor. "Guess who got out of bed on the wrong side this morning!"

Managing Your Own Anger

Sometimes we feel angry because of another's actions that we feel have threatened us in some way. Each of us has had the experience of being attacked by an angry person without warning and for no apparent reason. Whatever the trigger, we respond with fear and flood with adrenaline. This interferes with our ability to respond skillfully.

What Is Anger?
Anger is a useful emotion we all experience. It is biologically triggered by a similar chemical process to anxiety, but we interpret it differently. We are less likely to try to escape when feeling angry and more likely to act or confront. We feel angry when:

- our rights have possibly been violated
- we are threatened with loss
- we feel powerless and not respected.

Anger has a real purpose in our lives, but it needs to be managed, not just ignored. Learn to be realistic, let some of the anger go, and be assertive in situations where there is an issue that needs to be dealt with. In managing anger, get your body and emotions under sufficient control to decide reasonably and rationally how to handle the situation. Sometimes, after a rethink, you need to let it go because you have been incorrectly angry. Sometimes you conclude that, yes, you have a reason to feel angry, but you need to communicate your anger in a way that will "contain" rather than escalate the problem.

Body Calming

In many situations you have to deal with your angry feelings then and there. Try counting backward from 100 by twos, deep breathing, focusing on something in the room, or chanting to yourself in your head: "Stay cool" or "Chill out."

When possible, put some time between when you feel the strong emotions of anger and when you deal with them.

You can:

- practice controlled deep breathing until you feel calmer
- lie down or rest in a comfortable chair for a while
- play calming music. The endorphins (pleasure chemicals) gradually replace the adrenaline.
- use constructive physical activity to reduce the adrenaline-related chemicals in your body and increase the flow of endorphins instead. Go for a run. Swim. Walk around the block. Ride your bike.
- distract yourself for a while. Temporarily lock the issue away and focus on something more positive in your life.

These are only the first steps. Then you have to rethink the situation and decide what to do.

First, Check Your Facts

Many people initiate conflict while lacking information about what actually happened. Realizing halfway through that they are missing facts and that the situation is now looking very different, they may continue the conflict anyway. Too much "loss of face" is involved in backing down and admitting they were partly wrong. So, get as much information as you can. Don't jump to conclusions. You may need to wait awhile until you can get the information you need.

Rational Thinking

- Don't personalize the situation. It is not your weakness, it is a situation between people.
- Think rationally about who owned the original problem. It may belong, at least in part, to someone else.
- Remind yourself that the need to maintain the relationship or keep the situation well managed is usually the more important goal.
- While it is understandable that you want to express your angry feelings or retaliate, it is not helpful. Catharsis, or "letting it all out," can make the situation worse. If you are going to communicate that you are angry about a situation, do so assertively, not aggressively.
- Use lots of rational self-talk, such as, "It's not worth losing my cool."

Talk It Through with Someone Else

Ask someone you trust to help you do a reality check. You should be able to expect care and empathy from them, but also a check on how rational your thinking is about the situation.

Be Assertive

Anger can be constructively expressed if you act assertively rather than aggressively.

- Use "I-messages."
- Clarify, first, that you are looking for a friendly solution, not a fight. Use a goodwill statement, for example, "I value the professional relationship we have always had and would like to maintain that."
- Listen. Try to hear and see their point of view.
- Ensure that your body language is under control.
- Don't expect others to be pleased that you have been assertive.

Use Low-Key Language

Use low-key language so that you don't wind yourself up. "That so-and-so has infuriated me and I won't put up with it!" will wind you up. "I am upset over what she said to me" is less likely to get things out of proportion.

Keep Things in Perspective

Remind yourself to keep what has happened or what someone has done in perspective. Anger can make things seem much worse than they are.

Recognize That Stress Can Make Things Worse

Avoid the trap of letting stress and work overload make you more prone to anger over small things.

Are any other factors making you particularly angry at the moment? For example, feeling ill, tired, hungry, hurt by something else? If you are flooded with anxiety, try not to deal with angry feelings or situations till you have calmed down.

Own Your Own Anger

Use I-statements to locate the anger in you rather than seeing it as caused by someone else. For example, "I am feeling angry because of what you said" is better than "You made me angry."

Diagnose What You See as the Real Threat in the Situation

Anger usually relates to potential loss, violation of rights, or disrespect. However, you may regard a situation as threatening when it is merely one where two people see things differently. For example, you may be perceiving a partner's disagreement as a challenge to your expertise rather than just a difference of views expressed in an emotional manner.

Use Self-Talk for Managing Your Own Anger

- I'll focus on dealing with the problem and stay calm.
- This isn't about proving that I am right and they are wrong. I don't have to "win" this, I have to manage it.

- I need to keep reminding myself about what the ultimate goal is here.
- This isn't a disaster, it's a small problem to be solved.

Unsent Angry Letters

Write a really angry letter, but don't send it. Leave it for a day or so and then reread it. You may then want to modify it now that you are feeling calmer. Make the language more low-key and less inflammatory. Remind yourself of the goal to maintain the relationship. This helps clarify your feelings and allows you to practice what you want to say. Then you can send it, or not send it but accept it as a way of clarifying your feelings and thoughts. Refer to the section on conflict resolution (page 248) and the chapter on healthy self-assertion (page 232) for more detail and direction.

Don't deal with anger when you have consumed alcohol or some other mood- or mind-altering substance. Angry feelings escalate and perceptions become even more distorted when mood-altering substances are involved.

21

Managing Conflict

CONFLICT CAN BE simply defined as:

- when two or more people have currently incompatible goals
- when two or more people cannot agree but need to make a decision
- when one person feels their personal rights have been violated.

Conflict can be healthy in a personal relationship. Relationships are very much about reconciling differences. First, you need to recognize that differences always exist between two people, no matter how compatible or how much they love each other. Many differences just have to be acknowledged and accepted as part of who you are. Other differences cause conflict, which is often no more than seeing things differently and having clashing goals. This conflict needs to be satisfactorily resolved for both, and when achieved, the relationship grows stronger. By resolving the conflict, both have signaled their strong desire to maintain the relationship. It makes people feel more trust in the strength of the relationship. Resentments do not fester long term.

The ability to solve conflict is vital, and such skills may be the basis of your survival in a wide range of situations.

Conflict in personal relationships can range from something as simple as how glasses are stacked in the dishwasher to more serious issues such as purchasing a new house or the handling of family interactions.

In the workplace, conflict might occur in meetings, over project decisions, between colleagues with different management styles, with support staff, or in customer-service situations.

Conflict-positive organizations recognize that with conflict there is also the potential for growth, creativity, productivity, and better relationships. Conflict-negative organizations try to avoid it at all costs, believing that conflict is always a destructive force.

There are eight main actions you can use to deal with conflict. All are appropriate at various times but the four likely to result in constructive resolution of conflict are:

- being assertive
- smoothing
- apologizing/placating
- problem-solving negotiations.

You Need a Large Repertoire of Different Conflict Resolution Skills to Match the Skill to the Situation

The strategy that you use to resolve the conflict will depend on:

- your degree of distress and what kind of conflict it is
- the time available
- your level of skill
- the power balances in the situation
- how important the issue and the relationships are to you.

The Eight Strategies for Conflict Resolution

1. Forcing

This is not a good way to deal with conflict. Forcing means overpowering, cheating, hurting, threatening, lying, or putting others down in order to try to "win" when there is a disagreement. It risks alienating the other person, reducing future working effectiveness, and increasing the likelihood of a counterattack.

2. Avoiding or Withdrawing

Ignore a conflict only when it is over something trivial and unimportant. Little conflicts that are avoided often grow into big conflicts. Indirect expression of anger or fear through sulking, non-cooperation, sarcasm, or talking behind the person's back can create new conflicts. Temporarily withdrawing may be constructive so that you can deal later with the issue and the person after planning or when more information is available.

3. Asking for Support or Mediation

Try to handle a conflict by yourself first. Ask those in a senior position (in an organization) or friends or family members for support if you are being damaged, or if the situation is intolerable or really counterproductive to goals.

4. Agreeing to Disagree

If you don't agree about something, but you don't have to make a decision, you can say, "We will have to agree to disagree on this one." That doesn't mean you are wrong. Differing views are not dangerous.

5. Acting Assertively

You can be assertive. Ask someone to stop, or say what you want in a firm way. Use friendly assertion first and then move to firmer assertion. You should start what you say with "I" ("I want you to stop spreading that rumor about me because it is untrue"). If they don't listen you just keep repeating it in a firm way (the broken-record tactic). Make firm but not aggressive eye contact and don't look away. Stand tall. Use a strong voice. Don't smile.

Use less alienating low-key phrases to express your concerns, such as:

- I am troubled by…
- I am concerned about . . .
- I am disappointed with . . .
- I am uncomfortable about . . .
- We seem to have a problem/difficulty/blockage with . . .

Also refer to the section on assertion skills on page 232.

• • •

6. Smoothing

If you don't feel strongly or when you are prepared to let the other person have their way, you can choose to give in. This is called "smoothing." Smoothing should be done with good grace and without resentment. But if you smooth too much, or if the other person never smoothes for you, don't keep doing it. A little bit can be cooperative, but too much makes you a doormat and people will lose respect for you.

7. Apologizing and Placating

Apologize to the other person if you are wrong or mistaken, or just apologize for the part for which you were responsible. If it seems fair, make up for what you have done. Saying "Sorry" should be done genuinely and not in a sulky, resentful way. Sometimes, both people may be wrong in small ways. Don't apologize too much or people may see you as a pushover.

8. Problem-Solving Negotiation

This is the best tactic of all. You see the problem as belonging to both of you ("We seem to have a problem here"). Then you talk with the other person to find a way in which both of you can get a lot, but not necessarily all, of what you want. Aim for a "win some and lose some" solution, about which you both feel all right. For example, if two friends who are traveling together can't agree where to stay because one wants to stay in a bed-and-breakfast and the other wants to stay in an four-star hotel, they could alternate, staying in a cheap place one night and an expensive one the next.

Constructive Management of Conflict

Acknowledge That Conflict Can Be Constructively Resolved

Positives such as an improved relationship and greater trust may come from dealing with the conflict. Not everything that is faced can be changed, but nothing can be changed until it is faced.

Understand That Some People Are Very Frightened of Conflict

For some, conflict situations have always ended in negative outcomes, and so a state of "learned helplessness" results in which they believe that nothing they can do will solve the problem. Consequently, withdrawing seems easier.

Many fear that one of these negative outcomes will occur:

- they will "lose" and be "bested" in a disempowering way
- they will be damaged or look foolish
- the relationship will be weakened and the other person will terminate it and no longer like them
- they will be perceived as a nasty person.

People from backgrounds where there was much fighting and many destructive outcomes from conflict may be more frightened and avoid it more often. On the other hand, if you come from a background where there was an unspoken rule that conflict should be avoided at all costs, you may be just as apprehensive about it.

Jointly Define the Conflict as Mutual

If one person sees the other as having the problem, it is more difficult to get a resolution. The situation needs to be defined as mutual straight away. Say, for example:

- We appear to have a problem.
- It looks like we need to negotiate this.
- We don't seem to be seeing this in the same way.

Jointly Define the Conflict as Small and Specific

Keep the focus on specific issues rather than framing the situation as one where "we don't get on" or "we have a conflicted relationship."

Stay Calm and Manage Your Angry and Frightened Feelings

If you feel out of control because of angry or anxious feelings, you will probably handle things badly. Get your feelings under control first. Realize when they start to overwhelm you. Withdraw temporarily, but deal with the problem when you feel calmer. Suggestions on handling angry feelings are in the chapter on anger management on page 239.

Conflict Feels Uncomfortable

Yes, conflict does feel uncomfortable. Yes, there is a risk. But its resolution can also strengthen a relationship and produce better outcomes. Using conflict resolution skills well makes you stronger and more confident.

The Other Person May Have an Equally Valid Perception of the Situation

Listen to what they have to say and don't jump to conclusions. There are often several equally valid views on the same issue. Rarely is there an "absolute truth" in a conflict.

Time and Timing Are Important in Resolving Conflict

Remind yourself that it can take hours, days, or weeks to resolve some issues. If the timing is wrong (for example, you have to be elsewhere at a particular time, you are very tired, etc.), make an appointment to resolve it later. Make sure you follow through and don't forget about the postponement, or the other person will be angry and resentful. Temporarily withdrawing from a conflict may be constructive, so that you can deal with the person and the issue more thoroughly, at a more advantageous time, or when more information is available. But if you say you are taking some time out and will return to discuss it later, and then you don't, you will create even greater conflict and resentment. It is tempting later on, when things are cooler, to pretend it never happened. It is better, however, to return to the issue and say, "Let's have a chat about . . . now that we have both had some time to think things through."

Resist the Desire to "Hit and Run"

It is unfair and alienating to make your point, express your emotions about a situation and then leave before the other person has had a chance to state their position.

Focus on the Problem, Not the Person

Keep the discussion focused on the issue, not the other person's character, motives or past behavior. Avoid insulting or demeaning language. See FIND PEACE on page 256.

Keep Your Sense of Humor

Using humor to be patronizing, to wound, or to trivialize the conflict is not helpful. However, an appropriate use of humor can make a situation seem less threatening, though still important.

Protect the Other Person's Ego by Allowing Them to Save Face

Everyone needs to save face and appear respected, sensible, and reasonably powerful. People involved in escalating conflicts often forget the future importance of maintaining good relationships and concentrate only on winning in the present. Allow the other person to feel well treated and respected, even if there is some temporary conflict.

Start with a Goodwill Statement

Where it is true, ensure that the other person knows that your mutual relationship is important and you wish to resolve the situation amicably. Say, for example, "I really value our working relationship so I hope we can deal with this in a way that allows us to continue working well together."

Use Goodwill Retracking If Things Start to Get Heated

Make a statement to remind yourself and the other person about your vulnerabilities and the importance of the relationship to you.

- (to a coworker) "Look, we're both getting upset and we're starting to say things I suspect that neither of us really means. Can we put the brakes on for a minute?"
- (to a partner) "Honey, I want to work this out peacefully, because I don't want it to start affecting our relationship."

22

Skills for Maintaining a Strong Romantic Partnership

FACTORS SUCH AS common interests, shared values, affection, compatibility, shared time, appreciation, humor, a satisfying sex life, financial security, and the sharing of joy are important in any marriage or committed relationship. But they are not the main factors that predict whether the couple will stay together.

A lasting relationship results from a couple's ability to resolve the conflict that is inevitable in any relationship, and to deal with the resultant feelings. Most couples start their relationship with love and great expectations but get into trouble because they don't know how to handle the negative feelings that are an inevitable part of conflict.

Typically, the woman is the couple's emotional and social captain. She "reads," charts, navigates, debriefs, and draws attention to issues and crises. Without cooperation and communication from her partner, however, changes do not occur and the relationship stagnates. And if the woman signals unskillfully that attention is needed to deal with a relationship issue, the result can be resentment and alienation.

The basic rules and principles given in this chapter have been derived from the best and most recent research studies into relationship effectiveness. Identify which key areas you can work on to improve your relationship via changing your own behavior. You can't change another's behavior, only your own. Often, though, when you change yours, they change theirs.

The psychologist John Gottman and his associates carried out a sensitive study of couples interacting. They studied 150 couples at all stages of marriage for nearly a twenty-year period. It is probably the most extensive and respected research in this area. Using psychological, behavioral, and physiological (body reactions) measures they were able to predict with an accuracy rate of 94 percent which relationships would survive and which would not. In fact, they can now make this prediction with the same degree of accuracy after observing just three minutes of a session in which newlywed couples are in an argument. In general terms, the less effectively the couple handle the conflict, the more likely they are to break up.

John Gottman's book *Why Marriages Succeed or Fail* outlines much of this research. Here are guidelines and skills for effective relationship maintenance that have come, in part, from this research.

Rule One: Speak Up

Don't expect your partner to mind-read. Be gently assertive about saying what you want, need, or feel. Many people do not express their needs. Instead, they secretly wish their partner understood what they want. When eventually they do say what they want, after a long period of not getting it, they do so angrily. It goes like this: "If you loved me you would be able to read my mind, know what I need, and then you would do it. Since you don't do this, it must mean you do not care about me. So why should I care about you?"

Rule Two: Don't Sulk When Things Don't Go as You Want

Sulking is withdrawing, being cold, detaching emotionally, and reducing interaction. Sulking may give you power in the form of revenge or punishment. It may also make the other person reach out to you for fear of losing you, so you get some proof that they really do care. Sulking may sometimes force the other person to give you what you want. But it is an unhealthy power that damages good relationships. The healthy alternatives are outlined in the Introduction (page xi). The chapters on assertion (page 233) and rational thinking (page 222) will also be useful.

Rule Three: Be Optimistic about the Outcome of Conflict and Not Frightened by It

See conflict as an opportunity to "clear the air" and improve your relationship. If you handle it with a reasonable level of skill, the outcome will be positive. Good resolution of conflict can actually strengthen a relationship. It indicates commitment by showing a preparedness to maintain the relationship in a good state, and it clears the air of much resentment. It also affirms that the relationship is strong enough to withstand the occasional necessary conflict.

Rule Four: Always Try to Negotiate

In most cases you will maintain your relationship more effectively if you go for a win–win approach, where you have as your main objective a desire to find a solution to any conflict which provides mutual benefit. See the section on conflict resolution on page 248.

Rule Five: Close "Emotional Chasms" Quickly

Don't let an "emotional chasm" open up too far or you will find yourselves unable to cross back over to each other. When a couple does not handle conflict well, it tends to become an entrenched pattern. Unresolved issues become a source of resentment, which further opens up a distance between the two. This creates a kind of emotional chasm, which separates and reduces intimacy and closeness. After a while, even with good motivation, it becomes increasingly difficult to cross back over into intimacy. Eventually, as the chasm widens even further, the motivation to cross over lessens because it seems such an impossible task. As soon as an emotional chasm starts to open up between you, do something to close it.

The Nine Principles

The following nine basic principles for maintaining a satisfying relationship can be summed up by the acronym "FIND PEACE." A briefer version of the acronym appears on page 266 and can be used as a reminder once you decide on the improvements you wish to make in your relationship skills.

1. Flooding Damages Discussions and Needs to Be Controlled

Flooding with anxiety, and hence emotion, occurs when you are overwhelmed because of the release of adrenaline and cortisol into your bloodstream. Read the chapter on anxiety and its biological and emotional effects on page 96. When you flood with anxiety, this is what happens:

- your thoughts become disorganized and focusing is difficult
- you experience a strong desire to strike back at the threat (Fight!) or flee from it (Flight!)
- you feel angry toward the other person
- you become aware of a pounding heart and muscle tension
- you have difficulty with breathing as you inadvertently hold your breath when the flooding starts.

The speed of flooding is variable. Individuals with a predisposition to anxiety flood more quickly and more intensely, and take longer to recover. The more pressure you are experiencing from outside factors such as work or children, the more easily flooded you will be in relationship discussions. In general, men become flooded far more readily than women. When men "stonewall" (that is, refuse to discuss an issue and act like a "stone wall") in the face of a complaint from their female partner, it is usually because they are flooding with anxiety underneath their seeming indifference. They fear being made to look foolish or powerless, or losing control of themselves, and saying or doing things which will harm the relationship or that they will regret.

When women get angrier and angrier in the face of their male partner's stonewalling, it is usually because they are flooding with anxiety at not being able to resolve an issue. Underneath, they fear that their partner does not care about them or may leave them.

If flooding happens often enough, you respond to the situations where it has occurred before with dread (for example, when your partner says, "We have to talk" you think, *What now?*). You become hypervigilant. When you experience a particular facial expression or tone of voice, which previously has accompanied conflict, you feel as though you have already been attacked. In a relationship where one partner has become chronically flooded over time, the couple seems blind to evidence of the good things in the marriage and recognize only the bad.

What You Can Do

- Don't discuss emotional issues when you are not calm or when you have consumed a significant amount of alcohol
- If you are the one flooding with anxiety, go away till you calm down. This takes about 30 to 60 minutes, depending on how upset you are. It is essential that you come back to the discussion when you calm down and that you let your partner know you will come back to the issue, not just forget about it.
- If you recognize that your partner has become distressed and anxious but isn't aware of it, request that you deal with it when you are both calmer. "Let's take some time out because we're both very upset at the moment. We'll deal with it better when we are calmer." Don't be patronizing or insulting by saying things like, "I am not prepared to talk about this until you get control of yourself!" You both own the problem.

2. In the Here and Now. Don't "Kitchen-Sink"

It is unhelpful to continually refer to things which happened in the past, even if you feel justified in doing so. "Kitchen-sinking" is when you throw all your other unresolved grievances into the discussion when trying to deal with one specific grievance.

What You Can Do

- Don't throw in a whole collection of prior, unresolved grievances.
- Don't keep bringing up the past. It is understandable that you remember it, but it is not helpful to talk about it because none of it can be undone.
- Ask yourself how you would feel if every foolish, thoughtless, or inefficient thing you had done was continually resurrected each time an issue came up that focused on you.

3. Nobody Is Perfect

If you have unrealistic expectations about your partner, you will always be disappointed. See them as a real person, complex and with weaknesses and limitations. Everyone is flawed, but the trick is to focus on their positive characteristics. You are not perfect either and you want them to accept your limitations and weaknesses. Focus on what is really important. If you continually send "Be more perfect because you are not good enough" messages to your partner, they may feel constantly inadequate and resent you for it.

What You Can Do

When your partner disappoints you, remind yourself of all their good qualities and say to yourself, "Nobody is perfect, including me. I wonder what I do that disappoints them." Avoid "Be more perfect or I can't love you" messages.

4. "Difference" Doesn't Mean "Defect" or "Danger"

Reject the "difference" approach where you emphasize the differences between you each to try to establish that you are a better person than your partner. Focus on seeing differences as just that, not as defects or threats to your integrity or to who you are. The reality is that you cannot change anyone else's behavior. But by changing your own, for example, by being more accepting, sometimes others are encouraged to change.

What You Can Do

- Accept your partner's differences. They are entitled to be who they are, not who you think they should be. You are entitled to ask for small changes in areas that directly affect you. But it is only possible to change when you feel accepted as you already are. By accepting your partner's differences, they are more likely to feel free to change in some small ways.
- Remind yourself that a good relationship is about being your own person as well as about being part of a couple.

• • •

5. Positive Balance Sheet (1:5 rule)

Relationships that satisfy and last have five positive interactions to every negative. In a stable relationship, a couple sees each other through rose-colored glasses. The more you expect and search for positives, the more likely you are to find them and to highlight their significance in your mind.

What You Can Do

- Wear your rose-colored glasses as often as possible when thinking and talking about your partner. Love has to be a little bit blind.
- Use "pleasers" every day to make your partner happy. No one else knows what pleases your partner better than you do.
- Ask for what pleases you, too.

6. Express Goodwill and Respect All the Time

You need to handle conflict and difficulties within the context of your love for your partner and a desire for the relationship to continue and to be good. Successful partners operate with goodwill, that is, your motivations should be to:

- protect your relationship
- allow your partner to maintain face and be able to express their point of view
- find a solution that is mutually acceptable.

Once goodwill is lost, it is an uphill battle to maintain a relationship. Goodwill is not present if you are trying to do any of the following:

- "win" at all costs
- prove how righteous and good you are
- put your partner down
- always be the boss
- show no concern for your partner's well-being or feelings
- appear not to care whether the relationship is maintained or not.

What You Can Do

Show as much respect to your partner as you would to a stranger. Do not speak disrespectfully, insult, or lecture them. We have all had the horrible experience of overhearing a couple speak rudely to each other in public, and usually cringe as we recognize some of what we do ourselves and how dreadful it really is.

Agree before you disagree. For example, find an aspect of what they said which makes sense to you (even if it is only small) and say that first. Here are two examples:

- Yes, I realize how hard you work. But I need time with you, too.
- You're quite right, it would have been better if the car had been serviced this month. However, it has been a really busy time and I just couldn't get to it.

Remember that every behavior has two sides, and look on the bright side of any behavior that distresses you. For example, you may be troubled by your partner's difficulties with expressing positive emotions such as affection. However, the bright side of that could be stoicism, whereby when times are tough, your partner doesn't complain or express negative emotions.

Use charitable interpretations. When your partner hurts or annoys you, look for the kindest way to "frame" it in your own mind. For example, when they don't introduce you around at a work social function where you don't know many people, you can raise it as a mild complaint later, but say to yourself, "He didn't realize that I was feeling a bit intimidated," or "He was so anxious about impressing the senior partner, he forgot that I didn't know many people there."

Use goodwill retracking when it looks like things might be going downhill. These are reminders of your vulnerability and feelings, your mutual love, and the importance of your relationship and of maintaining it in a healthy state. Goodwill retracking allows you to refocus. It works best when accompanied by a hug, hand squeeze, or other act of affection. Here are some examples of typical expressions of goodwill retracking:

- Let's see if we can negotiate this. It's not important enough for us to fight about.
- I love you and I don't want this to cause a rift between us.
- We need to stay on the issue so we can get a resolution here.
- We can't stay upset with each other.
- You know I love you and I want to work this out.
- That really hurt my feelings.
- Can we try to talk about this without blaming each other, please?
- We both seem to be getting pretty upset, and that's not going to help us work this out without damaging our relationship. How about we take some time out to cool down and then sit down and discuss it more calmly?

7. Admit When You Could Be in the Wrong

Most of us get defensive when a complaint is made about us. This principle is about having the courage to accept that we may have been wrong, forgotten something, been thoughtless or offended in some other way, even if that wasn't our intention (and it usually wasn't!). None of us is perfect. But we all fear that admitting to a fault or mistake will give our partner a stick to beat us with. Usually the reverse is true. An admission of fault or partial fault defuses attack in most cases.

What You Can Do

- Avoid getting into a "Yes, you did," "No, I didn't" argument. It is better to have a healthy relationship than be self-righteously standing on the moral high ground. It is very lonely up there.
- Acknowledge things that are true, nearly true, or possibly true.
- Admit to mistakes you might have made. Remind your partner that it is hard to admit or acknowledge if they then follow up with an attack or if they act holier-than-thou. They must fulfill their side by accepting that you are not perfect (neither are they!) and by not dwelling on what you did.

- Accommodate, adapt, or apologize, depending on what is needed.

Avoid acting defensively in the face of complaint. Acting defensively means that you always play the role of the innocent victim who never does anything wrong. This can be done through:

- Denying responsibility ("I never said I would collect the dry cleaning. You must have misheard me.")
- Making excuses ("There were so many other more important things to remember than your dry cleaning.")
- Cross-complaining. Your partner's mistakes and weaknesses don't negate any mistake or imperfection on your part. ("You should talk! What about when you didn't pick up the supplies I asked you to get?")
- "Yes, butting"("Yes, I did forget to do it, but you had given me too much to do anyway.")

There is an old saying that sums this up perfectly: "When you're in the wrong, admit it; when you're in the right, shut up."

8. Control Criticism and Contempt

Complaints are a valid way of letting someone know that something is upsetting you. A complaint is a negative comment about something you wish were otherwise. It is a specific statement of anger, displeasure, distress, or other negativity. ("I don't like it when you don't consult me before you commit us to weekend outings.") Complaints are all right if they are made within a context of goodwill and respect. Complaints are about an action, behavior, or situation. They do not attack character or competence. While complaints are legitimate, criticism and contempt are not, and they can destroy relationships very quickly.

- Criticizing is when you air a complaint but at the same time throw in a negative remark about the other person's personality, character or ability. ("You are stupid and thoughtless.") Criticizing attacks the person instead of the behavior and focuses on blame. Criticism emphasizes "You should or shouldn't" and "always/never" ("You are so selfish. You never consider what I want on our weekend off.")

- Showing contempt is when you go one step further than criticism and use insults, sneering, put-downs, sarcasm, or hostile humor ("Here we have yet another example of your thoughtfulness toward me. Another weekend jaunt I don't want to go on.")
- It is hard but possible to withdraw from a pattern of ongoing criticism and contempt, and turn things around.

What You Can Do
- Confront gently when you are upset about what your partner has done or said, and use complaints, not criticism or contempt.
- Avoid put-downs, insults, and negative comments about your partner's character or competence.
- Don't see "wounding the other" as your main aim. It may feel powerful and righteous for a few minutes but it will feel awful when you think back on what you said and contemplate what long-term damage you may have done.
- Remind yourself of the long-term damage of criticism and contempt. Expressions of criticism and contempt can't be easily taken back and they thoroughly erode a relationship.

9. Engage in Discussion and Problem-Solve

When your partner has a complaint or there is a problem, you should be prepared to take part in any discussion they initiate about an issue that is important to them. Don't stonewall. When you act like a stone wall you don't listen, you walk away, or you refuse to discuss. Unresolved or ignored complaints gather momentum and can crush a healthy relationship.

What You Can Do
- Participate in any discussion your partner initiates about an issue that is important to them.
- Listen, validate (that is, allow and accept) feelings ("I can

see that you are upset over that" rather than, "That's ridiculous! Why would that upset you?")

- If you suspect you stonewall because you feel overwhelmed with fear and anxiety when "serious talk" is threatened, it is all right to temporarily withdraw from the discussion. Then you can calm down, but you must come back to the discussion voluntarily.

Prompting Cards

Prompting cards are a strategy to assist in training your brain to think more helpfully about situations and to improve your skills over time.

Write on the back of a business card or cut out a piece of cardboard the size of a business card. Keep the card in a plastic holder so it won't get damaged in your wallet or handbag. Most news agencies sell plastic train pass holders that will do the job.

Select the self-talk statements or summaries that will most help you. Write your selections on the card. Do not use too many because you will be less likely to remember them. Use a highlighter to remind yourself of which ones you want to work on. Then, several times each day, take out the card and read through the self-talk statements or the skill reminders. You can also use the card on the spot in circumstances in which you are confronted with a difficult situation. Eventually you won't need to read it, as the statements will become second nature to you.

The P Strategy

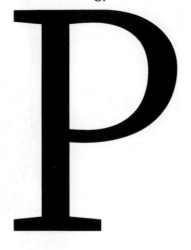

proof?
possibilities!
positive aspects!
perspective!
plainer language
personalizing?
panic paralyzes!
problem solving!
persistence!
put it aside!
physiology?
problem ownership?

FIND PEACE

Flooding damages and must be controlled
In the here and now. No kitchen sinking.
Nobody is perfect
Difference is not defect

Positive balance sheet of 5 to 1
Express goodwill and respect all the time
Admit when you could be in the wrong
Control criticism and contempt
Engage in discussions. Don't stonewall.

PART

VI

Following Up

Finding a Good Psychologist

MANY PEOPLE ARE confused about the difference between a psychiatrist and a psychologist.

A psychiatrist completes a medical degree and then adds further qualifications in psychiatry. A counseling or clinical psychologist usually completes a degree in psychology and usually adds postgraduate qualifications in counseling or clinical psychology. Generally, a psychologist works on a short-term basis to support and problem solve with the "worried well," whereas the psychiatrist is more likely to see those with a biologically based mental illness.

One major difference is that as a doctor, a psychiatrist is legally able to prescribe medication, which is sometimes needed in certain disorders. However, it is not uncommon for a psychologist to work with a medical practitioner who prescribes medication while the psychologist focuses on behavior.

Patients can be referred either to a psychologist or a psychiatrist. Both professionals select from a range of models in deciding which techniques to use with patients. It is necessary to gain a referral from a medical practitioner before visiting a specialist psychiatrist.

How Do You Tell If the Psychologist Is Any Good?

- Check their qualifications: you would normally expect that a psychologist has a master's degree or similar postgraduate qualifications in psychology.
- Ask if rational-emotive therapy is used, as this is the counseling model with the best success rate.
- Observe their manner with you. A good psychologist's

manner is empathic and supportive, but not judgmental. There is a difference between giving information and giving advice.

- Reflect on whether you are given a chance to tell your story.
- However good they are, it is possible that the first psychologist you try may not good for *you*. If you are not happy, look elsewhere.

Contact Details for Professional Organizations

American Psychological Association
Main website address: www.apa.org
For information about how to locate a psychologist in your area:
  http://locator.apa.org/

Canadian Psychological Association
Main website address: www.cpa.ca
For more detailed information about how a psychologist can assist you: http://www.cpa.ca/public/

Books You Might Like to Read

Anger Management and Conflict Management

Kotzman, A. & Kotzman, M. (2007) *Listen To Me, Listen To You: A Practical Guide to Self-Awareness, Communication Skills and Conflict Management* (2nd edition). Camberwell, Vic: Penguin Australia.

Harbin, T. (2000) *Beyond Anger: A Guide for Men: How to Free Yourself From the Grip of Anger and Get More Out of Life*, New York: Da Capo Press.

McKay, M., Rogers, P. & McKay, J. (2003) *When Anger Hurts: Quieting the Storm Within* (2nd edition). Oakland, CA: New Harbinger Publications.

Nay, W. R. (2004) *Taking Charge of Anger: How to Resolve Conflict, Sustain Relationships and Express Yourself Without Losing Control*. Farmington: University of Connecticut Health Center.

Paleg, K. & McKay, M. (2001) *When Anger Hurts Your Relationship: 10 Simple Solutions for Couples Who Fight*. Oakland, CA: New Harbinger Publications.

Anti-Social Personality Disorder: Sociopathic Behavior

Babiak, P. & Hare, R. D. (2007) *Snakes in Suits: When Sociopaths Go to Work*. New York: Harper Paperbacks.

Hare, R. D. (1999) *Without Conscience: The Disturbing World of the Psychopaths Among Us*. New York: Guilford Press.

Anxiety

Ellis, A. (2000) *How To Control Your Anxiety Before It Controls You*. New York: Citadel Press.

Rapee, R. P. (1998) *Overcoming Shyness and Social Phobia: A Step-by-Step Guide*. Lanham, MD: Jason Aronson.

Rapee, R. M., Wignall, A., Spence, S. H., Cobham, V. & Lyneham, H. (2008)

Helping Your Anxious Child: A Step-by-Step Guide for Parents (2nd edition). Oakland, CA: New Harbinger Publications.

Assertiveness

Alberti, R. & Emmons, M. (2008) *Your Perfect Right: Assertiveness and Equality in Your Life and Relationships* (9th edition). Atascadero, CA: Impact Publishers.

Bower, S. & Bower, G. (2004) *Asserting Yourself: A Practical Guide for Positive Change* (updated edition). Cambridge, MA: Da Capo Press.

Paterson, R. J. (2000) *The Assertiveness Workbook: How to Express Your Ideas and Stand Up for Yourself at Work and in Relationships.* Oakland, CA: New Harbinger Publications.

Small, B. (2006) *What About Me, What Do I Want? Becoming Assertive.* Victoria, BC: Trafford.

Borderline Personality Disorder

Chapman, A. & Gratz, K. (2007) *The Borderline Personality Disorder Survival Guide: Everything You Need to Know About Living With BPD*, Oakland, CA: New Harbinger Publications.

Friedel, R. (2004) *Borderline Personality Disorder Demystified: An Essential Guide for Understanding and Living with BPD.* New York: Da Capo Press.

Bullying

Randall, P. (1997) *Adult Bullying: Perpetrators and Victims.* London: Routledge.

The MBTI and Personality Types

Bayne, R. (2004) *Psychological Types at Work: An MBTI Perspective.* Florence, KY: Cengage Learning.

Berens, L. V., Cooper, S., Ernst, L. K. & Martin, C.R. et al. (2003) *Quick Guide to the 16 Personality Types in Organizations: Understanding Personality Differences in the Workplace.* Huntington Beach, CA: Telos Publications.

Kroeger, O. & and Thuesen, J. M (2002) *Type Talk: The 16 Personality Types That Determine How We Live, Love, and Work.* New York: Dell.

Laney, M. O. (2002) *The Introvert Advantage: How to Thrive in an Extrovert World.* New York: Workman Pub.

Pearman, R. P., Lombardo, M. M., Eichinger, R. W. (2005) *You: Being More*

Effective in Your MBTI Type. Minneapolis: Lominger Limited.

Tieger, P. D & Barron-Tieger, B. (2000) *Just Your Type: Create the Relationship You've Always Wanted Using the Secrets of Personality Type*. Boston: Little, Brown.

Tieger, P. D & Barron-Tieger, B. (2007) Do *What You Are: Discover the Perfect Career for You Through the Secrets of Personality* Type. Boston: Little, Brown.

Optimistic Thinking

Seligman, M. E. P. (2006) *Learned Optimism: How to Change Your Mind and Your Life*. New York: Vintage Books.

Rational Thinking

Ellis, A. (2001) *Feeling Better, Getting Better, Staying Better: Profound Self-Help Therapy For Your Emotions*. Atascadero, CA.: Impact Publishers,

Ellis, A. (2006) *How to Stubbornly Refuse to Make Yourself Miserable about Anything (Yes Anything!)*. New York: Citadel Press.

Ellis, A. (2003) *How To Keep People From Pushing Your Buttons*. New York: Citadel Press.

Ellis, A. (2005) *The Myth of Self-Esteem: How Rational-Emotive Behavior Therapy Can Change Your Life Forever*. Amherst, NY: Prometheus Books.

Tanner. S. & Ball, J. (2004) *Beating the Blues: A Self-Help Approach to Overcoming Depression*. New York: Oxford University Press.

Relationship Skills

Gottman, J. & Silver, N. (2000) *The Seven Principles for Making Marriage Work*. New York: Three Rivers Press.

Gottman, J. Schwarz Gottman, J. & DeClaire, J. (2007) *Ten Lessons to Transform Your Marriage: America's Love Lab Experts Share Their Strategies for Strengthening Your Relationship*. New York: Three Rivers Press.

Gottman, J. (2002) *The Relationship Cure: A 5-Step Guide to Strengthening Your Marriage, Family, and Friendships*. New York: Three Rivers Press.

Gottman & J. Schwarz Gottman, J. (2008) *And Baby Makes Three: The Six-Step Plan for Preserving Marital Intimacy and Rekindling Romance After Baby Arrives*. New York: Three Rivers Press.

McKay, M., Fanning, P. & Paleg, K. (2006) *Couple Skills: Making Your Relationship Work*. Oakland, CA: New Harbinger Publications.

General Reading

Cavaiola, A. & Lavender, N. (2000) *Toxic Coworkers: How to Deal with Dysfunctional People on the Job.* Oakland, CA: New Harbinger Publications.

Kraly, F. S. (2006) *Brain Science and Psychological Disorders: New Perspectives on Psychotherapeutic Treatment.* New York: W. W. Norton.

McKay, M. & Fanning, P. (2000) *Self-Esteem: A Proven Program of Cognitive Techniques for Assessing, Improving, and Maintaining Your Self-Esteem, (3rd Edition).* Oakland, CA: New Harbinger Publications.

Ratey, J. J. & Johnson, C. (1998) *Shadow Syndromes: The Mild Forms of Major Mental Disorders That Sabotage Us.* New York: Bantam Books.

Seligman, M. E. P. (2004) *Authentic Happiness: Using the New Positive Psychology to Realize Your Potential for Lasting Fulfillment.* New York: Free Press.

DSM IV-TR

DSM IV-TR: *Diagnostic and Statistical Manual of Mental Disorders,* Fourth Edition, Text Revision (2000). Arlington, VA: American Psychiatric Association.

Index

ABOUT THE AUTHORS

HELEN MCGRATH, PHD, is a clinical psychologist in private practice as well as adjunct professor at RMIT (Royal Melbourne Institute of Technology) University in Melbourne, Australia. A highly regarded consultant, conference speaker, and media commentator, Dr. McGrath is the author of numerous books and articles on social skills, relationships, and well-being for the general community, educators, and health and workplace professionals.

HAZEL EDWARDS, MED, writes nonfiction and fiction for adults and children. Her more than 200 books include the classic children's book *There's a Hippopotamus on Our Roof Eating Cake*, which is approaching its 30th anniversary. After Hazel Edwards' 2001 expedition to Antarctica as writer-on-ice, bases there use *Difficult Personalities* as a resource. More information about her can be found at www.hazeledwards.com.